# THE MAKERS OF
# TRINITY CHURCH
# IN THE CITY OF BOSTON

# THE MAKERS OF
# TRINITY CHURCH
## IN THE CITY OF BOSTON

Edited by James F. O'Gorman

University of Massachusetts Press
AMHERST & BOSTON

Published in association with
Trinity Church in the City of Boston

Copyright © 2004 by Trinity Church in the City of Boston
Printed in the United States of America
LC 2004001712
ISBN 1-55849-436-7
Designed by Jack Harrison
Set in Adobe Garamond with Weiss Titling display
Printed and bound by Sheridan Books, Inc.

Library of Congress Cataloging-in-Publication Data
The makers of Trinity Church in the city of Boston / edited by James F. O'Gorman.
    p. cm.
  "Published in association with Trinity Church in the city of Boston."
  Includes bibliographical references and index.
  ISBN 1-55849-436-7 (cloth : alk. paper)
1. Trinity Church (Boston, Mass.)
2. Church architecture—Massachusetts—Boston—History—19th century.
3. Romanesque revival (Architecture)—Massachusetts—Boston.
4. Richardson, H. H. (Henry Hobson), 1838–1886
5. Boston (Mass.)—Buildings, structures, etc.    I. O'Gorman, James F.
  NA5235.B75M35 2004
  726.5'09744'61—dc22

                       2004001712

British Library Cataloguing in Publication data are available.

This book is published with the financial assistance of
Trinity Church in the City of Boston and the Grace Slack McNeil Program in the
History of American Art at Wellesley College.

To the memory of

GEORGE MINOT DEXTER (1802–1872)

Architect, Senior Warden, and first Chairman of the Building Committee.

Had he lived he would have taken his place among

the Makers of Trinity Church.

# CONTENTS

# ILLUSTRATIONS

## COLOR PLATES    *(following page 112)*

# PREFACE

Architecture is not the expression of individual genius, despite the adoration given in our time to such magical names as Frank Lloyd Wright, Philip Johnson, and Frank Gehry. Although Howard Roark, the isolated and unbending hero of Ayn Rand's novel *The Fountainhead,* would never agree, architecture is a collective art. Buildings result from collaboration and compromise. They are the concrete manifestations of societal needs or desires expressed through (among others) client, building committee, designer, banker, engineer, contractor, decorator, and user. They are also altered by the remodeler. This definition of architecture justifies the bundling of the following essays.

We usually see the original Trinity Church on Copley Square, Boston (pls. 1–4), as H. H. Richardson's creation, but it is in fact the product of teamwork, of the collaborative efforts of many people including, originally, the client, Phillips Brooks; the chairman of the building committee, Robert Treat Paine; the architect, Richardson; the builder, O. W. Norcross; and the decorator, John La Farge. Its present condition is also the result of later glazing, importantly by Sarah Wyman Whitman, Margaret Redmond, and others, and of remodeling, most notably that of the chancel by the architectural firm of Maginnis & Walsh. The absence of any one of these contributors would have produced a different result. The absence, too, of other important figures who appear here but are given less space would have altered the church we now admire: the firms of Clayton & Bell, William Morris, and other glassmakers; engineers such as Ernest Bowditch, who worried about the sufficiency of the foundations and the weight of the tower; and the Reverend Arthur Lee Kinsolving, rector when Maginnis redid the chancel. But even that list is not complete, for supporting those historically visible leaders were the efforts of the not-so-visible and the anonymous: the members of Paine's committee, the draftsmen in Gambrill & Richardson's office (and in those of Ernest Bowditch and Maginnis & Walsh), Norcross's masons and millworkers, La Farge's and Sarah Whitman's many assistants. We may not know all their names or their individual contributions, but under the direction or inspiration of the key figures we do celebrate in this publication—here called the Makers of Trinity—all of them had a significant impact on the building standing on Copley Square. And that building is one of the glories of American ecclesiastical art and architecture.

In these chapters, Richardson shares the stage with some of his collaborators. After an overview of the place of the church in the history of its times, the reader will meet the principal early Makers of Trinity Church as well as some of its later embellishers. The founders came together in an extraordinary enterprise. They were remarkably young and relatively inexperienced for such an undertaking: Brooks, Paine, and La Farge were just thirty-seven years old in 1872 when the campaign began; Richardson was thirty-four; Norcross, a mere thirty-three. They came from varied backgrounds: Brooks and Paine were Harvard-educated Brahmins; Richardson was a Harvard-trained son of the slaveholding South; Norcross, a self-made Yankee; and La Farge, a New York–born, Paris-educated artist. Their collaboration was not without its rough moments and compromise not always easily reached, but in the end it went well, for each had a specific primary role: Brooks supplied the inspiration, Paine the implementation, Richardson the direction, Norcross the execution, and La Farge the initial decoration. The later works of stained glass designers (including those of female artists largely neglected until recently), sculptors, and remodeling architects enhanced the ensemble and brought the church to its present splendor. That splendor is admirably characterized in the second essay of this collection, and that splendor is being preserved and enhanced by the restoration project under way as this book goes to press.

The pages that follow briefly introduce each of these participants and outline their principal contributions to the making of Trinity Church.

But what of the essay on Henry Adams and his novel *Esther?* A puzzling inclusion perhaps. In what way does Henry Adams belong among the Makers of Trinity? Remember that I began with a definition of architecture as the manifestation of the needs or desires of society expressed through the client, architect, and so on, ending with the "user." The user is not just a person who lives, works, worships, swims, or studies in a building. A user can be someone who appropriates the history, image, or reputation of a work of architecture for his own ends. Edgar Allan Poe certainly "made" the House of Usher; Victor Hugo as surely recreated Notre Dame in Paris—which brings us back to Henry Adams, who made (or, if you prefer, remade) the decoration of Trinity Church the setting for his novel *Esther,* a pseudonymous publication of 1884.

The essay published here looks at *Esther* as a product of its time as well as of the specific history of Trinity. Basing his setting on the church ordered by his cousin, Brooks, and designed by his friend, Richardson, and on a building campaign under way as he taught history at Harvard, Adams spun a tale of Gilded Age religious uncertainty. The story lifts Trinity out of its site on Copley Square and imagines it as the locus for larger societal discourse. So Henry Adams was a significant user of Trinity, although not in the conventional role of communicant. In that sense, he too becomes a Maker of Trinity Church, a creator of its image beyond the physical realm.

This book originated in a symposium organized by the editor and held at the Boston Public Library on November 17, 2001, as part of the year-long celebration of the 125th anniversary of the dedication of Trinity Church on February 9, 1877. That symposium—and this publication—resulted from a collaboration between the church and the Grace Slack McNeil Program in the History of American Art at Wellesley College. The papers presented on that occasion have been augmented here in order to include other significant contributors to the church as it stands today. Since the creation of Trinity was an integrated effort of all the participants, the reader will find information about the role of each not only in the chapter devoted to him or her but throughout the text. The authors hope that this collection will help establish a balance in our thinking, talking, and writing about the making of architecture in general, and Boston's Trinity Church in particular.

JAMES F. O'GORMAN

# THE MAKERS OF
# TRINITY CHURCH
# IN THE CITY OF BOSTON

# INTRODUCTION

## *From the Parish to the World:*
## *The Architectural Context of Trinity Church*

KEITH N. MORGAN

LET'S BEGIN by resetting the scene. Established as the third Anglican parish in Boston, its first church erected in 1735, Trinity is one of the oldest Protestant congregations in the city. The importance of the church to Boston moved into a high register, however, when the young Phillips Brooks was called to the local pulpit in 1869. He quickly set in motion a series of initiatives that made Trinity Church the most dynamic religious institution in the city and one admired (if not envied) by Christians throughout the country. The most tangible of Brooks's visions was to move the church from its early nineteenth-century quarters on Summer Street in the business district to a larger and more visible site in the expanding Back Bay.

Here the story shifts from the charisma of a single individual to a dialogue among the forceful, progressive (and surprisingly young) men who pushed the new church into the realm of a masterwork. Having decided in 1870 to make the move, the parish announced a limited competition in 1872 for the design of the new building. Three established Boston architectural firms and three New York architects were invited to compete. In some ways, Henry Hobson Richardson, who won the competition, was the least likely man to carry the day. Although he had useful contacts from his undergraduate years at Harvard (as did some of his competitors) and had recently completed the prominent Brattle Square Church, at Clarendon Street and Commonwealth Avenue, he was also the youngest and least experienced of the group. As David Chesebrough writes in this volume, Richardson was clearly Brooks's choice for the job, the rector having invited the architect for a private interview before the competition designs were submitted. Richardson's ability to understand the needs of the parish and its dynamic pastor and to translate them into an innovative physical form brought him the prize that became the foundation for his subsequent international reputation.

To assess quickly the contributions and importance of the key figures we honor as the Makers of Trinity, I want to comment on six aspects of the creation of this church: the building program, its architectural style, construction technology, interior decoration, stained glass enrichment, and the international reputation of the building.

First the program. Although Trinity was nominally built for the parish, its character was heavily shaped by the figure of Phillips Brooks. The rector inspired the congregation to move to a new building, held firm ideas about the form that building should take, and was not reticent in sharing his prejudices. Brooks was probably the most compelling American preacher of his generation. Trained at Harvard and at the Virginia Theological Seminary, aware of progressive international trends in theology, Brooks was a key advocate for the Broad Church movement, a campaign by British and American clergy to overcome the traditional competition between high- and low-church Anglicanism. Similarly, he joined a group of liberal clerics who chose to engage aggressively the challenges of modern science and the industrialized world in order to develop a more dynamic and inclusive faith. In constructing a new church building, Brooks sought to create a structure that would reinforce and expand his mission: Since for him, preaching was the central act of worship, Trinity was designed as a modified Greek cross auditorium to allow him to exercise his exceptional talents as a preacher. As first built, Keith Bakker shows here, the church deemphasized a liturgical service. The chancel was quite severe, with a simple desk and lectern at the front edge of the space from which Brooks dominated his audience. Behind, a row of massive wooden chairs lined the chancel, and a wooden communion table stood where the high altar now stands. On this somewhat austere stage, Phillips Brooks cajoled, goaded, and inspired the large congregations that came to hear him preach. He insisted that the balconies accommodate 350 persons, those who did not pay for rental of pews on the main floor of the church; others often filled the seats around the chancel, creating an oratory theater in the round. The importance of this man to this building and his congregation is signaled by the many images of Brooks now found throughout Trinity—a standing statue by Augustus Saint-Gaudens beyond the north transept, the bust by Daniel Chester French in the baptistry (pl. 12) and the image of Brooks among the great preachers on the west porch of the building and on the massive pulpit, another among the reliefs on the chancel walls.

Beyond the program, Trinity Church provided H. H. Richardson an opportunity to explore and refine the potential for Romanesque—meaning early Medieval—style as a vehicle for modern design. Admittedly, a modest American tradition of using Romanesque architectural forms for Protestant religious buildings had begun in the 1840s. Kathleen Curran here carefully blocks in the influence of St. George's and St. Bartholomew's, New York City Episcopal churches in the Romanesque style, which Brooks repeatedly visited and recommended that Richardson inspect. Brooks saw the use of the Romanesque as a way to connect his church theologically to purer ideals of early Christianity. His architect had already experimented with Romanesque forms in the nearby Brattle Square Church of 1870, which may be why Brooks favored him in the competition. As the complex plans for Trinity evolved between 1872 and 1877, the building matured into a design mode that Richardson made thoroughly his own, based in a knowledge of Romanesque forms but modernized to match the spirit and the needs of the 1870s. Richardson wrote about wanting to achieve quiet in his buildings. Here he took an architectural tradition of thick walls, small windows, and long naves and massaged it into a composition of generous volumes, punctured by large openings, and restrained ornament both within and without. Indeed, it was in this commission that Richardson perfected a personal design manner that he further explored in his subsequent work and that deeply influenced the architecture of his generation.

The process of actually building Trinity Church is an important part of the story, even if the structure is not as innovative as the design. For the most part, Richardson was not a participant in his generation's exploration of new materials and methods of construction, especially the use of iron. Trinity Church is rather a supreme example of traditional building practices and how these were harnessed to accommodate a structure of this scale and weight. The most interesting technological question was how such a massive stone structure, the largest yet built in the Back Bay, could be successfully supported on gravel-based landfill. Much of Boston and all of the Back Bay are constructed on filled land. The foundations of this granite and brownstone pile are placed not on bedrock but on 4,500 wooden pilings that were driven into the clay and gravel of the site and impregnated and stabilized by the high water table of the Back Bay. The greatest challenge was the engineering of a system of weight distribution that would allow the construction of the central tower, which is key to the image of the church. Actually, Richardson's original competition design focused on a much taller and heavier octagonal tower. Because the building committee and the consulting engineer, Ernest Bowditch, repeatedly demanded that the tower be redesigned, it was radically altered after 1872. This debate continued a full three years until Richardson achieved the present square, broad tower whose reduced weight could be distributed more easily through four massive corner piers to enormous granite pyramids set upon the bed of pilings. (One of the most exciting features of the proposed excavation of the undercroft of the church for new social, administrative, and educational spaces, part of the current work on the church, will be the ability for all of us to see and appreciate the structural foundations of the building.)

Robert Treat Paine, the forceful chairman of the building committee, persistently pushed the architect to make these multiple changes. Paine, a boyhood friend of Brooks, deeply loved this parish and the ideals of this building; he and his wife had deserted King's Chapel and Unitarianism after coming to hear Brooks preach. His phenomenal devotion to the building project, as beautifully detailed here in Thomas Paine's paper, was one of scores of commitments that he made to religious and charitable efforts, both within the framework of Trinity Church and in the many separate humanitarian enterprises that he launched. He was a member of sixty charitable committees at one time.

The other important control and support for Richardson's building efforts was Orlando Whitney Norcross, the master builder of Trinity Church, whose fascinating career James O'Gorman's paper adds to this mix of powerful young men. The creator of general contracting in American architecture, Norcross was a paragon of organization, marshaling teams of craftsmen and providing all the materials needed for this job. He opened granite quarries in Dedham, Massachusetts, and Westerley, Rhode Island, and a brownstone quarry in East Longmeadow, Massachusetts, to provide the fabric for this church. Having cut his teeth on two earlier projects with Richardson, from the much more complex Trinity commission Norcross gained a national reputation as a contractor, estimator, and engineer.

Interior decoration also represented a field of experimental collaboration at Trinity. Richardson designed the interior woodwork and nearly all the furniture for the church, as Keith Bakker reveals in his essay. One of the first American architects to become a designer of the furnishings for his buildings, Richardson provided at Trinity a substantial suite of furniture, most of which is still in use by the church today. The earliest schemes of both Richardson and Brooks indicate that a colorful interior was always intended. Richardson's competition drawings show bands of colored decoration designed to reinforce the architecture and the window openings, as well as some figural decoration. Brooks was also a lover of strong colors and supported Richardson's choice of a Pompeian or Persian red as the dominant tone for the space. This was not a timid move in a culture still dominated by the serene whiteness of Puritan and Congregational meetinghouses, as Ted Stebbins reminds us.

To achieve his vision, Richardson convinced the young artist John La Farge to conceptualize and supervise the decoration of the church, and he enticed the already overextended building committee to support this key component of his concept. The interior decoration of Trinity is one of the great bargains in American visual culture. The building committee insisted that it be executed quickly and cheaply. La Farge undertook the project for a paltry $8,000 and completed the initial scheme within less than five months, executing the painted ornamentation and murals in winter in an unheated building and using the contractor's scaffolding. Although a small number of earlier Protestant churches had interior mural decoration, the scheme for Trinity was especially lavish and consistent. In addition to the geometric stenciling of the trefoil vaults over the nave and transepts and the walls of those spaces, La Farge and a team of talented artists (including the sculptor Augustus Saint-Gaudens) executed the monumental figures of the prophets, evangelists, and angels with banners on the walls of the crossing tower. He also painted in encaustic, a wax-based paint with a luminous surface, the scenes of *Christ Visiting Nicodemus* and *Christ with the Woman of Samaria* in the spaces between the balcony windows of the nave. The wall decoration beyond these set pieces equally demands attention: for example, La Farge converted the flat plaster walls of the interior into three-dimensional plasticity with the simulation of vaulting ornament around the balcony arcade of the nave.

The interior decoration of Trinity Church was immediately and expansively celebrated in the contemporary press as a new stage of cultural achievement in this country, a collaboration of architect and artist to produce a visually richer environment. Trinity set a new standard for the integration of all the arts—architecture, painting, sculpture, and stained glass—which later public buildings (such as the Boston Public Library on the opposite side of Copley Square) would seek to emulate and equal. The decorative painting of Trinity also inspired the novel *Esther* (1884), published by the historian Henry Adams under a feminine pseudonym, a love story in which religious faith is the obstacle to happiness. Charles Vandesee meticulously unpacks the thinly veiled portraits of Phillips Brooks, John La Farge, and Adams's wife, Clover, who provided the inspiration for the novel.

Turning from painted decoration to stained glass, one finds that the driving force initially can be credited to Phillips Brooks and Richardson, who set the program and character of this important component. They shared a desire for a colorful church and for the potential of stained glass to instruct and inspire congregants and visitors. We need to remind ourselves of just how extensive Trinity's stained glass collection (and I use that term in the sense of an art museum's holdings) actually is. The church and its parishioners commissioned twenty-two major and fifty smaller stained glass windows between the late 1870s and the late 1920s. Brooks traveled to London in the summer of 1874 to tour the principal English stained glass studios. He came away with an enthusiasm for the work of Clayton & Bell, and the church commissioned that firm to design the windows that fill the chancel—the only stained glass in place at the time of the dedication in February 1877. Perhaps the more important English windows are the ones designed by Pre-Raphaelite artist Edward Burne-Jones and executed by William Morris & Company—leaders of the English Arts and Crafts movement—in the upper level of the south transept and in the baptistry. La Farge also used Trinity as a launching pad for his own experiments in stained glass. As explained by Virginia Raguin in this volume, La Farge had hoped to install grisaille glass that would be sympathetic with his mural decoration; the wishes of individual donors, however, led to a more diverse collection of stained glass ornamentation. When commissioned to add his own windows to the church, La Farge experimented with opalescent glass as seen in his masterpiece *Christ in Majesty,* triple lancet windows in the west balcony. The shimmering and ethereal quality of opalescent jewel clusters in these intense blue panels must be the delight of any visitor to the Trinity pulpit. La Farge added four narrative windows, which are interspersed with the work of other English and American designers around the upper levels of the nave and transepts and in the parish house. In dramatic contrast to the red and green tones of many of the early windows are the cool blue, white, and gold hues of the dominant windows in the south transept, the work of the French artist Eugène Oudinot and given by a Trinity parishioner who "abominated" English glass. If they settle less easily into the otherwise uniform stained glass spectrum of the church, they nevertheless connect Trinity to major international trends at the end of the nineteenth century. Added to this catalogue of significant stained glass are the windows by Boston designers, especially women artists—Margaret Redmond in the nave aisle windows, and Sarah Wyman Whitman in the parish house. Erica Hirshler's essay assesses the work and the context for these women artists. And remember that the parish house has been as richly ornamented as the church with important stained glass, although these windows have often been hidden or neglected through subsequent renovations of that space.

Finally, there is Trinity's role beyond service to the parish: the importance this building holds for the larger world. The *American Architect and Building News,* the country's first architectural periodical, began publication in Boston in 1876. In June 1885 the journal conducted a poll of its readers to determine the best examples of architecture in the United States. One hundred and seventy-five buildings were nominated, fifty-six of which received more than one vote. Of the ten buildings receiving the highest number of votes, H. H. Richardson designed five, with Trinity Church as the undisputed favorite. More than a century later, Trinity Church was the only building from that original list that was ranked by the American Institute of Architects among the ten finest buildings in this country.

A second litmus test for American architecture appeared the year following the

*American Architect* listing. André Daly fils et Companie in Paris published *L'Architecture Américaine,* a collection of 120 large-format photographs of recent architecture in the United States and the first significant indication of an emerging European interest in American buildings. Not surprisingly, Trinity Church is prominently included in this selection, as are many other buildings by Richardson, including those that were listed in the 1885 poll. Sadly, the most dramatic event in establishing the international reputation of Richardson and the church was the architect's premature death in 1886. The international press suddenly recognized that one of the great designers of the nineteenth century had died before they had awakened to his talents. Trinity Church was uniformly singled out as the most significant of his projects and the turningpoint in his career. Foreign journalists began to speak of "the American style" or the "modern Romanesque" as a major new statement in architectural evolution, pointing to this building as the finest example of this ideal.

When Philips Brooks also died prematurely in 1893, two years after leaving Trinity to serve as the Episcopal bishop of Massachusetts, his death returned the church to international attention. James Bryce, the English politician and historian, remarked that "possibly no man in the United States since President Lincoln, has been so warmly admired or so deeply mourned." And Brooks's funeral, held both within Trinity and on Copley Square, closed the Boston Stock Exchange and brought the city to a halt.

On a national level, Trinity held the same importance for the career of John La Farge. He gained a broad reputation as a mural painter and stained glass artist from his work at Trinity. And the church remained a magnet for significant projects by other key visual artists, such as the statues of Brooks by Augustus Saint-Gaudens and by Daniel Chester French, the leading American sculptors of their generation.

Not only did Trinity's design evolve between 1872 and 1877, but the Trinity Church that was dedicated in the winter of 1877 was not the same building in which one worships today. Ideally, all buildings are organic. They grow and change through time. They require use and nurture, without which they can die. This vital structure has significantly evolved over the past century and a quarter and will continue to change to meet the expanding needs of the parish. When you enter Trinity from Copley Square, you pass through a deep porch fronted by an impressive sculptural program of religious imagery. Although Richardson envisioned a projecting porch, the actual space was created in 1897 by Shepley, Rutan & Coolidge, the successor firm to Richardson's practice, which continued to serve the needs of this parish for half a century. Similarly, the richly sculptural pulpit was designed in 1916 by Charles Coolidge of the Shepley firm and executed by

John Evans. The children of Robert Treat Paine gave it as a memorial to their father in remembrance of his love for this building.

Within the sanctuary the most significant change occurred in 1937, when a competition was held to redesign the chancel. The blind competition was won by Maginnis & Walsh, the leading Roman Catholic church architects in the country. Thus, two key figures in the interior decoration of Trinity—John La Farge and Charles Maginnis—were both Roman Catholics. Milda Richardson explains the significant role of the Trinity chancel design in Maginnis's career. He replaced the more restrained space and decoration of the original with a vibrant focus that is both respectful of the earlier building and honestly reflective of architectural ideals in the 1930s. The green marble walls at the base are enriched by incised and gilded decoration that hints at the geometric ornamentation typical of the Art Deco period. Above, the gold to green to red stenciled decoration repeats the basic intention of Richardson's and La Farge's program for the church but leaves no doubt about where our eyes and our minds should be focused during services. Together, the massive, suspended, wooden gilded cross and the white marble altar inlaid with a mosaic design of golden tesserae provide a magnet for our attention.

Since the period of the Depression, however, relatively little has been changed in this complex except for the unfortunate removal of Richardson's massive corona, which lighted the sanctuary. The parish house was modernized in 1952 to accommodate the changing educational, administrative, and social needs of the parish—changes that did little to enhance the original character of that building and that are now woefully inadequate for the needs of the parish. After celebrating the 125th anniversary of the building of Trinity Church, the parish needs to embrace the challenges that this building represents: to maintain that inheritance and to let the structure continue to evolve in response to contemporary needs. And, indeed, Goody Clancy & Associates now supervise exciting plans for both the restoration of the tower and many of the stained glass windows and for the creation of expansive new space at the basement level for meetings, lectures, and other work of the church.

The Reverend Samuel T. Lloyd III, the current rector, often refers to Trinity as Boston's cathedral. Certainly the power and the beauty of the building create a ministry of welcome and of inspiration that actively contributes to all that goes on within. Brooks, Richardson, La Farge, Norcross, Paine, and many, many others shared and realized a dynamic vision for what this church could be. The current generation of parishioners must now embrace this gift to the parish and to the world and thus join the ranks of the Makers of Trinity Church.

# 1

## Trinity Church at 125

THEODORE E. STEBBINS JR.

I HAVE BEEN THINKING LATELY about turning points in history, about economic or social or scientific revolutions, battles won and lost, or terrible events like the attacks on the World Trade Center and Pentagon of September 11, 2001. But I have come to realize that great works of art may themselves be turning points and that they may be more important in the long run than all the political and other crises. What do we remember, after all, of the changing regimes or wars in ancient Greece or China or Egypt? What we know best of these civilizations comes from their art and their architecture. A magnificent painting, novel, or play, a piece of music, or even a building can appear unexpectedly, overshadowing its contemporaries, drawing on the past while pointing to the future, marking a moment in time. Life so often seems to be a theater of the absurd, but then along comes something—often, a work of art—that helps us feel grounded again. Trinity Church is such a work. It has been called a masterpiece, but that overused term doesn't do justice to the significance and the beauty of this place, or the role it has played, and continues to play, in people's lives.

To attempt that, we need to examine not only the architecture and decoration of this majestic structure but the ambitious young men who built it and the culture that produced it.

On July 4, 1876, Boston's attention would have been not on the nearly completed Trinity but on widespread celebrations of the nation's centennial, the one hundredth anniversary of the Declaration of Independence with its promise of equality and freedom for all. It was the period when the country, with all its virtues and all its faults, matured and when modern America was born. Boston and the nation were booming. The first great American world's fair was under way in Philadelphia. Since 1869 the nation had been unified by rail. A huge expansion of the railroads, together with the Homestead Act, led to the settlement of the West. The rapid industrialization across the North made necessary by the Civil War, combined with efficient farming, had by the end of the war made the United States the wealthiest nation on earth.

But the 1870s were also a contradictory time. As the West was settled, the Native Americans were being systematically displaced and destroyed. Reconstruction had been a failure, and the former slaves continued to live in conditions of poverty and prejudice. Immigrants pouring in from Ireland (who made up a third of Boston's population by 1876) were despised because they were poor, uneducated, and Roman Catholic. After eight years of the Grant administration, corruption and scandal were everywhere in the government and on Wall Street. As Walt Whitman wrote in 1871, "Society, in these States, is cankered, crude, superstitious and rotten."[1]

Yet it was the same poet, perhaps America's most eloquent voice, who also proclaimed, "Any period one nation must lead/One land must be the promise and reliance of the future."[2]

In all of our history it would be hard to match the group of extraordinarily creative talents that sprang up from the troubled yet fertile soil of the 1860s and 1870s. Thomas Eakins of Philadelphia in 1875 produced his *Clinic of Dr. Gross,* perhaps the most powerful of American paintings. Its muscularity and pyramidal composition remind one of a Trinity Church in paint. Winslow Homer (from Cambridge), James Whistler, John Singer Sargent, Mary Cassatt, and many other outstanding painters were all at work in this decade. In the same years, Richardson's friend Frederick Law Olmsted pioneered the American park system and became our greatest practitioner of landscape design. Two major writers, Mark Twain and Henry James, were both at work, and Twain's book *The Gilded Age* gave a name to the era. It was an age of giants, and America was ready to support them.

During the 1870s the nation grew more sophisticated; travel to Europe became easier because of the steamships; and Americans began to lose some of their fear of the arts, some of their traditional mistrust of the senses and the sensuous (though one should add that this battle is not yet won). In 1874, Harvard became the first university in the nation to teach the history of art, and in 1876, William James opened his pioneering laboratory in psychology at the same institution. This was the time when the Metropolitan Museum in New York, the Museum of Fine Arts in Boston, and many other significant cultural institutions were founded. The MFA's brand-new Venetian Gothic building next door to Trinity, on the site of the present Copley Plaza Hotel, opened on July 3, 1876.

The Age of Sail was being supplanted by the Age of Steam, but Boston— though slow to give up the clipper ship—still prospered in the 1870s as the nation's second largest seaport. From a small merchant city it had become a great industrial center, with its abundance of capital and a large labor pool. It was a leader in the manufacture of iron, textiles, shoes, clothing, watches, and pianos, and its railroads provided efficient links to all of New England and to the West.

A perfect exemplar of the new Boston was Robert Treat Paine, head of Trinity's building committee. He graduated from Harvard in 1855 along with his great friend Phillips Brooks. Paine had deep Boston roots, as a great-grandson of a signer of the Declaration of Independence. He was a lawyer who had made a fortune in real estate, railroads, and copper mining sufficient for him to retire in 1870, at the age of thirty-five. He devoted the rest of his life to good works—with a special interest in the welfare and housing of working people—and to Trinity.

Boston's leading writer of the time was William Dean Howells, who devoted *The Rise of Silas Lapham* to the adventures of Colonel Lapham, a newly wealthy paint merchant who moves to the newly fashionable Back Bay. Architecture and architects were much on his mind, as they were on the minds of the Trinity family. On one occasion, the colonel recounts his problems with his architect to his future son-in-law: "I started out to build a forty-thousand dollar house. Well sir! that fellow has got me in for sixty thousand already, and I doubt if I get out of it much under a hundred. You can't have a nice house for nothing. It's just like ordering a picture of a painter. You pay him enough, and he can afford to paint you a first-class picture; if you don't, he can't."[3] The Trinity building committee faced similar problems, though with more sophistication than the good colonel.

Earlier American artists had trained in England and Germany, but this generation turned to France instead. For the next century, Americans regarded Paris as the center of the art world, as the essential place for a young architect or painter to study. Winslow, Homer, Eakins, Cassatt, and Whistler all went, as did the architects, beginning with Richard Morris Hunt. When the wealthy young southerner Henry Hobson Richardson graduated from Harvard in 1859 and decided on architecture as a career, he too naturally traveled to Paris to study. Richardson's technique, for the rest of his life, reflected the systematic methods he learned at the Ecole des Beaux-Arts, and his buildings demonstrate his love of French architecture, especially the Romanesque churches of central and southern France. This same American taste for all things French led within a few years to the unrivaled collection of the work of Monet and the French Impressionists at the Museum of Fine Arts.

It is well known that Trinity, in 1869, elected Phillips Brooks rector. Brooks was a Boston native who, after a term in Philadelphia, served Trinity for twenty-two years before becoming bishop of Massachusetts in 1891, two years before his death. He was widely regarded as the greatest preacher of his era; the church's decision to move was made in order to create a suitable new space for the preaching of Brooks. A Back Bay lot was purchased, and in March 1872 a building committee was formed. Six architects, including Richardson, competed for the job of designing a new church by submitting drawings and plans. Richardson, of course, was selected, and we wonder how this happened. In later years, even he professed amazement that it had, for his competition design was undistinguished. It featured a long nave and a high and ungainly octagonal tower; there was no inkling of the powerful massing that one finds in the church that was eventually built. At the same time, Richardson's design was probably no worse than the others, for American architecture in these years was at a low ebb. Even Mariana Van Renssalaer, Richardson's first biographer, described his work prior to Trinity as "nondescript." The one possible bright spot was his design two years earlier for the Brattle Square Church (now the First Baptist Church) at the corner of Commonwealth Avenue and Clarendon Street, just two blocks from the new Trinity site. That building is best known for its tall tower with a sculptural frieze by Frédéric Bartholdi, who later became famous for the Statue of Liberty. Brattle Square nevertheless proved a disaster, with terrible acoustics and major cost overruns that drove the parish into bankruptcy in 1876. Fortunately for Richardson, it was still incomplete in 1872 when Trinity was choosing an architect. Had it been finished by then and its problems known, it is unlikely that Richardson would have received his great opportunity at Trinity. As we all know, luck plays a role in history.

Still, one wonders why he was selected. Probably the Trinity building committee made its selection the way we all are likely to do when faced with hiring professionals in fields outside their own, that is, people are generally swayed by charm, character, and connections—and these were Richardson's long suits. The young architect was tall, handsome, and well mannered. The loss of the family fortune during the Civil War had had no outward effect on him, and he was said to carry himself in good times and bad with "an indescribable air of ease."[4] He had married an attractive and well-connected Bostonian, Julia Hayden. Moreover, the thirty-four-year-old possessed one great advantage over the other candidates: as a popular Harvard undergraduate he had been a member of several clubs, including the prestigious Porcellian; thus he needed no introduction to the rector, Phillips Brooks, or five of the eleven-man building committee—they were all fellow Porcellian members.

Before work began on the new property, the church bought the adjoining triangle of land where the parish house now stands, and Richardson quickly saw the great opportunities the enlarged site offered for a graceful, asymmetrical building, one whose superb location gave it the potential of becoming Boston's de facto cathedral.

Once Richardson had the commission, however, the old-boy network could no longer help him. What was needed now was a huge, flexible talent, the gift of being able to grow almost overnight. The Trinity we know today resulted from two years of engineering disputes, design debates, and high friction involving the architect, the rector, the contractor, and the building committee. Richardson's plans were redrawn, rejected, then redrawn again. The low estimate for construction came in from O. W. Norcross of Worcester, but it was for $355,000, as compared to the budget of $200,000. Another delay followed. Then the engineers reported that the architect's tall, octagonal tower would be unsafe. Thus, two years after winning the competition, Richardson was forced to prepare entirely new plans. By this point, tensions were running high between committee, builder, and architect, with Richardson at one point comparing Paine and his colleagues to England's infamous Star Chamber. Cancellation of the whole project became a possibility. Out of this crucible, miraculously, came the building we have today. Richardson somehow hit on the solution of a great square tower, inspired by the Old Cathedral at Salamanca, Spain. In the process, he invented Richardsonian Romanesque, the strong, round-arched building style in stone that quickly came to dominate American architecture. Even today, through all of Boston's suburbs one comes across churches, libraries, railway stations, and even the occasional home in Richardson's version of Romanesque.

I should add that once the new church was up, all the acrimony was quickly forgotten. We know this not only from the records but because Trinity just two years later turned to Richardson again for the design of the superb brick rectory, just a block away on Newbury Street. He later designed a country house for Mr. Paine, and he and Norcross went on to collaborate on numerous projects.

Richardson wrote that his new style "might be characterized as a free rendering of the French Romanesque."[5] Indeed, he drew not only on the Auvergne in central France but also on the south of France, on the twelfth-century porch at St. Trophime with its fine sculpted figures, and on the famous west front at St. Gilles with its three beautifully spaced doorways with round arches. He drew inspiration also from Spain as we've seen, and from English and German churches as well. But he did so freely and not derivatively, in the same spirit as that of Winslow Homer admiring Jean Millet, or Eakins and his love of Velazquez. No one from the eleventh or twelfth century would ever mistake Trinity for an old Romanesque church.

The massing of the forms, the extraordinary setting-off of the parish house, the perfect, seemingly inevitable placement of every window and every detail, the rough-hewn exterior stonework with walls of pale Dedham granite and trim of darker East Longmeadow sandstone, the invention of new kinds of tall, rounded arches, the replacing of the typical dome of a Romanesque church with a square tower, and the roof of orange tiles—all these were Richardson's, and his alone. As

Douglass Shand-Tucci observed of Trinity, this was "an American architecture that was the master, not the servant, of its sources: a building couched in terms of a venerable style, but a style suffused with a new vitality and power."[6] Walt Whitman had foreseen all this when he wrote:

> *Ages, precedents, have long been accumulating undirected materials,*
> *America brings builders, and brings its own styles.*
> *The immortal poets of Asia and Europe have done their work and passed to*
> *    other spheres.*
> *A work remains, the work of surpassing all they have done.*[7]

As the building neared completion during the summer of 1876, attention turned to its interior. Richardson designed the pews, and T. B. Wentworth of Osborn's Mill was contracted to make them for $18.50 each. O. W. Perry made a huge wrought iron chandelier that hung over the crossing, which, sadly, was removed many years ago.

Most important, Richardson, aided by Phillips Brooks, now argued for money and time in order to have the interior richly painted and decorated. The pressure against them must have been enormous: the parish had been homeless ever since its earlier church burned down in the Boston fire of 1872, and the project was over budget. Fortunately, rector and architect prevailed, and on September 15 the church hired John La Farge to decorate the entire interior in four months' time! He was paid $8,000, which included materials and pay for all his helpers. Richardson and Brooks had always conceived of Trinity as a color church, with Pompeian red, or "old rose," dominating, and they may well have had La Farge in mind from the beginning. In any case, the painter immediately gathered together a group of Boston's best young artists, who worked night and day throughout the cold months of that fall and winter to produce the extraordinary interior we see today. They finished their work on February 1, 1877; two days later the scaffolding came down, and the building was consecrated the next week, on February 9.

When we leave Trinity, what most of us remember is the interior, which is La Farge's. There is nothing Romanesque about it; instead, the huge square spaces remind us of the early Christian basilicas of Rome. Richardson provided an extraordinary blank canvas for the painters to work on in the symmetry of the great tower, which rises one hundred feet above us, the massive round arches and the four huge columns, the semicircular apse, and the short transepts and nave of the Greek cross design. Still, everything was bare when La Farge and his crew began. He deserves great credit as coauthor of the building.

La Farge himself was an aristocrat, the son of wealthy French émigrés, and a Roman Catholic; he was sophisticated, well traveled, and wholly versed in the art of the past. His intellect and his fluency in every medium were dazzling. He worked as an illustrator, watercolorist, painter, and engraver; he became a pioneer muralist and stained glass maker; and he was a poet, historian, and essayist besides. Though a New Yorker, he was already well known in Boston and a friend of the architect. But when he began his work at Trinity, there was no American precedent to rely on. As the nineteenth-century historian Henry Adams wrote, La Farge took Richardson's "solid, massive and unmodulated spaces" and through his art made them seem airy, unsubstantial, and multifaceted.[8] To a public used to the bare white interiors of Colonial churches or the cold stone surfaces of the nineteenth-century Gothic style, La Farge opened up a whole new realm of experience. For Trinity, he drew on the decoration of early Christian churches, on Venice and the Byzantine world, on medieval crafts, on Arabia, Egypt, and the Italian Renaissance. The result is what James F. O'Gorman called "a rainbow of different natural materials brought from around the world": Scottish granite columns supporting the arches, gilt-leather upper walls, oak timbering, imitation mosaic and jeweled crosses.[9] We see the gold-leafed Egyptian-style bases on the clustered columns, decorative Near Eastern arches at the sides of the nave, and a complex of interwoven, stylized floral patterns and astrological symbols on the farthest reaches of the ceiling. These American painters, like the architect, felt confident enough to take whatever they wanted from world art and make it their own.

The youthful painters executed La Farge's compositions directly on the walls, following ancient techniques. They worked in dangerous conditions on very high scaffolds in an unheated building, laboring beside the masons, carpenters, and plasterers who were finishing their own work. They portrayed Saints Peter and Paul high on the east wall, Isaiah and Jeremiah to the north, and David and Moses to the south; these figures are surrounded by representations of Old and New Testament scenes and figures and by biblical quotations. Considering that neither La Farge nor his assistants had painted on this scale or in this manner before, the results are remarkable. What the individual figures occasionally lack in terms of modeling is more than compensated for by the effects of the overall scheme. La Farge himself said, "I knew that our work at Trinity would be faulty, but this much I was able to accomplish—that almost every bit of it would be living."[10]

Times had changed. We recall how John Adams, writing from Versailles a century earlier, had told his wife, "I cannot help suspecting that the more elegance, the less virtue, in all times and countries."[11] The people who built Trinity did not agree; they thought that elegance and virtue went together nicely. This splendid setting with its glowing reds, golds, and greens, where no surface no matter how distant is left unadorned, has been compared to Aladdin's Cave, to the Alhambra, to San Marco in Venice, and to "an Arabian nights fairyland."[12] Yet all the luxuriant colors and materials are used so seamlessly that in the end one remembers not the details but rather the atmosphere of thoughtfulness and reflection, the warmth of the place, the sense of comfort.

Trinity's leaders knew exactly what they were doing. In 1875, Thomas Amory of the vestry wrote the parish, "It is naturally the wish of all of us, in creating for the purposes of public worship a costly structure wherein we hope will endure for ages, to render it as perfect as we can, not only in its special use, but also as a work of art."[13] This was a new idea in America: a building as a work of art both outside and in. Here at Trinity began the period ambitiously known as "the American Renaissance," implying the belief that the young nation could harness the combined talents of architects, mural painters, sculptors, and craftsmen to build structures worthy of a Rome or a Florence. Thus the great Florentine palace that we call the Boston Public Library, designed a decade later by two of Richardson's former assistants, could never have happened without Trinity.

When Henry Adams, a close friend of both Richardson and La Farge who had watched the whole process, described Trinity in his novel *Esther*, he cheerfully reported, "As a display of austerity, the show was a failure." For Adams, the pridefulness of the congregation was a match for the rich decoration: "Huge prophets and evangelists," he wrote, "looked down from the red walls on a display of human vanities that would have called out a vehement Lamentation of Jeremiah or Song of Solomon, had these poets been present in flesh as they were in figure."[14] But I should add that when Phillips Brooks's friend Dr. A. H. Vinton preached at the consecration services of February 9, 1877, he took as his text Revelation 21:22: "I saw no temple therein; for the Lord God Almighty and the Lamb are the temple thereof."[15] Perhaps this was his way of suggesting that people's pride in the great building be balanced with humility.

When the church was consecrated in 1877, only the seven rather conventional stained glass windows in the chancel, by the English firm of Clayton & Bell, had been installed; the rest were filled temporarily with clear or grisaille glass. But a call for donors was highly successful, and within a decade or so, all the other windows had been commissioned and installed, giving Trinity a virtual survey of the best stained glass of the era (except for that of La Farge's archrival, Louis Comfort Tiffany). Equally beautiful are the highly realistic windows in the south transept by Eugène Oudinot of Paris and the quite abstract foliate ones in the north, which were designed by Edward Burne-Jones—one of the most important English Pre-Raphaelite painters—and executed by the famous firm of William Morris &

Company in London. The unquestioned artistic-masterworks inside the church, however, are the four windows by La Farge himself. He had taken up stained glass only in 1875, when almost nothing of the tradition existed in the United States. Within a few years, he had invented a new glassmaking technology and had virtually reinvented the art. Innovative use of opalescent glass enabled La Farge to solve the great problem in this medium: how to create both brilliant colors and effective space and modeling in glass.

La Farge's masterpiece in any medium, to my eyes, is his extraordinary *Christ in Majesty,* the three-part window installed in 1883, high on the west end of the church, which during services is visible only to the preacher. The figure of Christ, his right hand raised in benediction, was inspired by the famous thirteenth-century sculpture on the central portal of Amiens Cathedral. The amazing blue-green background behind the figure and in the windows on either side evokes the mosaics of Ravenna; it was created through the use of individual, round nuggets of glass, each larger than a golf ball. The greatest French critic of the day wrote that this work's "astonishing brilliance surpasses, in its magic, anything of its kind in modern times."[16] Almost equally fantastic are La Farge's *Resurrection* window in the north transept, which has been cleaned in recent years, and his *New Jerusalem* window beside it, which has not. La Farge himself defined stained glass as "the art of painting in air with a material carrying colored light."[17] It is an art that can be seen supremely well at Trinity.

What is Trinity? One writer called it "the most original, the most poetic, and the most expressive church yet built in the United States."[18] James O'Gorman summed it up by saying, "Trinity represented American culture's coming of age."[19] We must remember that it was built by young men: Paine, Brooks, and La Farge were thirty-seven when it was begun; the architect was thirty-four, and the builder, O. W. Norcross, just thirty-three. In its rough, random ashlar, polychrome walls, in the powerful pyramid they form, in the calm, reflective, and luxurious interior, the church symbolizes the wealth and power and energy of the culture. It gives evidence of its builders' ambition and their confidence in themselves, in Boston, and in America. But it speaks also of the builders' faith, of their belief in the arts and the life of the mind. As these men worked here, they revolutionized American architecture just as surely as Homer, Eakins, Sargent, and Whistler at this time were remaking American painting, just as La Farge would remake stained glass, and as Saint-Gaudens—one of La Farge's assistants here—would bring new life to American sculpture.

Trinity today is much as Phillips Brooks knew it, though there have been changes, as this is a living building and not a museum. The richly carved porch, based largely on Richardson's designs, was completed only in 1897. A new pulpit in 1916 replaced the desk from which Brooks preached (without the aid of a sound system, one must add), though the eagle lectern, I should point out, was here from the very beginning. Finally, the chancel in 1937–38 was redecorated in an art deco manner with a green marble wall, relief sculptures in gold above, and a new marble communion rail and altar.

Each of the five primary builders, Brooks, Paine, Norcross, La Farge, and Richardson, went on to a highly successful career based at least in part on the extraordinary results they had achieved together at Trinity. In the decade left to him, Richardson came to dominate American architecture, and he prepared the way for the future: for Louis Sullivan, who watched Trinity as it was erected, and even for Frank Lloyd Wright. Some of Richardson's buildings, such as Sever Hall at Harvard or the Gate Lodge at North Easton, may be more polished and more nearly perfect than Trinity Church. But in the end, nothing he ever did was as powerful or influential, or has been as much loved, as this building.

Richardson himself died at the height of his success in 1886. He died insolvent, for he had always been reckless financially. He had huge appetites, even by Victorian standards, and he weighed 345 pounds at his death. People described him, as they describe many of us, in contradictory terms. One client reported, "He bullies and nags everybody; makes great demands upon our time and service" and is "a great deal of trouble."[20] But another, Frederick Law Olmsted, described the "eager, unselfish, and really vital interest" that Richardson took in other people and called him "the greatest comfort and most potent stimulus that has ever come into my artistic life."[21]

In the end, we remember him for his work, and his work here, in collaboration with La Farge and the others, was magnificent. Despite all the changes of taste and culture that have occurred since it was built, Trinity is still hugely admired. In the 1880s it was voted America's outstanding building. During the 1950s it was still thought to rank among the top six. For me, it stands as the greatest building in Boston—rivaled only by the Boston Public Library across Copley Square—and in the highest rank nationally. I believe that its only peers from across America are a handful of extraordinary houses—including Jefferson's Monticello, Frank Lloyd Wright's Falling Water, and Philip Johnson's Glass House—along with a small group of sublime public structures: the U.S. Capitol, Saarinen's Arch at St Louis, Louis Kahn's Kimbell Museum in Fort Worth, and Rockefeller Center in New York.

But finally, let us ask, how much does this matter? How can we pause to celebrate art in the troubled early years of the twenty-first century? I would say, how can we not? We remember that Londoners took faith every morning when they woke up to find St. Paul's miraculously still standing after the nightly bombing. And we recall Shakespeare asking the same question:

*Since brass, nor stone, nor earth, nor boundless sea,*
*But sad mortality o'ersways their power,*
*How with this rage shall beauty hold a plea,*
*Whose action is no stronger than a flower?* [22]

How with this rage shall beauty hold a plea?

## NOTES

1. Walt Whitman, "Democratic Vistas," in *Walt Whitman: Complete Poetry and Collected Prose* (New York: Library of America, 1982), 937.

2. Walt Whitman, "By Blue Ontario's Shore," in ibid., 471.

3. William Dean Howells, *The Rise of Silas Lapham* (1885; New York: Modern Library, 1951), 48.

4. James F. O'Gorman, *H. H. Richardson: Architectural Forms for an American Society* (Chicago: University of Chicago Press, 1987), 15.

5. "Description of the Church by H. H. Richardson, Architect," in *Consecration Services of Trinity Church, Boston, February 9, 1877* (Boston: Trinity Church, 1877), 13.

6. Douglass Shand-Tucci, *Built in Boston: City and Suburb, 1800–1950* (Boston: New York Graphic Society, 1978), 56.

7. Whitman, "By Blue Ontario's Shore," 470–71.

8. Henry Adams, "The Mind of John La Farge," in Henry Adams et al., eds., *John La Farge* (New York: Abbeville Press, 1987), 39.

9. O'Gorman, *H. H. Richardson: Architectural Forms,* 55–69.

10. John La Farge, quoted in Adams, "Mind of John La Farge," 39.

11. John Adams to Abigail Adams, April 12, 1778, in Charles Francis Adams, *Familiar Letters of John Adams and His Wife Abigail Adams, during the Revolution* (Boston: Houghton Mifflin, 1876), 329.

12. Adams, "Mind of John La Farge," 37.

13. Thomas C. Amory, "Trinity Church Memorial Windows, 1875," in *Trinity Church in the City of Boston,* ed. Arthur C. Chester (Cambridge, Mass.: John Wilson & Son, 1888), 73.

14. Henry Adams, *Esther,* in *Democracy, and Esther: Two Novels by Henry Adams* (Garden City, N.Y.: Doubleday, 1961).

15. *Consecration Services of Trinity Church, Boston, February 9, 1877* (Boston: Trinity Church, 1877), with the consecration sermon by Rev. A. H. Vinton, D.D., a historical sermon by Rev. Phillips Brooks, and a description of the church edifice by H. H. Richardson, architect.

16. Samuel Bing, *La Culture artistique en Amérique* (1895), quoted in Henry A. La Farge, "Painting with Colored Light: The Stained Glass of John La Farge," in Adams et al., *John La Farge,* 210.

17. John La Farge, quoted in Henry A. La Farge, "Painting."

18. William H. Pierson Jr., "Richardson's Trinity Church and the New England Meeting House," in *American Public Architecture: European Roots and Native Expressions,* ed. Craig Zabel and Susan Scott Munshower (University Park: Pennsylvania State University, 1989), 13.

19. O'Gorman, *H. H. Richardson: Architectural Forms,* 55.

20. Quoted in *ibid.,* 25.

21. Quoted in Mariana Griswold Van Rensselaer, *Henry Hobson Richardson and His Works* (Boston: Houghton Mifflin, 1888), 40.

22. William Shakespeare, Sonnet 65.

2-1. Phillips Brooks (1835–1893), ca. 1885. (Courtesy of The Archives of the Episcopal Church USA).

# 2

## Client: Phillips Brooks

DAVID B. CHESEBROUGH

Sydney E. Ahlstrom, the eminent historian of American religion, labeled Phillips Brooks and Henry Ward Beecher "the princes of the pulpit" during the nineteenth century, two men who "were in a class by themselves, envied and emulated the country over."[1] Phillips Brooks (fig. 2-1 and pl. 12), with an ancestry rooted in prominent seventeenth-century Puritanism on both his paternal and maternal sides, was educated at the Boston Latin School, Harvard, and the Virginia Theological Seminary. He received honorary doctorates from Harvard and Oxford Universities. His first two parishes were in Philadelphia (1859–69). His sojourn in that city was marked by his writing of the beloved Christmas carol "O Little Town of Bethlehem" and the delivery of his most famous sermon, "Abraham Lincoln," written upon the death of the sixteenth president. From 1869 to 1891 he served as rector of Boston's Trinity Church, his most productive and influential years. For the final fifteen months of his life, Brooks was the bishop of Massachusetts, a term that ended abruptly with his untimely death in 1893 (probably due to diphtheria) at fifty-seven years of age.

Two months after the consecration of the new Trinity Church in February 1877, the church's proprietors wrote a letter to their rector wherein they acknowledged and expressed their appreciation for his primary role in the construction of the magnificent edifice. "We cannot let this great epoch in the life of our ancient Parish pass," they wrote, "without placing on permanent record our sense of the deep obligations of us and our whole people to our beloved Rector, Mr. Brooks." The proprietors cited the building committee's report that during the five-year building project, "his taste and culture, his zeal and patience and faith have largely aided in the great result; that to him in large measure is due the beauty and the glory of the new Church; that he has been himself the inspiration of the Architect, Builders, and Committee."[2]

Phillips Brooks began his Boston ministry at the early nineteenth-century Trinity Church in late October of 1869. Three years later, on November 11, 1872, a fire destroyed that building and much of the surrounding area. The parish had already been planning to relocate and had purchased property in the fashionable Back Bay area a year before the fire. The evidence is clear that Brooks was instrumental in the selection of the site at Clarendon Street and St. James Avenue. His name was not listed on the roll of the building committee, but as in many ecclesiastical organizations, the pastor is an ex officio member on all committees of the church, and Brooks proved to be far more than an unofficial appendage. He was the committee's guiding light and its inspiration, his fingerprints everywhere to be found upon the structure. A biographer of Brooks has written: "From the very beginning the preacher impressed himself upon the building in which his words were most frequently to be heard . . . and it were well for all who look upon the finished structure to realize how largely the living personality of Phillips Brooks concerned itself with every detail of the building, from the preliminary drawings of the architect to the final interior decorations of his other friend, Mr. John La Farge."[3]

One of the first tasks of the building committee was the selection of an architect. On March 12, 1872, the committee sent an invitation to six architectural firms to participate in the competition for the designing of Trinity Church. On June 1 the committee selected the young architect Henry Hobson Richardson. The evidence again indicates that Richardson was Brooks's choice from the beginning. The two men had met at the pastor's residence two weeks after the March 12 invitations; as nearly as can be determined, none of the other competitors was awarded a similar privilege. At this meeting, apparently, Brooks told Richardson what he envisioned in a church structure, and not surprisingly, therefore, Richardson's competitive design most closely resembled the dream of the renowned rector: Romanesque rather than Gothic, an octagonal tower rather than a spire, and a somewhat boxy sanctuary conducive to preaching.[4]

The two men were different in many ways, but their talents and personalities complemented each other. Alexander Allen, the first serious compiler and editor of Brooks's papers, has noted: "It was impossible to bring together two such personalities as Richardson and Phillips Brooks without something great and unique as the product of their joint discourse. Mr. Richardson was not a man with ecclesiastical convictions, who endeavored to turn his religious musings into architectural expression, but endowed with a rich and generous nature, who appreciated the large-hearted rector of Trinity and responded to his suggestions. Mr.

Brooks was not an architect, but he came near being one." Allen further observed that when Brooks had traveled in Europe, he visited historic churches wherever he went, "and by his intelligent interest in the subject had prepared himself for the tuition which Richardson could give." As to style, Allen emphasized that Brooks "was clear, that the first condition was to break away from the so-called Gothic style, whose introduction into England and America, following in the wake of the Oxford Movement, was owing in a measure to the attempted return to medieval religion which had characterized the Anglican Church for the last generation."[5]

In his journeys to England and western Europe, Brooks had observed the Gothic architecture of the late Middle Ages, characterized by pointed arches, rib vaulting, and flying buttresses. For Trinity's rector, such a style was too ecclesiastical and gave the impression of creating too great a line of demarcation between the church and the world, between the clergy and the laity, and between the sacred and the secular. Brooks advocated a more inclusive theology where barriers, as much as possible, were broken down. In one sermon he spoke of this comprehensive theology: "We are all God's children, whether the best or the worst of us, those who are living the most upright lives, as well as those the most profligate, are all Christ's children. . . . Men are commonly preached to that they are a great deal wickeder than they are, that they must not set so high worth upon humanity. I tell you we want another kind of preaching along with that. There is in every man something greater than he has begun to dream of. Men are nobler than they think themselves."[6]

With his inclusive theology, marked by the idea that "we are all God's children," Brooks sought for an architectural style that would convey such ideals. He found what he wanted in the Romanesque, an architectural style prominent in Europe from the ninth to the twelfth century.[7] Marked by round arches, massive walls, and mosaic ornament, it was a style closer, Brooks thought, to an earlier and more authentic Christianity, a style that was replaced in the latter Middle Ages by the ecclesiastical Gothic. The Romanesque would be revived in Germany in the late 1820s and in the United States during the mid-1840s. The new Trinity Church would not be pure Romanesque, for in reality it was a mixture of several styles, something that James O'Gorman and others have labeled "Richardsonian Romanesque."[8]

Part of the Romanesque style was that instead of Gothic high spires pointing to the heavens above, churches were adorned by shorter towers, often squared off at the top. The concept was important to Brooks because the tower was more earthbound than the otherworldly spire. At Boston's Trinity Church there was little, if any, debate on the subject: a massive central tower would become the dominant exterior feature of the building.[9]

The tower expressed Brooks's theological conviction that ecclesiasticism was not something opposed to or set apart from the world but something that must be integrated into the very nature of existence. The idea that spirituality is not a separate entity of our earthly journey but an essential part of it was expressed in an address that he delivered before the annual Church Congress in 1875, titled "Best Method of Promoting Spiritual Life": "The spiritual life of man in its fullest sense is the activity of man's whole nature under the highest spiritual impulse, which is the love of God. It is not the activity of one set of powers, one part of the nature. It is the movement of all the powers, of the whole of his nature under a certain force and so with a certain completeness and effect."[10]

Theologically, Brooks was a Broad Churchman who tended to stress the one-ness of religious expressions rather than their differences. He was a liberal who was open to various theological perspectives. His Christianity could accommo-date the latest discoveries of science, and he was a student of biblical criticism. He received and accepted many invitations to preach in Baptist, Reformed, Presby-terian, and Unitarian houses of worship. Such inclusiveness caused Brooks some problems and disputes with the more conservative elements of the Episcopal Church, but although the opposition was sometimes loud, it was never great in numbers, and he could usually ignore it. There were times, however, when the criticisms irritated him. Smarting under some recent attacks, he once wrote to his brother William, "a nice free church this is of ours."[11]

His Broad Churchmanship affected Brooks's concepts of architecture and other art forms. His choice of the Romanesque style and of towers rather than spires were attempts to lay sectarian and other differences aside, to restore a more basic Christianity, one with fewer divisions within and fewer boundaries against the outside world and culture. Brooks wanted to disarm society's suspicions of ecclesiasticism.

A part of Brooks's Broad Church view is discovered in his concept of preach-ing as it related to worship. For him, preaching was the central act of worship, the conveying of truth to others through the spoken word. In his renowned "Lectures on Preaching," delivered at Yale in 1877 and subsequently published, Brooks shared his still popular definition: "Preaching," he asserted, "is the communica-tion of truth by man to men."[12] This simple definition has been cited in almost every book on homiletics since the late nineteenth century. True to his ancestral Puritan and evangelical background, the sermon, for Brooks, was the focal point of worship—not the liturgy or the sacraments, as some would have it. John Woolverton has summarized Brooks's position on the centrality of preaching in the worship of God: "He believed the right words, emotionally and intellectually charged, could reach many and change their relationship to God and to each other. . . . The transcendent Other comes to listeners through the artistry of the true preacher. . . . It is the daunting task of the preacher to awaken his auditors to such a reality, to let himself—and now herself—be used as a channel for the reality that brings him to this place."[13] Such a concept of preaching influenced the interior architecture of the house of worship. The boxy sanctuary of the Romanesque style, as opposed to the long and narrow naves of most Gothic churches, brought the worshipers closer to the preacher. It was designed to be free of all obstacles that might prevent the worshipers from seeing and hearing the proclamation of the Word.

Since his preaching drew many outsiders to the church every Sunday, Brooks urged Richardson to design a gallery that would seat at least 350 people. Here would sit those who did not rent pews, the throngs from all walks of life, of varying belief and unbelief, who wanted the experience of listening to a sermon from Phillips Brooks. These gallery seats, writes Curran, were "some of the best seats in the house," sometimes "to the chagrin of those who did pay pew rents."[14] The gallery seats were always filled, and many of the attenders had to stand. A letter to Brooks from a young woman, dated April 8, 1881, described those who were not of the congregation who came to hear the great preacher at Trinity: "I wish you could watch as I do from my pew near the door of Trinity Church, the crowds who come after all the regular congregation are seated, hundreds of young men, Harvard students and many others, who do not mind at all standing up for hours, if they can but hear your words, and people who impress me more than these eager young men even are the crowds of older men and women, looking very weary with the hard struggle of life who come in, and listen with breathless attention, and at last go home, with such a look of rest in their faces."[15]

The emphasis on preaching did not, however, dwarf the administration of the sacraments, though a table rather than an altar symbolized an invitation to all, an effort to diminish ecclesiastical barriers between the sacred and secular, between the chosen few and the rest of humanity. Allen has described the purpose and the place of the Lord's Supper in Brooks's Trinity Church: "Its motive was to represent the idea of Christian communion and fellowship as one great end which the Lord's Supper was designed to promote. In the center of the apse stood the Lord's table,—a table according to the original institution of the feast, not an altar or a sideboard, but a table, whose importance to the Christian imagination was not obscured or dwarfed by other ornament, not even by the chancel windows."[16]

The interior decorations of Trinity Church were truly magnificent. John La Farge, an eminent American artist, was hired to superintend a staff of artists who would paint basically biblical scenes upon the interior walls. For example, the church's nave contained two panels, *Christ Visiting Nicodemus* and *Christ with the Woman of Samaria*. Brooks, inspired by his observations of European churches, chose the subjects of the many murals; La Farge and his assistants carried them out. La Farge was quick to acknowledge the contributions of Brooks, writing to the rector that the internal decorations were "a part of the church so distinctly yours."[17] La Farge began his duties with the intention he would only paint a few pictures on some of the walls. Those first attempts were so captivating, however, that La Farge, Brooks, and Richardson "saw their opportunity to attempt something never before accomplished in America."[18] Murals were painted in luxurious color wherever wall and ceiling space could be found. The only real problem for La Farge was time: twice he was granted extensions, and the work was completed only a few days before the service of consecration.

Trinity was alive with color, red being predominant. It was the favorite color of both Richardson and Brooks, and the two of them brought their love for red into the church. Henry Van Brunt wrote that the "desire of the architect for a red effect was accepted as a starting point." Allen has written that Brooks loved color and "red was his favorite color. . . . [W]hen ordering prayer books and hymnals for Trinity Church, he specified that they must be bound in red."[19]

During the five years of construction between the burning of old Trinity and the move into the new Trinity, the congregation met in Huntington Hall, which they rented from the Massachusetts Institute of Technology. During this sojourn, Brooks delivered a sermon on the relationship between external beauty and the growth of the inner spiritual life. The sermon was in part a justification for the time, effort, and expense of the new building. External beauty had sacramental value because it represented and expressed something internal and spiritual. God, Brooks emphasized, "would rather tempt us with his beauty than bind us with his bands. It is better to be urged on by the inspirations than to be driven with the compulsions of holiness."[20]

The new Trinity Church was consecrated on the evening of Friday, February 9, 1877. It was a glorious moment for the congregation and specifically for its rector. Phillips Brooks had held the congregation solidly together during the construction process, an experience that has too often divided some churches. The vestry acknowledged "how deeply we all feel indebted to him, for holding our parish so firmly united by his devotion to us, through all the dreary interval between our old home on Summer Street and our new church."[21]

It was Brooks who inspired and motivated the congregation to share generously of their finances in order to build the church. It was an expensive undertaking, and the preacher knew how to justify the expense. Upon the completion of the edifice, there was an overrun of $60,000. Once more the rector appealed to his people, and the debt was quickly erased. He led in this regard not just by words but by example, of which the vestry also took note: "We appreciate most deeply his noble generosity in contributing so largely to the treasury of the Parish, and in thus setting an example which was followed by our people so liberally that we have been able to present our church free from debt and consecrated to God. And we accept his gift as one more proof among many of his ardent love to his parish." The vestry further acknowledged Brooks's guiding role in both the exterior style and the interior decoration of the new building. "Trinity Church in his lifetime was popularly known as Phillips Brooks's Church," wrote Allen only a few years after Brooks's death. "There is a sense in which it may be regarded as his monument."[22]

The consecration service that Friday evening was almost as majestic as the building itself. Episcopal bishops from around the nation, adorned in their finest vestments, added to the pageantry. The governor of Massachusetts and the mayor of Boston were among the many honored guests. More than one hundred clergymen, representing various denominations, walked in the procession. Broad Churchmanship at its highest and best was on display. One of the clergymen in the procession was James Freeman Clarke, a prominent liberal Unitarian and a friend of Brooks. Some Unitarians criticized Clarke for participating in the observance of communion, and some conservative Episcopalians denounced Brooks for allowing Clarke to partake of the sacrament. From Philadelphia, an Episcopal clergymen wrote to the bishop of Massachusetts protesting the "admission to Holy Communion of those [specifically Clarke] who avowedly deny and deprave the faith." (Brooks, annoyed by what he perceived as narrow sectarianism, wrote to his brother Arthur, also an Episcopal rector, about the Philadelphia clergyman: "What a pig——seems to be."[23] More people, however, approved Brooks's display of Broad Churchmanship. As one biographer has written: "Because he represented the spirit of liberalism and warm sympathy toward all Christian people, many persons beyond his parish counted him their pastor and personal friend. When he entered the temporary pulpit in Trinity Church the Sunday morning after the consecration service he stood there with a new significance even for his closest friends who could sense in him a new power for right and good."[24]

For Phillips Brooks the new Trinity Church was an expression of what was important in theology. The Romanesque style, he thought, reflected early, authentic Christianity. The tower, in contrast to the spire, signified that the church must be related to the here and now. The boxy sanctuary, without impediment to sight, emphasized the importance of preaching in worship. The communion table, as opposed to an altar, represented an invitation to all to partake of the sacraments. The large gallery was yet another expression of openness. The splash of color, especially red, communicated the joy, passion, and hope of faith. Finally, the biblical murals were an attempt to draw Christianity back to its roots.

## NOTES

1. Sydney E. Ahlstrom, *The Religious History of the American People* (New Haven: Yale University Press, 1972), 740.

2. Stephen G. Deblois, Clerk of the Corporation, to Phillips Brooks, April 4, 1877: Alexander V. G. Allen, *Life and Letters of Phillips Brooks*, 2 vols. (New York: E. P. Dutton, 1900), 2:139. It was not unusual in the nineteenth century for local pastors to play such a prominent role in church design and construction. When the Plymouth Church in Brooklyn was destroyed by fire in 1849, the new building was designed according to the desires of its famous pastor, Henry Ward Beecher. He instructed the architect: "I want the audience to surround me, so that they will come up on every side and behind me, so that I shall be in the center of the crowd, and have the people surge all about me." Robert T. Oliver, *History of Public Speaking in America* (Boston: Allyn & Bacon, 1965), 376. When the Broadway Tabernacle in New York City was under construction in 1835–36, the noted evangelist Charles G. Finney informed the architect, Joseph Ditto, that he wanted a sanctuary where a large congregation could easily view the preacher and the preacher feel a closeness with his audience. Ditto, trained in one of the older schools of architecture, complained that it "would injure his reputation to build a church with such an interior." Finney, however, prevailed, and the "Akron Plan" of sanctuary design would be popular for at least the next hundred years. L. Nelson Nichols, *History of the Broadway Tabernacle of New York City* (New Haven: Tuttle, Morehouse, & Taylor, 1940), 60. See also Keith J. Hardman, *Charles Grandison Finney, 1792–1875, Revivalist and Reformer* (Syracuse, N.Y.: Syracuse University Press, 1987), 302.

3. M. A. DeWolfe Howe, *Phillips Brooks* (Boston: Small, Maynard, 1899), 44.

4. Kathleen Curran, "The Romanesque Revival, Mural Painting, and Protestant Patronage in America," *Art Bulletin* 81 (December 1999): 708.

5. Allen, *Life and Letters,* 2:124–25. Brooks published an article on Richardson in the *Harvard Monthly,* October 1886: see Phillips Brooks, *Essays and Addresses: Religious, Literary, and Social,* ed. John Cotton Brooks (New York: E. P. Dutton, 1895), 482–89.

6. Recorded in Edgar Dewitt Jones, *Lords of Speech: Portraits of Fifteen American Orators* (Chicago: Willett, Clark, 1937), 192.

7. An excellent article on the influence of Romanesque architecture in America, and specifically on Trinity Church, is Curran, "Romanesque Revival," 693–722.

8. James F. O'Gorman, *Three American Architects: Richardson, Sullivan, and Wright, 1865–1915* (Chicago: University of Chicago Press, 1991), 26.

9. In Brooks's previous pastorate, Holy Trinity Church in Philadelphia, when there was a need for some kind of tall structure to complete the building, Brooks was at odds with the members of the vestry of Holy Trinity who wanted a spire. At one point, Brooks thought the vestry had won, and in discouragement he wrote to a friend: "I have just broken my head against my vestry in an at-

tempt to put a tower harmonious and solid on my church. I have failed. It is to be a spire, taller than anything in town, not bad and not good" (Allen, *Life and Letters,* 1:587). Brooks eventually prevailed, however, and a tower was erected (fig. 3-10).

10. Brooks, *Essays and Addresses,* 21.

11. Raymond W. Albright, *Focus on Infinity: A Life of Phillips Brooks* (New York: Macmillan, 1961), 127.

12. Phillips Brooks, *Lectures on Preaching* (New York: E. P. Dutton, 1877), 5.

13. John F. Woolverton, *The Education of Phillips Brooks* (Urbana: University of Illinois Press, 1995), 99.

14. Curran, "Romanesque Revival," 708.

15. Quoted in Albright, *Focus on Infinity,* 217.

16. Allen, *Life and Letters,* 2:126–27.

17. Quoted in Albright, *Focus on Infinity,* 184.

18. Allen, *Life and Letters,* 2:134. A *Boston Transcript* reporter, allowed a preview of the interior just days before the consecration, exulted: "Only seeing can realize the superb beauty of the decoration, rich not garish, elaborate and not 'piled on,' magnificent in splendor, yet noble and dignified, artistic yet religious and fitting for the place. . . . There is nothing like it this side of the ocean. Trinity is the first church in this country to be decorated by artists, as distinguished from artisans. The result must be to make an era in American art and Church building" (February 5, 1877). See also Allen, *Life and Letters,* 2:261.

19. Henry Van Brunt, "The New Dispensation of Monumental Art," *Atlantic Monthly* 43 (1879): 635; Allen, *Life and Letters,* 2:249. See also Curran, "Romanesque Revival," 712–13; she makes the interesting observation that "red was the late nineteenth century's color of artistic but cozy domesticity, and the decision to apply it at Trinity must have been a somewhat defiant gesture by Richardson, with Brooks's obvious endorsement (or vice versa), to render an ecclesiastical space domestic. Certainly the vision of a crowd-packed church and chancel united by a warm 'Persian' red atmosphere was the antithesis of formality. It was at once homelike, theatrical, and passionate. The glaring and top-heavy gold of the chancel today, the result of massive renovation in 1937, separates it from the nave and crossing in a way that undermined Phillips Brooks's original intention that the chancel remain bare and undistinguished from the rest of the church."

20. Quoted in Albright, *Focus on Infinity,* 176. Such a sermon relays a pervading characteristic of Brooks's utterances—a spirit of optimism. Archdeacon Farrar from England wrote shortly after Brooks's death, "I think he must have been born an optimist." Frederick William Farrar, "Phillips Brooks—An English Estimate and Tribute," *Review of Reviews* 7 (March 1893): 177. Sermon after sermon from Brooks radiated optimism. In one sermon titled "New Starts in Life," he proclaimed: "O my young friends, the world is beautiful and every breath of your young life is happiness. You have a full right to feel that! And life is full of promise." In another, "The Preeminence of Christianity," he blended a somewhat dour note with an even more optimistic one: "Christianity will make the man suffer very often, but she will fulfill his life; she will make him perfect." Phillips Brooks, *New Starts in Life and Other Sermons* (New York: E. P. Dutton, 1897), 11, 327.

21. Allen, *Life and Letters,* 2:139.

22. Ibid., 139, 125, 251.

23. Albright, *Focus on Infinity,* 422–23 n. 87.

24. Ibid., 186.

3-1. Robert Treat Paine (1835–1910) as a thirty-year-old real estate lawyer during the Civil War. (Author's collection.)

# 3

## Chairman of the Building Committee: Robert Treat Paine

THOMAS M. PAINE

ROBERT TREAT PAINE (figs. 3-1, 3-10) lived to the full the distinctively Victorian idealism of his era. The least well known among the Makers of Trinity Church, Paine not only managed the delicate matters of raising funds and negotiating with architect and builder, as chairman of the building committee, but also practiced beyond the walls of the church what Phillips Brooks preached, to the lasting betterment of the wider community. A friend of Brooks since childhood, Paine collaborated with him at the intersection of architecture and philanthropy, where faith and hope meet charity, where uplift meets outreach. Their friendship has been described as "high spiritual fellowship."[1] Here is what one half of this friendship said of the other in a letter penned the day after Trinity Church was dedicated: "The Church would not be standing there, the beautiful and stately thing that it is, except for your tireless devotion. How I have wondered at your undiscouraged faith; and all my life as I look back on these years of anxiety and work, I shall see a picture of constancy which I know will make me stronger for whatever I have to do."[2] The man of faith described is Paine, and the man who had his doubts, the man writing the letter, is Brooks. Surely, though, the sentiment was fully reciprocated.

Getting Trinity Church built tried men's souls. It took longer to design and longer to build than anyone had anticipated, ran far over budget, contended with national economic crisis, threatened to put the parish into debt, and cost three workers their lives.[3] Sometimes friendships are not strained by great stress but strengthened. For Brooks and Paine, each was the other's flying buttress. Though central to their story, Trinity Church is only one among several monuments to their friendship-as-collaboration, for Paine was also instrumental in building three other churches and hundreds of affordable houses, as well transforming the very nature of philanthropy in the nation's then most philanthropic city.

Named for his great-grandfather, a signer of the Declaration of Independence, Paine was Boston born and bred to the bone, the third of nine children of Charles Cushing Paine and Fanny Cabot Jackson, who lived quietly, or as quietly as so many children allowed, in a modest townhouse in Bedford Place between Summer Street and Bedford Streets, and between the First and Second Churches.[4] Nothing could disturb the toddler's sunshiny disposition or loquacity described in entries in his parents' "Memoranda of the Children," mirroring a similar journal of the Brookses, who moved into the neighborhood in 1842.[4] Young Robert's sunniness grew over the years into the boundless optimism that was to serve his parish so well and even in his old age make him seem still young and eager for what the next day would bring.

As he got older, his at-home father taught him both a classics-inspired morality and shooting, with lots of practice in each in the idyllic setting of their working farm in the area of Beverly Farms, to which they were able to escape for country air in the summers. Though the four brothers returned to Boston late in the school year each fall, they were, thanks to their parents' home schooling, still at the head of the class when they got there.[5]

More than his brothers, Robert took away from his mother something that looms large in the story. To Fanny, a judge's daughter, he owed his deep Christian devotion. Like so many mothers, she early taught her children prayer, but beyond that, in her church activism among the needy, Fanny became a role model of dedication. In 1861 she was to write a pamphlet, *Christian Work the Most Precious Privilege of the Christian Disciple,* printed by the Boys Home, West Newton, in which we see the direct inspiration for Paine's later motto, "not alms but a friend." She argued for involvement with the needy then crowding in the cities, for giving not money but time, for hands-on rather than arm's-length involvement, and concern not just within one's social class but inclusive of all—down paths wherever they led, no matter how narrow the alley, how dark the stairs, how foul smelling the air of the dwellings, to paraphrase her pamphlet. Through the First Church she was active in the Children's Aid Society, founded in 1863.[6] A year after her death in 1878, Robert would take her at her word. Serving as vice president of the Children's Aid Society would be the least of it.

At age fifteen, Robert entered the Latin School, around the corner on Bedford Street, where Philly Brooks was a classmate, one without a trace of academic or athletic prowess. Perhaps they had already met through the First Church, where Dr. Nathaniel Frothingham preached a conservative form of Unitarianism, before the Brookses converted to Episcopalianism and began worshiping at St.

Paul's across from the Boston Common. In the class of 1855 at Harvard, Paine and Brooks had four more years together. Graduating at the top of their class, Paine delivered a commencement oration titled "The Man of Purpose." For the next fourteen years, Brooks and Paine went their separate ways. Robert attended Harvard Law School for a year, before joining his family in Europe.[7] Charles Cushing Paine sold his Boston house, full of high hopes that a prolonged stay in the best cities in Europe would do them all—and his failing marriage—a world of good. Robert studied law in Dresden and Paris. His sisters, in their teens, enrolled in schools in Paris and Rome, and one and all explored the cathedrals, civic monuments, and galleries, and climbed in the Alps, though all the while the parents were not speaking to each other. Meanwhile, Brooks was undergoing failure as a schoolteacher before entering the seminary.

After a year abroad, Robert returned to Boston in 1858 at age twenty-three, eager to get ahead in the world professionally and personally. He joined the law offices of Richard Henry Dana and Francis E. Parker, and he began courting Lydia Williams Lyman of 6 Joy Street, Beacon Hill, and the Vale in Waltham (fig. 3-2). A year later he was admitted to the bar; two years after that, he and Lydia became engaged, just months before his parents separated once and for all in 1861. Perhaps because of that disaster (divorce was still uncommon), none of his four sisters ever married. One would later become an Episcopal nun; the other three shared housekeeping and become active in church work, one at Trinity.

During the Civil War years, Robert's three brothers all fought for the Union.[8] Even his college roommate, Francis Barlow, with whom he tied for first rank at Harvard, went on to distinguished service as a general. Robert went his own way, ultimately becoming a dedicated pacifist. In 1861, though, Robert was focused on making money. As he wrote forty years later, he was proud to have made all his money himself, except for a $200 gift from his father.[9] Through the Civil War years he practiced real estate law with enough success that on April 24, 1862, Robert Treat Paine and Lydia Williams Lyman were married in King's Chapel, and went to live across the street from her parents, at 6 Mt. Vernon Place. The first of seven children, five of them daughters, was born in 1863.

In 1864, Robert took leave of his young family to accompany his sister Fanny to England, where she entered the Community of St. John Baptist, Clewer, Windsor, as a Sister of Mercy. Fanny was the first of Robert's siblings to leave Unitarianism behind. As Sister Francis Constance, she later returned to the re–United States to found the order's first convent in New York City and rose to become the first mother superior of the order in America, an inspiration to all who knew her. She, too, set Robert an example.

As soon as the war was over, Paine went west with Harvard classmate Alexan-

3-2. Lydia Williams Lyman (1837–1897) about the time she married Robert Treat Paine. (Author's collection.)

der Agassiz to investigate the Calumet and Hecla Copper Mine in northern Michigan and begin "thinking large." Under Agassiz the mine prospered and provided its workforce with model housing, schools, churches, and an employee aid fund—an ideal of corporate beneficence that in its way later inspired what Paine would do in Boston, fed by the staggeringly profitable Calumet and Hecla dividends that made Bostonian investors feel both smug and guilty.[10]

Most of Paine's fortune came from two Boston-backed railroads, the Chicago Burlington & Quincy, and the Atchison, Topeka & Santa Fe. In 1865 he went west with Charles Perkins, president of the then Burlington & Missouri Railroad, to the end of the line and traveled on by wagon three days across Iowa to the Missouri over the most fertile soil a Yankee could imagine. Paine invested and went west again and again. He was good with numbers, and a few good deals worked magic. By 1866 he was able to build a country house in Waltham—the first of many building projects.[11] His most profitable deal was in Nebraska, considered a desert by lazier investors. Paine poured all his money into Nebraska land bonds, held his breath, and cashed out handsomely. As he wrote in his autobiography, "The gains I made in these railroads I always attributed to my habit of thorough personal inspection, forming my own deliberate judgment and acting on it boldly"[12]—not the stuff of the coupon-cutting, trust-fund beneficiaries of the next generation.

After Phillips Brooks's return to Boston in 1869, Robert and Lydia Paine wasted no time in coming to Trinity Church to hear him preach.[13] For Brooks they gave up a church, King's Chapel, and a faith, Unitarianism. A year later, they were confirmed as Episcopalians, and Paine retired from business. Thereafter, the Paines simply could not get enough Brooks, typically attending both of his Sunday services and the Wednesday night service as well, and, "overcome with emotion, would walk the mile homeward without saying a word."[14]

Something about Brooks's power with the spoken word transcended the mere texts we are left to read now at so far a remove from that era, but this we know: Brooks was a master at "word painting." As a reconciler, not a polarizer, he was inclusive. His medium was common language; his subjects were contemporary issues (he was early on abolition, early on women's suffrage, read Darwin and Spencer; and his message was to celebrate through Christ what he called "the glory and the richness and the sweetness of all life."[15] When he spoke from the pulpit, words flowed like a mountain cataract, spoken with more intensity and more intimacy than he was comfortable with in speaking one-on-one. This eloquence and passion, more than any high-church ritual, was what was to fill Trinity's galleries to overflowing.

Before their collaboration on Trinity Church, Brooks and Paine collaborated on a building project of a different sort. As early as 1870, concerned about the tenement problem—which he later called "that worst curse of city life"—Paine began documenting slums that he described as "beastly" and a "jumble" with "floors rotten."[16] Deciding to take action, he began in an infamous dark West End slum called, with bitter irony, the Crystal Palace, where he had skylights installed, just as his mother might have wished. With Brooks and Dr. Henry Ingersoll Bowditch, who had founded the State Board of Health the year before (the first in the country), Paine established the Boston Cooperative Building Company. In his diary he described its seven model houses, built on Tremont and Kenney Streets, as "my houses" and enjoyed "working out plans for the greater comfort and decency of the occupants."[17] Hundreds more houses were to follow over the next three decades, as Paine's architectural ambitions kept growing. Also foreshadowing his involvement at Trinity, Paine was active in the building of Grace Episcopal Church in South Boston. Later the City Episcopal Mission was based there. The wood-framed church stood on the west side of Dorchester Street just south of Old Colony Street.

When Trinity Church itself needed a new home, consistent with his forward-looking ministry, Brooks had, as Paine wrote, "given decisive impulse to the scheme of moving Trinity Church from its ancient site on Summer Street to the Back Bay."[18] At the end of 1870, the church voted to make the move. On January 1, 1872, the church bought a rectangular lot on the east side of the future Copley Square. The arduous five-year process of building the new church began in earnest, in which Paine would, at several stages along the way, earn Brooks's gratitude for what he called Paine's largeness of ideas. On March 6, with several building projects behind him, Paine was made chair of the eleven-man building committee, which was to work closely with Brooks and be collectively accountable to the parish for the best design that prudent funding could buy.[19]

Within a week, the committee invited six architectural firms to submit designs. On June 1 the committee selected Gambrill & Richardson—then of New York City—over five competitors, and a week later, no doubt with the winning architect's suggestion, bought the abutting triangle of land fronting on then Huntington Avenue, owned, happily, by a parish member, Franklin Evans. As Paine later wrote in the final report: "The building committee were at once impressed with the importance of purchasing the triangle of land which now forms the Huntington Avenue front of our estate. An appeal was made to the parish for gifts of money, and a generous response enabled the committee to make the purchase. . . . The church thus completed its title to the whole domain of over an acre, enclosed by four public streets, and making the church visible in all directions. So far as the committee knew, this was the only site of the Back Bay where these advantages could have been secured."[20] But in the privacy of his autobiography, written in 1904, Paine recalled:

> I think it was owing to me that this location, almost of back land, was enlarged into our present superb site. It seemed to me such a rare chance to add to the original St. James Street lot the triangle of 14,687½ square feet and completing the whole area within two streets, Huntington Avenue and [what is now] Copley Square, that I urged the Vestry and the Building Committee the purchase of this triangle. The price was $75,000. I had secured from the State Commissioners their agreement to release and discontinue to us without cost the intermediate street of 6345 in area. The Vestry agreed to the purchase, provided the money could be raised. This task I undertook.
>
> I had a lithograph made showing the striking advantages of the enlarged site from 24,809 feet to 45,842 feet. This I took with me on my begging campaign [fig. 3-3].
>
> I started it with my own pledge of $2,000, and secured several more pledges of like amount, all payable in three annual sums. Trinity Church ought to know its great obligation to Mrs. G. Howland Shaw, who, as a result of my calls on her, signed her name for $9,000, and, inspired by this superb gift, all the $2,000 donors raised their pledges to $3,000. Next Sunday, when I called on Brooks, he threw up his arms with excitement, and his delight knew no bounds at my report of over $50,000 in one week. The subscription did not pause till $105,000 was pledged in my little red book.
>
> I must not claim too much of this success. I started the idea, and secured its passage and the pledges; but it was Brooks's glorious personality that made all his people so ready to give.[21]

By then, Paine was hooked, gave up his law practice, and took it on himself "not only to watch the progress of the work in all its supremely interesting details, but to . . . secure a quorum at our incessant meetings. I gave these duties a priority over business, so that once I failed to secure a ten-year lease of an estate of mine at $3,000 a year; after which I concluded I might as well abandon trying to carry on law. This I regretted for many years. Yet at length I reached the conviction that as we had this life on earth only once, I was not willing to devote the last half of it to the mere business of making money."[22] So it was that Brooks's visions of the beautiful church and the purposeful life inspired Paine, very flush at the extraordinarily young age of thirty-seven, to devote his resources and talents full time to Trinity and other good works, both sacred and secular. Over time he became convinced that the only way for one's will to be done in this world was not in a will but in one's lifetime.

Lydia Lyman Paine, too, who had been active in the Children's Aid Society since 1866, was busying herself with the Trinity Employment Society and would later become involved in charities benefiting Pine Farm, a halfway house of the Boston Children's Aid Society for homeless or wayward children, and home libraries.[23] Both husband and wife exemplified what historian Gertrude Himmelfarb calls "the combination of religiosity and rationality that informed the social

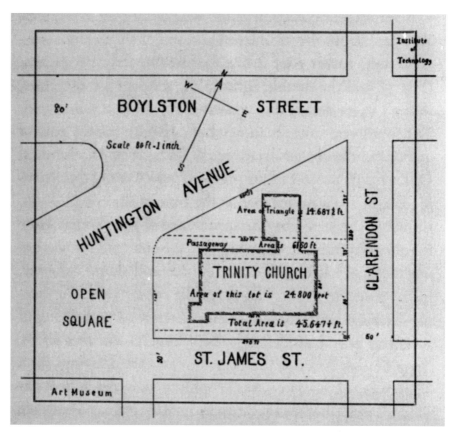

Within the map image:
BOYLSTON STREET
80'
Scale 80 ft - 1 inch
N
W
E
S
HUNTINGTON AVENUE
Institute of Technology
CLARENDON ST
Area of Triangle is 14.687½ ft.
Passageway
Area is 6180 ft
TRINITY CHURCH
OPEN
SQUARE
Area of this lot is 24.800 feet
Total Area is 45.647+ ft.
50'
ST. JAMES ST.
Art Museum

3-3. Lithograph made for Paine's "begging campaign" in 1872. It shows the virtues of a freestanding building lot long before Copley Square further dignified the church's setting. (Courtesy of Trinity Church Archives.)

consciousness of the late Victorians." Humanitarianism became a religion by other means.[24]

In the summer of 1872, while an ailing Richardson was redesigning Trinity Church in his New York office, Paine and Brooks took the first of three trips to Europe together over the next eleven years, this time visiting Norway; they shared a love of the mountains. It was on this trip that Brooks, who had been no less sheltered than Paine, first identified with the downtrodden.[25] Back home, after the loss of old Trinity on Summer Street in the catastrophic Boston fire of November 1872 removed all discord in the parish about the move, the building committee directed Paine and fellow member John Ropes to check up on Richardson in New York, where his bodily ailments could diminish neither his clear vision nor his enthusiasm for designing to the new expanded site.

Paine was also doing his homework, as recorded in his diary: his design due-diligence first appears in the form of comparative church plans (fig. 3-4).[26] When Richardson presented his revised design in April 1873, the committee, Paine wrote in his report, was concerned about such weighty design issues as tower safety—this before cost considerations intervened.[27] Even after Richardson reduced the tower weight by 25 percent, the committee voted in June not to accept the design and appointed an executive committee of three, including Paine, which in July approved new plans that were ready for bid by September.[28] The low bid by Norcross Brothers came in far above expectations at a time when Boston was still rebuilding from the fire, and panic was roiling the financial markets. Richardson went back to the drawing board, and when Norcross Brothers reduced their bid 20 percent, the committee signed on October 10, although final drawings were delayed until April 1874, and even then the tower was too heavy to suit the committee. If this was the moment of crisis, it also led immediately to the anticipated moment of high ritual when, on Thursday, May 20, 1874, at 10:00 A.M., as Paine noted excitedly in his diary, Brooks laid the cornerstone for a church whose broad mass seems so fitting an embodiment of his Broad Church Episcopalianism.

The advocate of hands-on personal inspection in personal investments, Paine could do no less for his church in the months that followed. Doubtless, he wanted to be doubly sure that the financial disaster that befell Richardson's Brattle Square Church—cost overruns forced that congregation to disband in 1876—would not happen here. By now, Paine's services had earned him the title of vestryman, a post he would cherish for the rest of his life.

Taking nothing for granted along the way, Paine calculated pier volumes in his diary.[29] Indeed, his diary records not only bids and donors and bills paid but also architectural details such as dimensions for naves, steps, pews, and galleries from comparable churches, plans for lighting and the organ case, and calculations for tiling and flag paving outside the church.[30] At least one building committee meeting with Richardson, Norcross, and T. M. Clark, the superintendent architect, was held at Paine's country house in Waltham. Though known for his salesmanship and consensus-building skills, Paine was meticulous in his duties to the point of interference, once incurring the displeasure of Norcross, who ordered him off the job.[31]

When the parish house, or "chapel," was completed in 1874 in the lightning speed of eight months, Paine's son George Lyman Paine, future minister, was the first child baptized there. In August, Richardson moved to Brookline, and Brooks was back in Europe. From Tours, France, he wrote Paine: "O my dear Bob, such old glass as one sees in these Churches little and big . . . would make our new Trinity the glory of America forever. . . . I should like to be with you at Waltham now. My kindest love to Mrs. Paine and the children."[32]

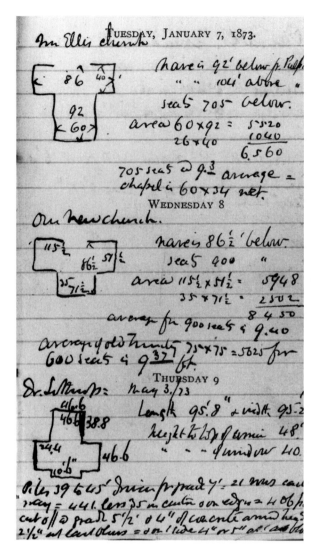

3-4. Paine's pocket diary documenting his involvement in design as well as fund-raising. (Courtesy of Stonehurst, Robert Treat Paine Estate, City of Waltham.)

At last, on November 10, construction began on the church itself. In April 1875, three years into the design process, Richardson produced the brilliant solution in the shorter tower—designed like that of Salamanca Cathedral in Spain—which was to become the signature element of Trinity. As construction costs mounted, however, there were moments of agony, prompting Brooks to urge Paine to look beyond the "vexations" to the "clear sailing before us. . . . One of these days we will look back on it all and be thankful that we struggled through all this."[33]

Paine's diary records both near-tragedy and triumph: "Thurs Nov 2 [1876]. Mr. Brooks had a narrow escape from being killed, a box falling down the Tower inside & he just escaped by jumping aside. I yelled, but he heard the noise in time to save himself"; [December 29] We try acoustics and are delighted, low reading heard easily everywhere."[34] Almost thirty years later, however, Paine would sum up the process glowingly; note the wording of the first sentence:

I wonder if any Building Committee ever took more pleasure in their task than did I. Five years; Brooks always on fire with interest and delight in all the great questions; Richardson a noble genius in architecture, with infinite patience in making plan after plan, as we rejected them in turn, declaring that art was infinite, and he could go on improving time after time. Then, too, Richardson had a rare faculty for attracting men of genius to work with him. Norcross Bros., our builders, have worthily achieved a great name and fame. La Farge took the contract for painting and decorating the interior, and gave a new and grand impulse to interior decoration in America with artistic mural figures. Augustus Saint Gaudens painted, as a labor of love for La Farge, the St. James in the north transept. Several other painters, afterwards distinguished, aided La Farge. . . . Richardson tremendous in his enthusiasm for art and architecture, quickly rising from deep gloom over his physical infirmities to exultant delight in his designs for the Church. . . .

In the last year or two a constant struggle had gone on of economy against extras. As the end drew near, $65,000 of debt had piled up to prevent the consecration of the church. Again I was forced to take up the task of a subscription book. Only $50,000 could be got. Then came that glorious Sunday when, with previous circulars telling the story and asking all to join, Brooks preached to his people and took up the collection. . . . The plates piled high with money, pledges, and checks; which Brooks and the vestry all gathered eagerly to count: $16,000. Delight knew no bounds.[35]

By February 1877 the essentials so long in the making were ready; all that remained to be done was peripheral. On the appointed day of consecration, February 9, five months after the original contract completion date and five years after the competition, Paine noted in his diary: "Consecration Friday Feby 9/77 Fine clear cool day. A glorious Day," and he wrote Brooks:

And now, my dear old Friend, at the close of this great day, which has brought the glorious consummation of our hopes and prayers, I want to send you a few words to say how this long five years' labor, working with you and for you and for our noble church, has been to me an inexpressible pleasure. . . .

On one matter, that of involving the Parish in debt, I have always been moved in two directions, feeling in the one hand that we were bound not to load the future of the Church with a heavy debt, and that as an agent of theirs I *must* be faithful to this obligation, and yet on the other hand unable myself to tolerate the idea that, in carrying out the great work of transplanting the church from one site to another and building our new church to stand for centuries we trust, we should strive or even be willing only to use the resources of the past.

Here, too, God seems to have been with us. And the debt, which in spite of our efforts to keep it down rolled up so large a sum, has only given us all an opportunity to show the love of the whole people to you, and their readiness to follow your example of great generosity, and their devotion to our glorious new House of God. The eager and noble response to your appeal shows better than any words, not only their love to you, but how much you have done in them.

Not one of the donors, large or small, but must always love it more as *his* church, now that he has taken part in its completion. And surely we must feel more worthy to have it and enjoy it, when we have added so largely to make it broad and beautiful and rich.

May the spirit of the Living God go with us into our new Home, and fill it and you and all of us full of His presence and power and blessing in this generation and many future generations, and make it a mighty power for good so that we shall not have builded it in vain,—this is the prayer of one whose rare privilege it has been to be in this matter your co-worker, and always your friend.

Brooks's reply on February 10 (excerpted in my opening paragraph) began on an emotional note: "I wish I could tell you, my dear Bob, something of what yesterday was to me, and how my deep gratitude and love to you mingled with the feeling of every hour. May God bless you is all I can say."[36]

It was Paine who wrote the report of the building committee's activities over the five years from competition to construction.[37] The first child Brooks baptized in the church was Paine's daughter Lily, even as Paine contemplated donating a window to be called "Jesus Blessing the Little Children."[38] That summer, Brooks, who so loved church ornament—the gold, mosaics, and glass—was in England conferring with stained glass makers Clayton & Bell and, on behalf of Paine, Henry Holiday.[39] The Paine window, originally in the south nave where La Farge had placed a grisaille window to subdue the harsh light obscuring his murals, is now in the north nave. In these years, before La Farge invented opalescent glass in 1879, Paine and Brooks were more keenly focused on the didactic possibilities of English pictorial glass.[40] (The particular theme of the Henry Holiday window held some personal significance for the Paines, because their four-year-old daughter Florence had died in 1872, and would hold even more significance when their sixteen-year-old daughter Fanny died, two years after the glass was installed, in 1881.)

Almost overnight, the realization in Trinity Church of such a multifaceted largeness of ideas gave it its place as one of the buildings most admired among both architects and general public and its pivotal role in the rapid evolution in architectural design across the land. In its more immediate purview, the Copley Square we take for granted was a long way off. It was by no means a foregone conclusion in 1877 that this church would one day face a grand square in place of two triangular undeveloped lots at the intersection of Huntington Avenue and Boylston Street. Within three years, the combined forces of Trinity on the east of the future square, the original Museum of Fine Arts (completed in 1876) to the south, and the Second and New Old South churches to the north together attracted the Boston Public Library to the west, for whose relocation the city donated the site in 1880. Three years later the city purchased the triangle in front of the library, and finally in 1885 the triangle in front of Trinity, naming the intersection, ahead of its actual form, Copley Square. It took almost a full century after Trinity Church was completed before the rectangular park replaced the first block of Huntington Avenue and at last caught up with the name. Like an extension of Trinity, Copley Square gives the church the grandeur of a cathedral close, beyond the wildest dreams of Trinity's building committee. All of this owes something to Trinity's pioneering purchase of its triangular lot (fig. 3-5).

The making of Trinity Church on such ambitious architectural terms symbolized, at least for Paine and Brooks, something more: the parish leaders' new and more ambitious covenant, or involvement, with the community. Paine bought 13 Burroughs Place, where the church ran "industrial charities" under the name of Trinity House and where Lydia Paine was also active; Paine agreed to donate the house, provided the church agreed to donate to those charities and to a mission in China as well.[41]

3-5. The Trinity Church that Phillips Brooks knew, before the west porch was added in 1897 and years before there was a Copley Square. (Keystone stereoview, 1883; Author's collection.)

Philanthropic support of existing institutions was not enough for Paine; the issue was to borrow the best ideas, adapt them, and, if need be, create new institutions to meet the challenges of rapid industrialization and urbanization. His flair for organization would serve him well as a social reformer and, indeed, community builder. Through Paine, the philanthropic movement to eradicate urban pauperism that had begun in England, championed by John Ruskin and philanthropist Octavia Hill, and spread by way of Buffalo and Philadelphia, came to Boston.[42] Perhaps borrowing a contemporary British slogan, "Not money but yourselves," Paine took pride in the slogan he coined, "Not alms but a friend," especially when he heard it repeated in New York, Chicago, Baltimore, New Orleans, and other places where he spread his gospel.[43]

Among philanthropic organizations in Boston the time had come for coordination, filling in gaps, avoiding overlap and waste, yet building bridges between faiths. To do this, with Brooks's blessing, Paine organized the Associated Charities in 1878, the year that his mother died.[44] This organization owed much to Octavia Hill's Charity Organization Society, founded in 1869. Paine initially had to fight to end mutual suspicion and petty jealousy between charities. He must have succeeded in great measure, for he remained president until 1904. Brooks was on the board.

A year later, in 1879, Paine organized the Wells Memorial Institute, the largest so-called workingmen's club in the country, where Lydia Lyman Paine too was active, and where Paine did the unthinkable—allowed trade union meetings to take place. Named for the Reverend E. M. P. Wells, missionary of the Episcopal City Mission in Boston, the Wells Memorial was soon affiliated with a Workingmen's Building Association, a Workingmen's Loan founded to combat the evils of pawnshops and loan sharks, and, perhaps Paine's favorite, the Workingmen's Cooperative Bank. Paine was president of them all, and Brooks often spoke at their meetings, consistent with a vow he had made as early as 1874 to "help the workingmen."[45]

As might be inferred from his housing ventures dating back to 1870, Paine's other philanthropic motto must have been "Own your own home." He fervently believed that along with thrift, home ownership afforded by the cooperative bank was "the most effectual agency in these ways of improving the economic condition of the masses of plain people that I have ever known."[46] The Workingmen's Building Association built hundreds of affordable single-family homes in Roxbury—which continue to be well maintained—on winding streets with names like Sunnyside Terrace.

Paine even helped set up a network of 662 private citizens, "friendly visitors" to blanket the whole city, household by household, and find out who was in what trouble; with his mother's exhortations ringing in his ears, he became such a visitor himself.[47] Paine and fellow philanthropists believed that friendly visitors could approach, indeed befriend, those in need, not simply by throwing money at them but by helping them to sort things out and develop prudent habits. Self-reliance, so-called self-help, was the key.[48] As a contemporary account has it:

> It is a most significant fact about all of Paine's work that he followed out in action the implication of every position taken by him. Is it found that the source for employment is too large a problem for the friendly visitor? He helps to establish the Industrial Aid Society. Are the housing conditions bad not only in isolated cases but in areas? He creates the Better Dwelling Society which finally gets the city beyond the attitude of waiting for a pestilence before instituting sanitary reforms, and by periodically prodding the Board of Health secures the destruction of all the worst slums in the oldest parts of the city.
>
> Not many know that for a period of twenty-five years not many weeks passed when Mr. Paine did not spend one or two evenings with a little group or committee of workingmen, taking counsel with them on an equal footing as to investments of the funds in the homes which some of them were building.[49]

In retrospect, such paternalistic methods are easily criticized, and they have been. The term "workingmen" seems antiquated, but historian Gertrude Himmelfarb's recent charitable assessment of the charitable Victorians is persuasive. The practical man of business, if he saw charity as an act of love in the spirit of St. Paul, also believed that "the mere sentiment of charity is impotent and often harmful."[50] For Tocqueville, in his still compelling *Democracy in America,* the formation of private associations to further joint purposes was one of the wonders of America.[51]

In 1882, while Paine pursued his philanthropic projects, an exhausted Brooks left for a fifteen-month tour that was to take him from Europe to as far as India. In the company of Richardson, also exhausted, he looked at the French Romanesque prototypes firsthand, as well as Chartres. Before going on to India alone, Brooks wrote Paine, "You will find Richardson glowing with splendid projects for Trinity. A front porch, a Chapter House, and the great Piers covered from top to bottom with mosaics."[52] Brooks returned to Boston in 1883, in the company of Paine—but not before Paine had met with Octavia Hill and toured model tenements, the Charity Organization Society, dispensaries, even police stations—all grist for his own charities.[53] They also visited Chartres together, where Brooks wanted Paine to see for himself whether the design of one of the cathedral porches could be adapted for Trinity.[54] In August, Paine was coincidentally sketching floor plans in his diary for an addition to his Waltham house—plans that in many details anticipate the end result that Richardson designed for him a year later.[55] Also in 1883, Paine's Wells Memorial Building was completed, an elaborate Queen Anne–style, six-story structure offering "innocent amusements, social pleasures, reading rooms, and class instruction." Its imposing facade included ornamental brick and lively fenestration.[56]

Elected in 1883, Paine represented Waltham in the General Court for all of one year, 1884, and served on its committee of charitable institutions. Although Democrat Paine hated politics, he became a Mugwump Republican, supporting Grover Cleveland over Blaine; later he supported William Jennings Bryan, taking the pro-silver bimetallist position, consistent with his liberal social policy leanings. Moreover, he was a candidate for Congress in 1888 and nominated for mayor of Boston in 1899.

Brooks, who tried to get to Europe every other summer, in 1885 joined the entire Paine family, including the five children aged nine to twenty-two, in touring Germany, merrily climbing in the Alps (fig. 3-6), and filling three gondolas in Venice. For this friendship of Brooks and the Paines, perhaps it was the apogee. This was the year that social realist artist and Richardson client Hubert von Herkomer began portraits of both the architect and the Paines.[57] The latter two works still hang in Stonehurst, the Paines' country house in Waltham; as redesigned by Richardson, it was then under construction and almost complete at Richardson's untimely death in April 1886. Brooks was very likely one of the first guests to sit on the Olmsted-designed terrace that next summer, as well as stand for his height to be recorded on the closet door—at six-four, towering over the Paines.

As early as 1886, Paine was filling the great hall of Stonehurst with activists from the philanthropic community. In October, on behalf of the Associated Charities, he hosted one hundred guests in what may have been the first such fund-raiser.[58] In 1887, he gave Harvard $10,000 (worth perhaps $500,000 now) to fund a fellowship for the "study of ethical problems of society, the effects of legislation, governmental administration and private philanthropy to ameliorate the lot of the mass of mankind."[59]

Paine was just reaching his stride. He chaired the committee to build St. Andrews Mission, 27 Chambers Street, West End (fig. 3-7) to minister to the desperate, the hospitalized, even the incarcerated. Paine seems to have been making his own architectural drawings, which he sent on to Brooks in Europe during the summer of 1887. The result, as built, was decidedly Richardsonian, a truly urban church, its design—and therefore its visual outreach—reading as almost secular. The letter that Brooks wrote Paine from Heidelberg, alluding first to St. Andrews and then to Trinity, is a key document in their ongoing mutual admiration:

3-6. Phillips Brooks (left, standing), Robert Treat Paine (second from right, standing), Lydia Lyman Paine (in front of him), and Paine progeny in the Alps, 1885. (Courtesy of Stonehurst, Robert Treat Paine Estate, City of Waltham.)

Your letter, which I was very glad indeed to get this week, made me see you at home, dining on the terrace, and keeping the Fourth of July. It was a pretty picture. I wish I had been there. And then came your very interesting account of the discussions about the new chapel, and your delightful architectural drawings, which gave me such a clear idea of how it ought to be done and how it ought not to be done. It would make a very interesting summer if I could have been at home and talked all these things over with you all. I need not tell you that I like the largeness of your ideas. Many a time, in these last twenty years, you have saved us from doing things on a small scale, and kept us large. We shall never forget—I hope history will not let it be forgotten—that we owe it to you that Trinity Church is big and dignified, and not a little thing on a side street, which one must hunt to find, and think small things of when he has found it. . . . [I]t will be pleasant when I take you by the hand again on your own porch. I send my love to Mrs. Paine and Edith and John and Emily and Robert and Ethel and George and Lily, and am, ever and ever, Affectionately yours.[60]

The loss of the asymmetrical Richardsonian facade of St. Andrews in the evisceration of the West End has not been sufficiently mourned.

In the ten years following completion of its building, the parish tellingly spent

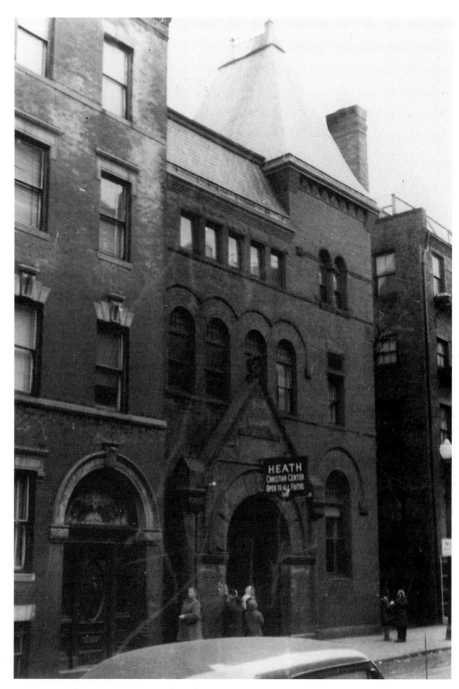

3-7. St. Andrews Mission, 27 Chambers Street, in Boston's West End, a project spear-headed and partially funded by Paine. (Photo by John B. Little, January 1956; Courtesy of the Society for the Preservation of New England Antiquities.)

as much on outreach as it had on its building.[61] In 1889, Paine funded construction of the Peoples Institute for Workingmen. Far less architecturally distinguished than the Wells Memorial, this now demolished panel brick–style, flat-roofed building later (if not originally) featured shops at ground level and meeting rooms in the two upper stories.[62]

In 1890, Paine and his wife joined in endowing, with $200,000, the Robert Treat Paine Association, a family-run foundation to promote the spiritual, moral, and physical welfare of the "working classes" through such organizations as the Peoples Institute, Peoples Coffee House, Windsor Home for Aged Women, Working Girls Club and Trinity House. A contemporary observed another picturesque aspect of Paine's hands-on philanthropy: "Mr. Paine's own home has always been hospitably open to all who shared his interests, and many a hopeful plan has had its inception under his roof among a group of guest-friends such as would hardly have come together at any other house. One of the most pleasurable experiences in the lives of any who have been fortunate enough to participate, were the annual receptions given in June at the Waltham place to the entire body of the membership of the Wells Memorial and the Peoples Institutes" (fig. 3-8).[63]

The last time Brooks committed his feelings about Paine to paper, he summed up a lifetime: "And you know something, you cannot know all, of how this great happiness and delight in all these years has had the most sacred and close connection with you and yours. What you and your wife and your children have been to me it would be impossible to try to tell. But the great years never could have been without you. How it all comes pouring on my recollection. What a million of little and big events. And how thankful to you I am you will never know. God bless you for it all!"[64]

At his tragically premature death in 1893 (then bishop, he caught a cold preaching in a drafty church), it might have been fitting to remember Brooks's own words about the premature death of Richardson not seven years before: "When some men die it is as if you had lost a pen knife and were subject to perpetual inconvenience until you could get another. Other men's going is like the vanishing of a great mountain from the landscape and the outlook of life is changed forever."[65] For Paine, losing Brooks was like losing family. A large charcoal portrait of Trinity's rector still hangs in the great hall of the Waltham house.[66] Paine also served on the committee for a memorial to Brooks, which commissioned Saint-Gaudens's statue outside the church.

Despite the shock of the panic of 1893, work on the west front of Trinity Church went forward and was completed in 1897. But the memorial to Brooks that mattered even more than a statue took a bit longer, and that was Phillips Brooks House at Harvard, for which Paine again chaired the committee.[67] At the

3-8. An annual summer reception ca. 1890 of Wells Memorial and Peoples Institute membership at Stonehurst, Paine's estate. The house, designed by H. H. Richardson and F. L. Olmsted, incorporated his older Waltham house. (Courtesy of Stonehurst, Robert Treat Paine Estate, City of Waltham.)

dedication in 1900, Paine spoke as plainly about Brooks as Brooks himself did in his sermons, giving us a portrait of his friend that eluded the official biographies:

> When he graduated he had not been confirmed in church and he had no profession in view. He took up school teaching as a temporary means of livelihood, and he failed. I sat with him one day at his desk in the Latin School in 1856, and saw that he could not control the boys. Disheartened, he sought the counsel of friends, and with their advice devoted himself to the ministry of God. Never have we seen the powers of a noble life expand, irradiate, grow dominant, as in those years and decades of the life of Phillips Brooks. He who could not speak at school became, some of us think, the greatest Christian preacher of all ages. He who failed to control a schoolroom of boys developed such powerful influence over all ranks and ages of life, that whether speaking to a crowded gathering of plainest people on a Sunday evening in Faneuil Hall, or preaching to the students of Harvard and meeting them in his room as college preacher the dominance of his personality was felt by all.[68]

All told, as one of Brooks's star parishioners, Paine was a member of sixty committees and felt "over-committed." Yet he not only held numerous offices in his church but was active in many organizations (fig. 3-9), ranging from the Episcopal City Mission to the now infamous Watch and Ward Society, the People's Institute, the Prison Association, and the Congress of Workingmen's Clubs. He was an admirer of General Samuel C. Armstrong, leader of black troops, and supported his development of Hampton Institute in Virginia (founded in 1868) as well as the Tuskegee Normal School in Alabama.[69] He had over two hundred modest single-family dwellings built in the South End, Roxbury, and Jamaica Plain, many sold at cost, often on installment.[70] In 1891 he became president of the American Peace Society and served for many years (fig. 3-10). In 1896 he chaired the effort to build Christ Church in Waltham.[71] He supported the YMCA, the Society for the Prevention of Cruelty to Children, McLean Hospital, the American Sunday School Union, and the National Education Association.[72]

The address Paine gave at the International Congress of Charities, Correction and Philanthropy in Chicago, published as *Pauperism in Great Cities: Its Four Chief Causes,* brought him international recognition as an authority on social re-

3-9. Some of the numerous nonprofits that Paine founded and ran over a forty-year period, thus enlarging Trinity's mission in its community. (*Boston Sunday Globe,* January 4, 1903; Courtesy of Stonehurst, Robert Treat Paine Estate, City of Waltham.)

3-10. Robert Treat Paine, the philanthropist, holding a pacifist tract, 1890s. (Author's collection.)

form and philanthropy.[73] In all his writings, his language, to twenty-first-century ears, exudes confidence to the point of arrogance. We do well to recall that when his, the Civil War generation, came of age, such things as virtue and moral rectitude and respectability were subject to none of the skepticism and outright assault that became commonplace a century later. In 1904, at a statewide conference the year he retired as president of the Associated Charities at age sixty-nine, Paine still espoused the "new charity"—philanthropy infused by personal connection and, as ever, personal inspection—and dedicated the last of his published writings to the memory of his mother.[74]

After his own death in 1910, his children—one then a minister, another married to an architect—gave Trinity Church its magnificent pulpit, adorned with carvings of great preachers, Brooks among the rest.[75] It is inscribed as follows:

> *Robert Treat Paine,*
> *Classmate and Friend of Phillips Brooks,*
> *Vestryman and Warden of this Parish*
> *1874 to 1910.*
>
> *To the great preacher*
> *he gave the friendship of a lifetime.*
>
> *To the parish*
> *he rendered loyal and generous service*
>
> *to the glory of God*
> *and in loving memory of their father*
> *his children erect this pulpit*

In the making of the Broad Church, Paine's contribution was an aesthetic different from that of the artists: to keep the dream alive, raise the money, check the math, and make the dream come true. And in the broad community, Paine's achievement as a social reformer, community builder, and philanthropist owed much to the synergy of a friendship between two lads who grew up together and, as adults full of both boyish enthusiasm and gravitas, almost outdid each other in good works.

## NOTES

Thanks to Lorna Condon, librarian of the Society for the Preservation of New England Antiquities, for assistance in tracking down Paine's now-lost Boston institutional buildings; to Anne VanDusen of Trinity Church; and especially to Ann Clifford, director and curator of Stonehurst, for many kindnesses and for the additional research that appeared in her December 2001 slide lecture in honor of Trinity Church. I am also indebted to the other authors in this volume and to my wife, Lynn Sharp Paine, for many insights. My favorite general published sources on Trinity Church and

Stonehurst are Margaret Henderson Floyd, *Henry Hobson Richardson: A Genius for Architecture* (New York: Monacelli Press, 1997); and James F. O'Gorman, *Living Architecture: A Biography of H. H. Richardson* (New York: Simon & Schuster, 1997).

1. Brooks to Paine, February 10, 1877, Massachusetts Historical Society Collections, quoted in Alexander V. G. Allen, *Life and Letters of Phillips Brooks,* 2 vols. (New York: E. P. Dutton, 1900), 2:138.

2. Allen, *Life and Letters,* 2:138.

3. T. M. Clark, "Building-Accidents at Trinity Church, Boston," letter to the editor, *American Architect and Building News,* February 24, 1877, 62. Paine alludes to the "terrible accident" that resulted in the death of William Hurd, on July 10, 1874, in his diary, Archives of Stonehurst, Waltham, Mass., owned by city of Waltham and Robert Treat Paine Historical Trust, Inc. (hereafter cited as "Stonehurst Archives" and "Paine Diary"). Note that diary dates are those printed on the pages used, typically earlier in year than Paine's actual entries.

4. Paine was all too well aware that he was also descended from two Pilgrims, three Puritan governors, thirteen Puritan ministers (no match for Brooks's roster), five judges, and three lawyers, as well as Anne Hutchinson and Anne Bradstreet. Bedford Place became today's Chauncy Street, east of Kingston Street.

5. Robert's father, Charles Cushing Paine (1808–1874), did not seek the prominence that could so easily have been his; he gave up law practice for four months of the year and finally abandoned law altogether for managing small investments and conducting historical research. Perhaps part of his unengaged approach to life could be explained by the lack of a father figure in his own childhood, since he was two when his mother was widowed and thereafter raised him and three older sisters as a single parent with limited income opportunities. He gave his sons and daughters the father he never had and was active in raising his nine children. See Thomas M. Paine, *Growing Paines: Paternal Patterns and Matrimonial Matters in a Family Boston Born and Bred* (Wellesley, Mass.: privately printed, 1991).

6. The society merged later with other charities to form today's Boston Children's Services.

7. His grandfather Charles Jackson (1755–1855), a retired State Supreme Court justice, bequeathed to him and his first cousin, Oliver Wendell Holmes Jr., his law library.

8. Paine's eldest brother, Charles Jackson Paine (1833–1916), found himself leading black troops to glory in New Orleans and Richmond and, as the youngest major general in the Union army at war's end, won the affections of an orphaned heiress fourteen years his junior. His next older brother, William Cushing Paine (1834–1889), a brilliant West Point graduate, was a career army engineer who married soon after Robert did but died young, of alcoholism. The only younger brother, Sumner (1847–1863), the leader of his sophomore class at Harvard (class of 1865), left college and was killed at Gettysburg at age eighteen, the youngest of Harvard's Civil War dead.

9. Sarah Cushing Paine and Charles Henry Pope (hereafter cited as Pope), *Paine Ancestry* (Boston, Mass.: privately printed, 1912), 280.

10. Allen Forbes, *Other Industries of New England* (Boston: State Street Trust, 1924), 22.

11. Brooks was a houseguest in Waltham as early as September 1871, when he stayed overnight and walked an hour in the woods: Paine Diary.

12. Paine, autobiographical sketch dictated in 1904, contained in Pope, *Paine Ancestry,* 276–309; quote on 280.

13. Indeed, it may well be that Paine, along with his brother General Charles J. Paine, attended the Commemoration Day at Harvard in 1865, honoring the ninety-seven Harvard Civil War dead. On that occasion his classmate Brooks, then an unknown clergyman from Philadelphia, delivered a morning prayer of such profound spiritual power that overnight he became a household word in Boston, and people like Paine began to wonder what it would take to get him to come to Boston to preach. Regrettably, the text of that prayer has not survived.

14. George Lyman Paine, unpublished reminiscences in Stonehurst Archives.

15. Quoted in Raymond W. Albright, *Focus on Infinity: A Life of Phillips Brooks* (New York: Macmillan, 1961), 206, 215, 275.

16. Paine Diary, several dates, 1871; and "Address at the first public meeting of the Waltham Coop. Bank," October 21, 1880, 9, Stonehurst Archives.

17. Paine Diary, April 26 and August 4, 1871; Pope, *Paine Ancestry*, 303. Other members of the company were artist Sarah Wyman Whitman (1842–1904), who assisted John La Farge on minor aspects of the interior decoration of Trinity Church, painted a portrait of Brooks, and created a stained glass window in the parish house; architect-builder George W. Pope (1822–1896), with whom Paine worked over the next quarter-century; and Paine's sister Sarah Cushing Paine (1838–1924). I am indebted to Ann Clifford for this and several other points duly noted from her slide lecture on Robert Treat Paine, given at Trinity Church Parish House, December 2001.

18. Pope, *Paine Ancestry*, 281.

19. The committee, appointed by the vestry, comprised William P. Blake, secretary (1846–1922, Harvard '66, lawyer); Martin Brimmer (1829–1896, Harvard '49, son of George Brimmer, architect of the 1828 Trinity Church, cofounder of Boston Museum of Fine Arts, Boston legislator); Charles R. Codman (1829–1918, Harvard '49, lawyer); John G. Cushing; Stephen G. Deblois, treasurer; George M. Dexter (1802–1872, architect); Charles G. Morrill; Robert Treat Paine, chairman (1835–1910); Charles Henry Parker (1816–18??, Harvard '35, banker and lawyer); John C. Ropes (1836–1899, Harvard '57, lawyer, Civil War historian); and Robert C. Winthrop (1808–1894, political leader, orator, historian).

20. Allen, *Life and Letters*, 2:7. Compare Paine's language in his solicitation letter: "If we build without the triangle, we lose the open space among the church, the shrubbery, trees and lawn, with the seclusion and beauty, and peace, the splendid exposure on all sides, in short the best opportunity yet offered in Boston for a grand church-site." Quoted in Theodore E. Stebbins Jr., "Richardson and Trinity Church: The Evolution of a Building," *Journal of the Society of Architectural Historians* 26, no. 4 (December 1968): n.p.

21. Pope, *Paine Ancestry*, 281.

22. Ibid., 282.

23. Ibid., 316.

24. Gertrude Himmelfarb, *The De-Moralization of Society, from Victorian Virtues to Modern Values* (New York: Alfred A. Knopf, 1995), 148.

25. Allen, *Life and Letters*, 2:153.

26. Paine Diary, January 7, 1873.

27. Stebbins, "Richardson and Trinity Church," n.p.

28. On the executive committee besides Paine were C. H. Parker and C. W. Galloupe (replacing Dexter). Parker, twenty years Paine's senior and the member most concerned with tower safety, was made chair; he appears frequently in Paine Diary as CHP. See also Allen, *Life and Letters*, 2:8.

29. Paine Diary, March 4, 1874.

30. Paine Diary, January, June 27, 1873; February 4 and 26, March 4 and 18, December 31, 1874; January 16, February 6 and 10, March 7, 15, and 19, April 16, May 8, 1876, among other dates.

31. Diary of T. M. Clark, superintendent architect of Trinity Church, Archives of Trinity Church, quoted in Jeffrey L. Dodes, "Summary of Research: Robert Treat Paine House, Waltham, Massachusetts, Dining Room Woodwork," unpaginated manuscript, Stonehurst Archives. Clark wrote C. H. Parker and Paine on July 22, 1874: "Norcross is quite upset with me because I give directions which cost him more money, and materials. He said I would have to pay for them personally. I resign my post of superintendency today, if a directive about my authority is not made in paper by the building committee." It was made, and Clark stayed.

32. Brooks to Paine, August 4, 1874, Massachusetts Historical Society collections, quoted in Allen, *Life and Letters*, 2:96–97.

33. Brooks to Paine, April 17, 1875, Massachusetts Historical Society collections.

34. Paine Diary, entries written on pages for June 19 and August 1, 1876.

35. Pope, *Paine Ancestry*, 282. The $65,000 debt is equivalent to $2.5 million today. For financial details, see Stebbins, "Richardson and Trinity Church." The donor committee members were Brimmer, Deblois, Dexter, Galloupe, Paine, and Parker. Brooks donated one-quarter of his salary. In fact, Franklin Evans, the parish member who sold the triangle and took back a note, remained the creditor of what may be termed "nonvexatious" debt, since he extended the term beyond this date. (Coincidentally, Paine's grandson John H. Storer Jr. was to marry John La Farge's granddaughter Elizabeth Claxton.)

36. Allen, *Life and Letters*, 2:137–38.

37. Robert Treat Paine, "Report on the Activities of the Trinity Church Building Committee, 1872–1877," unpaginated typescript, Archives of Trinity Church.

38. Brooks to Paine, June 22 and July 7, 1877, Stonehurst Archives. For background on glass, see Susan Fondiler Berkon, "Stained Glass in Back Bay Churches," in *Victorian Boston Today: Ten Walking Tours*, ed. Pauline Chase Harrell and Margaret Supplee Smith (Boston: New England Chapter of the Victorian Society in America, 1975), 120–31.

39. Henry Holiday (1839–1927), painter and stained glass designer, studied at the Royal Academy Schools from 1854, becoming friends with Pre-Raphaelites Rossetti and Burne-Jones. He became chief designer at Powell & Sons, a stained glass maker, in 1863 (after Burne-Jones had left the previous year) and fulfilled more than three hundred commissions, many for American clients. As a painter, he excelled in drapery, producing cold-faced figure subjects close in spirit to the work of Rossetti.

40. Berkon, *Stained Glass*, 122–24.

41. Pope, *Paine Ancestry*, 305; $250 went to the charities and $550 to the foreign mission, which after the Boxer Rebellion was divided between Japan and the Philippines.

42. Paine knew of Ruskin's Working Men's Colleges. Octavia Hill (1838–1912), philanthropist and innovator in low-income housing reform, followed Ruskin's advice to put housing on a sound financial footing, ultimately managed some two thousand housing units, pioneered Paine's not-alms-but-a-friend philosophy, and cofounded the National Trust based on the prototype of the Massachusetts Trustees of Reservations. Paine's sister Helen (1851–1933) worked with Hill in London in 1888. Ann Clifford, slide lecture at Trinity Church, December 2001.

43. The date of coinage was December 29, 1879, in Paine's address to the Baptist Union. See Himmelfarb, *De-Moralization of Society*, 158; and Pope, *Paine Ancestry*, 295.

44. Pope, *Paine Ancestry*, 296. Martin Brimmer of the building committee also served.

45. Albright, *Focus on Infinity*, 178.

46. Pope, *Paine Ancestry*, 303. See also Robert Treat Paine, "Homes for the People," *Journal of Social Science*, February 1882, 115.

47. In 1884, Oliver Wendell Holmes Jr., Paine's first cousin and another relative of the Boston Civil War generation who had chosen to fight, delivered a Memorial Day address at Keene, N.H., saying "I think that, as life is action and passion, it is required of a man that he should share the passion and action of his time at peril of being judged not to have lived." Holmes enlarged the dialogue beyond battlefields. Each generation's battlefield would be its own. He exhorted the new generation to remember that living a good life, living fully, meant engaging in the higher spirit of the times by doing one's job. Paine, who had chosen not to fight, became fully engaged in trenches of his own.

48. Himmelfarb, *De-Moralization of Society*, 165–66.

49. Robert Treat Paine obituary, *Boston Evening Transcript*, August 12, 1910.

50. Pope, *Paine Ancestry*, 299.

51. Alexis de Tocqueville, *Democracy in America* (1835, 1840), ed. J. P. Mayer and Max Lerner (New York: Harper & Row, 1966), 485.

52. Allen, *Life and Letters*, 2:336.

53. Himmelfarb, *De-Moralization of Society*, 162–63. Hill's charities organized programs analogous to Paine's Associated Charities with their own cadres of "friends." In 1882, Paine chaired that

institution's Committee on Dwellings of the Poor. See also Robert Treat Paine, "Immediate Duty of Every City to Organize its Charities," in *Report of a Committee of the Churches Associated in the Boston Quarterly Charity Lecture* (Boston: John Wilson & Son, 1885), in Stonehurst Archives.

54. Pope, *Paine Ancestry,* 287.

55. The house survives as Stonehurst, the Robert Treat Paine estate, owned by the city of Waltham and open to the public. Paine Diary, pages dated August 22 and 29, 1883.

56. Pope, *Paine Ancestry,* 304. No longer standing, it was located at 987–89 Washington Street, just south of the present Amtrak/Massachusetts Turnpike corridor.

57. Hubert von Herkomer (1849–1914), active in Germany and England, Slade Professor of Fine Art at Oxford, also painted such social themes as the indigent women consigned to a workhouse in *Eventide, a Scene at Westminster Union* (1878), now in the Walker Art Gallery, Liverpool. Richardson agreed to a portrait when the artist suggested that the long dimension of the rectangle be horizontal—surely a reflection of the architect's own approach to design. The Paine portraits, traditionally vertical, are owned by the city of Waltham. Von Herkomer also painted Ruskin.

58. *Waltham Tribune,* October 7, 1886, Stonehurst Archives, courtesy of Ann Clifford, slide lecture at Trinity Church, December 2001.

59. Obituary, *Boston Globe,* August 12, 1910.

60. July 24, 1887, in Allen, *Life and Letters,* 664–67 and Pope, *Paine Ancestry,* 284.

61. Conversation with Ann Van Dusen, Trinity Church Programs, March 2001.

62. The building was located at 1161–75 Tremont Street in Roxbury, corner of Ruggles Street. See Pope, *Paine Ancestry,* 305.

63. Paine obituary, *Boston Evening Transcript,* August 12, 1910. Membership of the Wells Memorial Institute, mostly "working people," was approximately two thousand in 1897.

64. Boston, May 14, 1891, in Allen, *Life and Letters,* 2:851–52.

65. *Harvard Magazine,* October 1886, n.p.

66. The charcoal portrait is signed Almira Noa and dated 1894. It is owned by the city of Waltham.

67. Pope, *Paine Ancestry,* 289. The architect of this contextually sensitive building in the northwest corner of Harvard Yard was Alexander W. Longfellow; it is complemented by a statue of Brooks by Bela Lyon Pratt (1867–1917).

68. Pope, *Paine Ancestry,* 291.

69. Emily Lyman Storer, "Happy Memories," typescript, March 24, 1952, Stonehurst Archives. Hampton Institute—now Hampton University, Hampton, Virginia—pioneered in educating both blacks and Native Americans.

70. Paine obituary, *Boston Globe,* August 12, 1910.

71. Designed by Peabody & Stearns in the glacier boulder style Richardson had used at Stonehurst, with stones supplied by Paine from Stonehurst.

72. Priscilla R. Ritter, "Robert Treat Paine Papers, 1882–1910," typescript, 12 June 1967, Massachusetts Historical Society.

73. Robert Treat Paine, *Pauperism in Great Cities: Its Four Chief Causes,* (Chicago: N.p. 1893), 42 pages, had been preceded by Paine's other works on charity organization, cooperative banks, housing, and "not alms but a friend." Stonehurst Archives.

74. Robert Treat Paine, *The Inspiration of Charity* (Boston: W. B. Clarke, 1905).

75. Donors were Edith Paine (1863–1924), who married John Humphreys Storer (1859–1935); Robert Treat Paine Jr. (1866–1961), who married Mary Louise Mattingly (1872–1916), Ethel Lyman Paine (1872–1954), who married John F. Moors and Charles E. Raven; Rev. George Lyman Paine (1874–1948), who married Clara Adelaide May (1872–1948); and Lydia Lyman Paine (1876–1958), who married Charles Kimball Cummings (1870–1955), an architect whose father was an architect (Charles A., of Cummings & Sears). Designed by Shepley, Rutan & Coolidge and carved by John Evans, the pulpit was dedicated December 10, 1916.

4-1. Henry Hobson Richardson (1838–1886). (Photo by Marian Hooper "Clover" Adams, 1884; Courtesy of the Massachusetts Historical Society.)

# 4

## Architect: Henry Hobson Richardson (Gambrill & Richardson)

KATHLEEN A. CURRAN

IN 1885, THE YEAR BEFORE THE death of Henry Hobson Richardson (fig. 4-1), Trinity Church, Boston, was voted the best-liked building in the United States.[1] One hundred and six years later, in 1991, it was still in the top ten, voted ninth by members of the American Institute of Architects. In this same poll, Richardson placed third in the category of "top all-time American architects," following Frank Lloyd Wright and Louis Sullivan.[2] Despite the vicissitudes of time and taste, the building and the architect are still revered as national treasures. Why Trinity Church? Because it was at Trinity Church that the Richardsonian Romanesque was born. Margaret Henderson Floyd described the process as something like nuclear fusion, where "separate elements are combined in a special way to produce not merely the sum or melding of parts, but are transformed to release the expanded visual energy of a cohesive work of art."[3] The result of that burst of creation still elicits a visceral response from those who see it for the first time. What becomes clear, however, is that the Richardsonian Romanesque happened at Trinity by dint of a collaboration of which Richardson was the great impresario. He authored the style, but not without team effort.

Richardson was born on September 29, 1838, at Priestley Plantation in St. James Parish, Louisiana, the son of Henry Dickinson Richardson and Catherine Priestley.[4] Priestley Plantation stood near Oak Alley, perhaps Louisiana's most famous antebellum plantation, which neared completion in 1838, the year Richardson was born. Oak Alley's sybaritic classicism was the polar opposite of the direction Richardson would later take, yet its overwhelming presence oddly foreshadowed Frank Lloyd Wright's description of him as a "grand exteriorist" who had a "robust appetite for romance."[5] Richardson seems to have imbibed a taste for monumental architecture and its potential to move the senses.

His education was extraordinary for an architect coming of age in the mid-nineteenth century. After a year at Tulane University, he entered the freshman class at Harvard in 1856, where by all accounts he displayed no small share of southern charm and vivaciousness. Following Harvard, Richardson was only the second American to study architecture at the prestigious Ecole des Beaux-Arts in Paris. He began his studies there in 1860 and remained until the Civil War's end in 1865, with only one interim trip to Boston in the winter of 1861–62.[6] For one who was southern-born but northern-bred, Paris obviously served as neutral territory during one of the worst crises in this nation's history. He wrote to his fiancée Julia Hayden, whom he met while at Harvard, that he was "just waking up to the value of time" and vowed to study his profession "in such a manner as to make my success a surety and not a chance."[7] Richardson's words were not empty. When he returned to the United States in the fall of 1865, he was determined to be a success, and he did make the most of his days in his short life, living only to the age of forty-seven.

Richardson settled neither in Boston nor in New Orleans but chose instead to open an office in New York. He didn't have to wait long before receiving his first commission, in November 1866, to design the Church of the Unity in Springfield, Massachusetts. This instant success made marriage possible, and the Richardsons lived on Staten Island, where they remained until relocating to Brookline, near Boston, in 1874. Richardson kept an office in Manhattan, where in 1867 he had formed a partnership with Charles Gambrill, which continued until 1878, throughout the design of Trinity Church.[8]

In the six years between the Church of the Unity and Trinity Church, Boston, Richardson recognized that although he had studied in Paris, he had returned to a country with Anglo-Saxon architectural traditions. It would have been difficult for any American architect practicing in the 1860s and 1870s to avoid the popular interest in English Gothic architecture, and his Church of the Unity showed the influence of English Gothic parish churches on American ecclesiastical design. Although Gothic was new to him, the Springfield church (which was destroyed in 1960) evinced a promising talent. Mariana Griswold (Mrs. Schuyler) Van Rensselaer, author of his first biography (1888), wrote that "this first work reveals the essential qualities of Richardson's art, . . . that what he thought most about was the building as a whole—the mass, the body—and not any one feature or any question of treatment or decoration."[9] Van Rensselaer understood the architect's instinctive talent for pulling together parts to form an integrated composition.

The Church of the Unity was a very good start, but Richardson did not pursue the direction of the Gothic Revival. He chose instead to study the Romanesque period of medieval architecture directly preceding the Gothic. The word Romanesque had been introduced into the English language by William Gunn in 1813 to describe eleventh- and twelfth-century architecture which was like that of the Romans (thus "Romanesque").[10] It is characterized by round arches, masonry barrel vaults, thick walls, bold massing, and clearly articulated parts. These features resonated with Richardson's architectural tastes more than the Gothic, which tended to perforate and dematerialize walls. It was thus the round-arched Romanesque, not the pointed-arch Gothic, that inspired—and named—Richardson's personal style, to which he adhered until his death in 1886.

The Richardsonian Romanesque was born in the planning of Trinity Church, Boston. The building of Trinity was officially inaugurated on March 12, 1872, when the building committee of eleven men, chaired by Robert Treat Paine, invited six architectural firms to compete for the prized commission.[11] The firms were William A. Potter, Peabody & Stearns, Ware & Van Brunt, John Sturgis, Richard Morris Hunt, and Gambrill & Richardson. The deadline for entries was May 1, 1872. A rectangular site had already been purchased earlier that year in the Back Bay area—east of what is now Copley Square—at Clarendon Street and St. James Avenue.

When Richardson received the invitation, he set quickly to work. On the back of the letter he sketched two ground plans offering widely different solutions: one was for a long basilica with central nave and side aisles; the other was for a squat, compact cross with four equal arms. Richardson's French training had taught him to compose quickly and accurately by means of such sketches or *esquisses*, which, once amplified, would still contain the germ of the initial conception.[12] A drawing executed about three months later, in June 1872, shows that Richardson chose the compact cross or cruciform plan with the addition of a semicircular apse at the east end and towers at the front, or west end. This study also shows the addition of a parish house, made possible through the purchase of an adjacent piece of property on Huntington Avenue, which transformed the original rectangular site into a trapezoid.[13]

In the end, Richardson had, in fact, no other choice than to go with the compact cross. The reasons were twofold, having to do with topography and, in an entirely different vein, with theology. First, the trapezoidal site presented both structural and visual challenges. The soil was marshy, necessitating the construction of a foundation consisting of 4,500 wooden piles.[14] Visually, the church was surrounded by streets on all sides and would inevitably be viewed from a variety of perspectives. Each elevation was therefore of strategic importance, the rear and side views as much as the front. Indeed, the west or front elevation was the last one to be resolved; it remained incomplete until a decade after Richardson's death; its porch was added by his successor firm, Shepley, Rutan & Coolidge, between 1894 and 1897. Even Van Rensselaer chose to illustrate Trinity not from the front but, to handsome advantage, from the southeast (fig. 4-2).

Given this set of physical conditions, Richardson recognized that the building must be concentrated in mass and piled high, providing attractive vistas on all four sides. Coincidentally, a number of projects on which he was working at the time offered a similar challenge and solution. For example, in the same month, March 1872, that Richardson received the invitation from Trinity, he was also working on the competition for the Connecticut State Capitol. There the site was open and elevated above Bushnell Park in downtown Hartford, and he opted for a pyramidal shape with a cruciform plan similar to the second one he scribbled on the Trinity competition letter.[15] A tall central tower anchored that design and bestowed upon it a bold but graceful silhouette, recalling the grand chateaux of France's Loire Valley.

But Trinity was a church, not a state capitol, and so Richardson turned to the Romanesque ecclesiastical architecture of the central region of France called the Auvergne for ideas of how to deal with the compact, weighty massing demanded by the site. Among the churches that Richardson studied was St. Paul in Issoire (ca. 1130–50).[16] French Romanesque churches of the Auvergne are, with few exceptions, photographed from the rear, because they share a peculiar eastern arrangement: a semicircular apse out of which billow smaller apisidioles containing chapels. Looming above the apse is a high-shouldered tower crowned by a lantern, in this case, of octagonal shape.[17] Explaining why the Auvergnac churches appealed to him, Richardson later wrote that "the central tower became, as it were, the Church, . . . the apse, transepts, nave and chapels forming only the base to the obelisk of the tower."[18] At Trinity, the tower would "become" the church as well.

The competition drawings for Trinity that Richardson submitted in June 1872 show how the French Auvergnac churches inspired his thinking at that point (figs. 4-3, 4-4). The tall tower became the overriding feature, its striking octagonal lantern set within a square base that was equidistant from front and rear. The apse, in particular, revealed an affinity to St. Paul in Issoire, but the architect relinquished the small radiating chapels—not needed for an 1870s American Episcopal church—and opted instead for a single apse with a walkway or ambulatory along its lower half.[19]

The pyramidal composition was the right choice for the multivistaed site, and it proved just as desirable for the inside workings of the church. That brings us to the theological style of Richardson's mighty client, Phillips Brooks, and his legendary fame as one of the country's great preachers. A compact interior would

4-2. Trinity Church from the southwest, Gambrill & Richardson, Architects. (Mariana Griswold Van Rensselaer, *Henry Hobson Richardson and His Works,* 1888.)

provide the most effective environment for his words to be heard, and this condition was implicit in the invitation letter to the six architectural firms: generous galleries to seat 350 persons were a requested feature, along with an interior "with good acoustic qualities," unimpeded by columns.[20] The galleries, which were not taxed, formed what Alexander Vinton, Brooks's biographer, called "a church within a church."[21] Richardson's competition ground plan shows the sheer amount of space allotted to Brooks's galleries, encompassing roughly one-third the seating capacity of the building. In fact, Brooks allowed the throngs to saturate his church, including the chancel, so that he stood surrounded—not in the

FRONT ELEVATION

4-3. Trinity Church. Competition drawing for the west elevation, 1872, Gambrill & Richardson, Architects. (H. H. Richardson Papers, TC B1, Department of Printing and Graphic Arts, Houghton Library, Harvard College Library.)

REAR ELEVATION

4-4.  Trinity Church. Competition drawing for the east elevation, 1872, Gambrill & Richardson, Architects. (H. H. Richardson Papers, TC B3, Department of Printing and Graphic Arts, Houghton Library, Harvard College Library.)

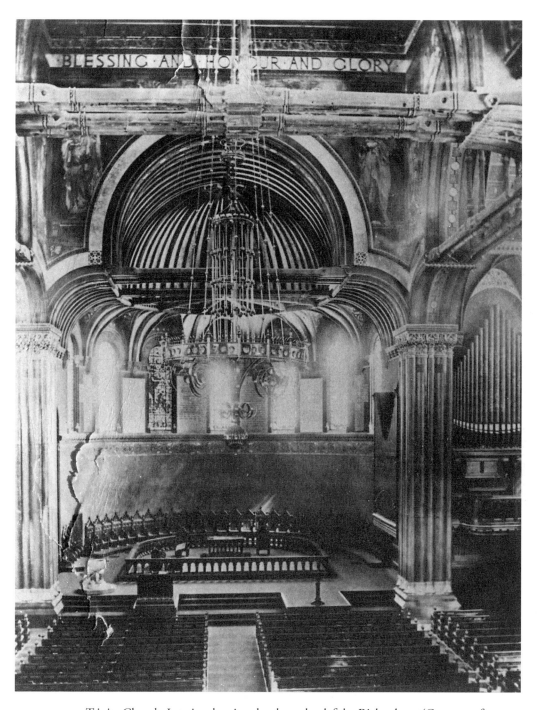

4-5. Trinity Church. Interior showing the chancel as left by Richardson. (Courtesy of Trinity Church Archives.)

present-day pulpit (which was installed in 1916 in memory of Robert Treat Paine) but at a temporary reading desk on the chancel steps (fig. 4-5).

Phillips Brooks's preaching style, then, was a major consideration in the choice of plan and interior arrangements. Although he was not an official member of the building committee, his diaries from 1872–74 reveal that he was present at every building committee meeting, including the one on June 1, 1872, when Richardson was selected.[22] Thereafter, Brooks remained involved at every stage, with frequent visits to the building site. His diaries, for example, record meetings with Richardson in New York throughout the heady planning years of 1873 and 1874. But he went to New York also to inspect other churches, often with building committee members. In some cases, they would then travel to Staten Island to discuss the architectural plans with Richardson.

Among the New York churches that Brooks visited, two were of formative influence for Trinity: St. George's Episcopal Church in New York, which stands on Stuyvesant Square and was built in 1846–49 to the designs of Eidlitz & Blesch (fig. 4-6), and St. Bartholomew's Episcopal Church (now destroyed), which was completed in 1872 to the designs of James Renwick Jr. (fig. 4-7).[23] It is not surprising that St. George's and St. Bartholomew's would have been of keen interest to Brooks. Like Trinity, they were both established, socially prominent Episcopal churches affiliated with the low-church wing of the American Episcopal Church. The rector of St. George's was Stephen Tyng, a renowned Evangelical. When it was completed, St. George's received national attention. In 1853, *Putnam's Monthly* declared it to be "the most chastely designed and most sincerely built church in New York City."[24] Tyng and Brooks were well acquainted and even felt a certain bond in that the old Trinity Church on Summer Street had been Tyng's church when he was growing up in Boston. When the relocated Trinity was dedicated on February 9, 1877, Tyng traveled to Boston to see Brooks's "new and grand church."[25]

St. George's and St. Bartholomew's shared one other important feature with Trinity Church: they were both Romanesque. In fact, when it was built between 1846 and 1849, St. George's was one of the earliest Romanesque Revival churches in the United States and the only one housing an Episcopal congregation. It was among the small cluster of churches of the mid-1840s that were commissioned by ambitious ministers of Calvinist persuasion—Congregationalist, Baptist, and low-church Episcopalian—who wanted to distance themselves from the Gothic, the quasi-official style of the high-church wing of American Episcopalianism. Evangelical ministers such as Tyng, who preferred a service that was preaching-based, admired the "primitive" simplicity of the Romanesque, as they would have described it.[26] Tyng distrusted such accoutrements of Catholic worship as altars

4-6.  St. George's Episcopal Church, New York, 1846–49, Eidlitz & Blesch, Architects.
(*Putnam's Monthly* 2, no. 9, 1853.)

4-7. St. Bartholomew's Episcopal Church, New York, 1872, James Renwick Jr., Architect. (Courtesy of the Museum of the City of New York.)

4-8. St. George's, New York, interior after renovations in 1869. (Henry Anstice, *History of St. George's,* 1911.)

and their regalia. He demanded of his architects that his communion table not be mistaken for an altar: "Make me a table, do you understand, a table that I can walk around and see under."[27] That table is relegated to the chancel in the photograph of the interior of St. George's taken in 1869, and Tyng's pulpit takes pride of place, edging into the congregation's space (fig. 4-8). It is this arrangement that Brooks witnessed in 1872 and that the chancel arrangements at Trinity so closely mirrored.

Brooks was particularly enamored of the elaborate tablets containing biblical texts that Tyng had implemented in St. George's in 1869 (visible in fig. 4-8). Brooks vowed to have them at Trinity, too, and they are visible in the original chancel walls between the clerestory windows (fig. 4-5).[28] The addition of these tablets, though, forced abandonment of Richardson's original double-volume apse, inspired by St. Paul in Issoire. As built, Trinity's apse took the shape of the apse at St. George's, with its high blind walls and clerestory windows (compare figs. 4-2 and 4-6).

It is hard to overemphasize the difference in appearance between the competition drawings for Trinity Church and the finished building. An incredulous Richardson later observed "I really don't see why the Trinity people liked them [the competition drawings], or, if they liked them, why they let me do what I afterwards did."[29] Besides the revised apse, an important architectural and liturgical feature, among other sweeping changes to the competition drawings were those made to the front elevation—again, partly explicable by examination of St. George's and especially St. Bartholomew's (fig. 4-7). For example, a design development drawing for Trinity, which probably dates between April and June 1873, shows that Richardson relinquished the rose window for a register of five arches, with a series of ascending arches in the gable above (fig. 4-9). This combination had appeared at St. Bartholomew's. Both churches also have an entryway much like that of the French Romanesque cathedral at St. Gilles-du-Gard, but this entrance was not the one Richardson saw there, so it could not have been the direct inspiration for Trinity. (Stanford White, Richardson's former apprentice, added it to St. Bartholomew's in 1900–1903.)

These revisions indicate that after he won the competition, Richardson immediately began to alter Trinity's appearance, no doubt at the building committee's and Brooks's urging. But what are we to make of the most striking change, that of the tower, the controlling feature of the church? The tall, ungainly tower and octagonal lantern were transformed into what is surely one of the most memorable church towers ever built, rivaling those of the great cathedrals of Europe. For some clues to that strategic transformation, which so altered—and arguably saved—the design of the church, it is useful to step back for a moment and summarize the design development process so far.

Theodore Stebbins has shown that in the four years between the competition drawings of 1872 and the construction of the church in 1876, Richardson made many sets of "final" plans.[30] In 1873 alone, he presented mature plans in April, in June, and in September, the third being the set shown to contractors to solicit bids. During this fertile gestation period he worked closely with Brooks and members of the building committee such as George Dexter (who died early on), Robert Treat Paine, and C. W. Galloupe. The dozens of drawings from this intense period (fig. 4-9 is one example) point out in painstaking detail how much Richardson's vision was maturing and his signature style developing. He continued to study French Romanesque architecture by perusing photographs and acquiring books such as Henri Revoil's *Architecture romane du midi de la France* of 1873, which contained plates of the two churches—St. Gilles-du-Gard and St.

4-9.  Trinity Church. West elevation drawing of ca. April–July 1873, Gambrill &
Richardson, Architects. (H. H. Richardson Papers, TC B7, Department of Printing and
Graphic Arts, Houghton Library, Harvard College Library.)

Trophime in Arles—on which he based the western porch and entrance.[31] He developed a sophisticated handling of ornament based on French Auvergnac mosaic masonry, employing for the first time the elaborate colored decoration that that one finds in the upper stages of the facade and rear apse.[32] And, Richardson began to exaggerate his trademark stone or "lithic" style, achieved by mixing walls of light Dedham granite with dark Longmeadow sandstone trim.[33]

On October 10, 1873, a contract was signed with Norcross Brothers, Richardson's "master builders," who, as James F. O'Gorman has shown, became key players in the making of a Richardson building.[34] As the pieces fell into place, though, persistent fears resurfaced about the weight of the building and particularly the tower. In April 1874, Richardson was informed by the executive committee (three members of the building committee) that the tower had to be lightened greatly on the recommendation of the new consulting engineer, Ernest Bowditch. The committee had aesthetic as well as practical objections to the octagonal lantern and wanted the tower wholly redesigned.[35] Richardson had no choice but to follow their directive.

The rest of the story is near-legendary. Van Rensselaer relates that one day when Richardson was ill in bed, looking at some photographs sent to him by John La Farge, he saw one of the tower at Salamanca Cathedral in Spain and declared, "This is what we want." The story may or may not be true, but there is a drawing of the tower in George Edmund Street's *Some Account of Gothic Architecture in Spain* (1865), a copy of which Richardson owned; Street declared that the Salamanca tower solved "better than the lantern of any church . . . the question of the introduction of the dome to Gothic churches."[36] Richardson had already used a Salamanca style tower for his Connecticut State Capitol competition in 1872. With Street's good advice, he probably decided to pull it out again and put to rest the nagging concern over Trinity's tower.

This explains Richardson's actions, but it does not explain why the executive committee had aesthetic concerns about the octagonal lantern. Once again, the evidence points to Phillips Brooks. Before he came to Trinity in 1869, he had served as rector at the Church of the Holy Trinity in Philadelphia. That church, designed by John Notman between 1856 and 1859, was another early example of the American Romanesque Revival (fig. 4-10). When Brooks arrived at Holy Trinity in 1861, the corner tower had not yet been built. In 1866 the vestry empowered him to oversee its construction, but Notman, the architect, had died the year before. Notman's proposed tower was virtually the same as the one added in 1867 by John Fraser except for one important difference: it was crowned by a tall spire.[37] Brooks did not like the spire, especially after having seen the majestic square tower at Durham Cathedral during a grand tour of England and Europe

4-10. Church of the Holy Trinity, Philadelphia, 1856–59, John Notman, Architect. Tower added 1867, John Fraser, Architect. (Author's collection.)

in 1865–66.[38] He thought that the spire would make the tower too tall and probably too Gothic (giving it religious connotations). At first the vestry insisted on the spire.[39] Brooks eventually prevailed, however, and got the square, spireless tower he preferred, the one at Holy Trinity today. When he left to take the job in Boston, he wrote to his brother William of his attachment to Holy Trinity: "I don't care a pin for the old granite tower [on Trinity Church, Summer St.], while the brownstone tower in Walnut St. [Philadelphia] is dearer than ever." Brooks obviously cared deeply about towers and their significance, and the square Salamanca lantern with its four corner turrets was much more in the spirit of his beloved Philadelphia church.[40]

That the tower was not his only memory of Holy Trinity brings us to the interior design and decoration of Trinity Church. Two strategic changes between the original plans and the final product reinforce the role played by Brooks and by earlier Romanesque Revival churches. Richardson originally intended an arched wooden ceiling for Trinity, perhaps something in the manner of his later small-town libraries. In the competition drawings the roof is visible in the transverse section (fig. 4-11), but he abandoned this idea, replacing the wooden ceiling with plaster and wood vaults of trefoil section. Holy Trinity in Philadelphia had a similar tripartite ceiling, and so Brooks again probably instigated the change.

As for the interior decoration, Richardson's original intentions were entirely different from what we see today, as evidenced by the competition drawings (fig. 4-11). The walls were dominated by stenciled patterns of Romanesque ornament: punched checkerboards with bands of medieval ornament surrounding the round arches. The source for his ideas was Stephen Tyng's St. George's in New York, whose walls had undergone extensive mural decoration in 1869 by Leopold Eidlitz after a fire had destroyed the original interior (see fig. 4-8). When Brooks visited St. George's in the early 1870s, he obviously took careful notes. Following John La Farge's hire in 1876 on Richardson's recommendation, though, Richardson decided to subordinate stenciled decoration to an overall background of deep Persian red, one of his *and* Brooks's favorite colors.[41] The red interior, with highlights of green and gold, imparted a sumptuous and domestic warmth, far removed from the stone exterior. La Farge and his crew filled the red background with Old and New Testament figures and two biblical history paintings in the nave. When that work was completed, it was considered as great a work of art as the church itself.

In the end, Trinity Church was a complex amalgamation of French and Spanish Romanesque sources,[42] Ecole training, and American Romanesque Revival churches, combined with a personal handling of materials, ornament, and architectural elements such as the round arch. It was nineteenth-century eclecticism at its most masterful.

If the best architecture is achieved through collaboration—of clients who are focused but know when not to interfere with the design, of talented contractors who take pride in their craft, and of gifted designers who are practical but can make a building sing at the same time—then Trinity Church was the perfect collaboration.[43] Richardson developed into a brilliant architect, but his collaborators aided in that transition, and Trinity was where that happened. The great impresario was lucky in life and lucky in his team.

4-11. Trinity Church. Competition drawing of longitudinal section, 1872, Gambrill & Richardson, Architects. (H. H. Richardson Papers, TC C1, Department of Printing and Graphic Arts, Houghton Library, Harvard College Library.)

# NOTES

1. "The Best Ten Buildings in the United States," *American Architect and Building News* 17, no. 494 (1885): 282.

2. Stephen P. Rentner, "Memo: The envelope, please . . . ," 6–7, October 1991, American Institute of Architects, Washington, D.C. This information was given to me by Douglas E. Gordon (Hon. AIA; director, AIA Editorial Development). According to him, the 1991 poll was the most recently accurate because "it was the result of a telephone polling of more than 800 AIA members, selected at random and called by an independent polling service" (e-mail exchange, June 4, 2001).

3. Margaret Henderson Floyd, *Henry Hobson Richardson: A Genius for Architecture* (New York: Monacelli Press, 1997), 15.

4. Monographs on Richardson that discuss his early life are Mariana Griswold Van Rensselaer, *Henry Hobson Richardson and His Works* (New York: Houghton Mifflin, 1888); Henry-Russell Hitchcock, *The Architecture of H. H. Richardson and His Times* (1936; Hamden, Conn.: Archon, 1961); James F. O'Gorman, *H. H. Richardson and His Office: Selected Drawings* (Cambridge, Mass.: Dept. of Printing and Graphic Arts, Harvard College Library, 1974); Jeffrey Karl Ochsner, *H. H. Richardson: Complete Architectural Works* (Cambridge, Mass.: MIT Press, 1982); James F. O'Gorman, *H. H. Richardson: Architectural Forms for an American Society* (Chicago: University of Chicago Press, 1987); James F. O'Gorman, *Living Architecture: A Biography of H. H. Richardson* (New York: Simon & Schuster, 1997); Floyd, *Henry Hobson Richardson*. Individual monographs and articles that deal with Trinity Church include Edgar D. Romig, *The Story of Trinity Church in the City of Boston* (Boston: Wardens and Vestry of Trinity Church in the City of Boston, 1952, 1964); Bettina A. Norton, ed., *Trinity Church: The Story of an Episcopal Parish in the City of Boston* (Boston: Wardens and Vestry of Trinity Church in the City of Boston, 1978); Theodore E. Stebbins Jr., "Richardson and Trinity Church: The Evolution of a Building," *Journal of the Society of Architectural Historians* 27 (December 1968): 281–98; Ann Jensen Adams, "The Birth of a Style: Henry Hobson Richardson and the Competition Drawings for Trinity Church, Boston," *Art Bulletin* 62 (1980): 409–33; William H. Pierson Jr., "Richardson's Trinity Church and the New England Meetinghouse," in *American Public Architecture: European Roots and Native Expressions,* ed. Craig Zabel and Susan Scott Munshower, Papers in Art History (University Park: Pennsylvania State University Press, 1989), 12–56; Kathleen Curran, "The Romanesque Revival, Mural Painting, and Protestant Patronage in America," *Art Bulletin* 81, no. 4 (December 1999): 693–722.

5. Frank Lloyd Wright, *Frank Lloyd Wright Collected Writings,* ed. Bruce Brooks Pfeiffer, 5 vols. (New York: Rizzoli with the Frank Lloyd Wright Foundation, 1992–95), 4:97, 361.

6. For an exhaustive study of Richardson's activities at the Ecole, see Richard Chafee, "Richardson's Record at the Ecole de Beaux-Arts," *Journal of the Society of Architectural Historians* 36 (October 1977): 175–88.

7. Richardson to Julia Hayden, April 25 and May 23, 1862, quoted in Van Rensselaer, *Henry Hobson Richardson,* 11, 12.

8. O'Gorman, *H. H. Richardson: Architectural Forms,* 16–17.

9. Van Rensselaer, *Henry Hobson Richardson,* 47–48.

10. Georg Germann, *Gothic Revival in Europe: Sources, Influences, and Ideas* (Cambridge, Mass.: MIT Press, 1972), 44–45.

11. Stebbins, "Richardson and Trinity Church," 281. In addition to Paine, the building committee consisted of George M. Dexter, Martin Brimmer, Charles H. Parker, Charles R. Codman, Robert C. Winthrop, John C. Ropes, John G. Cushing, Charles D. Morrill, Stephen G. Deblois (treasurer), and William B. Blake (secretary). C. W. Galloupe was added a year later on the death of Dexter.

12. O'Gorman, *H. H. Richardson: Architectural Forms,* 57–58.

13. Norton, *Trinity Church,* 31.

14. O'Gorman, *H. H. Richardson: Architectural Forms,* 59.

15. Charles Price, "Henry Hobson Richardson: Some Unpublished Drawings," *Perspecta* 9/10 (1965): 201–2.

16. Floyd, *Henry Hobson Richardson,* 47. Richardson would later (in 1882) visit the Auvergne but had not yet done so when designing Trinity.

17. Kenneth John Conant, *Carolingian and Romanesque Architecture 800 to 1200* (Harmondsworth, U.K.: Penguin Books, 1959), 176; Julius Baum, *Romanische Baukunst in Frankreich* (Stuttgart: Julius Hoffmann, 1910), 9–10; Xavier Barral I Altet, *The Romanesque: Towns, Cathedrals, Monasteries* (Cologne: Benedikt Taschen Verlag, 1998), 118–26.

18. H. H. Richardson, *A Description of Trinity Church,* talk given at the dedication in 1877 and printed as a pamphlet handed out at the church, 13.

19. I thank Virginia Raguin for pointing out to me that in twelfth-century France the radiating chapels were for celebration of multiple masses.

20. The letter is reproduced in Adams, "Birth of a Style," 410 n. 7.

21. Alexander V. G. Allen, *Life and Letters of Phillips Brooks,* 2 vols. (New York: E. P. Dutton, 1900), 2:142.

22. Brooks's diaries for the years 1872, 1873, and 1874 (partial) are among the Phillips Brooks papers at Houghton Library, Harvard College, bMS Am 1594.I (635), box 21. They offer an important account of events leading to the selection of Richardson. Curran, "Romanesque Revival," discusses Brooks's role at Trinity Church, incorporating information from these diaries.

23. On April 8 and 9, 1872 (that is, before the winner was announced on June 1, 1872), Brooks traveled to New York with George Dexter to see St. George's and St. Bartholomew's. They went back eight months later, on December 20, to revisit St. George's and later that day "went to Staten Island and spent several hours with Richardson over plans of the new church" (Brooks Diary, 1872). On November 30 of the following year, Brooks noted that he spent the evening at "Tyng's church" (St. George's), and the next day he called on the rector (Brooks Diary, 1873).

24. "New York Church Architecture," *Putnam's Monthly* 2, no. 9 (1853): 236–37.

25. Stephen Tyng to Phillips Brooks, February 25, 1877, Phillips Brooks Papers; Charles Rockland Tyng, *Record of the Life and Work of the Rev. Stephen Higginson Tyng, D.D.* (New York: E. P. Dutton, 1890), 25.

26. Curran, "Romanesque Revival," 694–98.

27. Quoted in Montgomery Schuyler, "A Great American Architect: Leopold Eidlitz," pt. 1, "Ecclesiastical and Domestic Work," *Architectural Record* 24 (September 1908): 167–68.

28. Brooks brother Arthur, who was rector at the Church of the Incarnation in New York, designed the tablets for him. P. Brooks to A. Brooks, December 21, 1876, Phillips Brooks Papers.

29. Quoted in Van Rensselaer, *Henry Hobson Richardson,* 63.

30. Stebbins, "Richardson and Trinity Church," 298.

31. James F. O'Gorman, "Documentation: An 1886 Inventory of H. H. Richardson's Library, and Other Gleanings from Probate," *Journal of the Society of Architectural Historians* 41, no. 2 (May 1982): 150–55.

32. Van Rensselaer, *Henry Hobson Richardson,* 63–64.

33. O'Gorman frequently uses the term "lithic" to describe Richardson's style.

34. James F. O'Gorman, "O. W. Norcross, Richardson's 'Master Builder': A Preliminary Report," *Journal of the Society of Architectural Historians* 32, no. 2 (May 1973): 104–13.

35. Stebbins, "Richardson and Trinity Church," 290.

36. Van Rensselaer, *Henry Hobson Richardson,* 64; O'Gorman, "Documentation," 155; George Edmund Street, *Some Account of Gothic Architecture in Spain* (London: J. Murray, 1865), 81–82. Street criticized the towers of French Auvergnac churches as "dark, savage, and repulsive."

37. Constance M. Greiff, *John Notman, Architect: 1810–1865* (Philadelphia: Athenaeum of Philadelphia, 1979), 211.

38. Brooks wrote of Durham, "I shall come back to Holy Trinity feeling that if the architecture perhaps is not quite as perfect Norman as Durham nor Mr. Clark's music quite as fine as York Minster, there is a great deal better chance to do the work of a minister in it than if I were Dean of York or Durham." Phillips Brooks to his brother Fred, September 26, 1865, Phillips Brooks Papers. Brooks recorded aspects of the 1866 journey in personal notebooks held in bMS Am 1594. 1 (635) (Box 20), Houghton Library. For Brooks's dislike of Notman's spire, see Allen, *Life and Letters,* 1:587.

39. Brooks wrote in frustration to a C. A. L. Edwards that "I have just broken my head against my vestry in an attempt to put a tower harmonious and solid on my church. I have failed. It is to be a spire, taller than anything in town, not bad and not good" (quoted in Allen, *Life and Letters,* 1:587).

40. Brooks to William Brooks, 30 July 1869, Phillips Brooks Papers. Stebbins ("Richardson and Trinity Church," 290) writes that Brooks did take the lead on the Trinity tower, indicating that he may very well have been behind the decision to relinquish the octagonal lantern on aesthetic grounds.

41. Curran, "Romanesque Revival," 711–18. In his notes, held in the Archives of Trinity Church, John La Farge described the color as "Persian red."

42. Richardson, "Description of Trinity Church," 13, called the style a "free rendering of the French Romanesque."

43. O'Gorman, *Selected Drawings,* 27–30, emphasized the collaborative aspect of Richardson's work.

BLESSING · AND · HONOUR · AND · GLORY ·

5-1. Trinity Church. The chancel in 1888. (Monographs of American Architecture V.)

# 5

## H. H. Richardson's Furnishings

KEITH BAKKER

ONE OF THE signature characteristics of H. H. Richardson's architecture is his well-documented attention to even the smallest details of his buildings. His contemporary and first biographer, Mariana Griswold Van Rensselaer, informs us that "no feature was too small, no object too simple to engage his thought."[1] Throughout Richardson's career, this attention to detail usually extended to the design of the furniture as well as the interior woodwork for his buildings, especially the public ones. Trinity Church is no exception, even though it is among his earliest works and was designed and built as Richardson was just beginning to establish his reputation as the preeminent architect of his day. Indeed, Richardson's ability to design furnishings that captured the spirit of his buildings may have played a critical role in confirming that reputation.

With the exception of two lecterns that probably had an earlier history with the church, all of Trinity's original wooden furnishings—both furniture and architectural woodwork—were designed by Richardson and his assistants at the firm of Gambrill & Richardson. A suite of carved walnut furniture for the chancel is the most significant in the development of Richardson's vocabulary in wood. This suite exhibits a distinct Romanesque influence in style and form, although none of the pieces can be said to be directly copied from Romanesque models. In addition to a communion table and altar rail, furniture in the chancel included a row of thirty-four sedilla (built-in chairs placed against the back wall of the apse), a pair of freestanding chairs flanking the communion table, a lectern designed for Phillips Brooks, and at least two carved stalls or benches with matching reading desks and kneelers. A few other tables and benches still used by the church appear to have been designed by Richardson's office, but so far, evidence for conclusive attribution is lacking.

Most published work on Richardson has paid scant attention to the furniture at Trinity Church other than to note its removal, but recent research commissioned by the church has revealed that most of it has been preserved. Much of the chancel furniture was removed from its original setting during renovations in the first half of the twentieth century, but a few pieces are still in use in the chancel, and almost all the original pews are still in place. Other pieces from the chancel suite are in storage or in use elsewhere in the church buildings; three signature pieces, the communion table and its flanking chairs, were donated to another Episcopal church in Massachusetts. Only the sedilla and a few kneelers are unaccounted for.

Fortunately, all this furniture can be seen clearly in early photographs of the church interior (fig. 5-1), and the determination of which pieces of the church's present furniture are original is based on comparisons of these nineteenth-century photographs with written records and with design drawings from Richardson's office. Especially helpful is a series of photographs taken for the fifth volume of the Monographs of American Architecture series, published in 1888 (e.g., fig. 5-2).[2] The interior of the church was not quite complete at its consecration in 1877, and so a few pieces of furniture in the 1888 photographs, as well as the first pulpit, were added some time afterward. Church documents show that Richardson worked closely with the church on changes to the interior at least through 1881, so the attribution as "original" of some furniture that does not appear in 1877 photographs is not unreasonable.

All the furniture and most of the woodwork in the church and parish house were constructed of black walnut. The Gambrill & Richardson design specifications for the interior of Trinity describe walnut wainscoting, doors, and door trim, with ash and oak for the stairways. Chestnut, at first specified for the parish house woodwork, was later changed to walnut and ash in many areas.[3] The walnut woodwork was a critical component of the decorative scheme that Richardson planned. From the start, he was adamant that the interior walls of the church be plastered and painted, though the building committee argued for saving money by using the stonework of the load-bearing walls as a finished interior surface. Richardson clearly realized that such a choice would not complement the painted murals that he envisioned as a critical element of the final design. His view eventually prevailed, and the interior walls were plastered and painted. The walnut wainscot and trim were finished to produce a rich reddish-brown appearance that would be in harmony with the red paint chosen for the plaster walls that filled the space between the wainscot and the murals. The furniture was designed and finished to match, even as La Farge and Richardson painstakingly tested numerous shades of red paint on the walls and ceilings until Richardson was satisfied with the final color.

5-2. Trinity Church. Close-up of the "Sedilla" in 1888, no longer extant; bust of Arthur Stanley by Mary Grant, ca. 1885. (Monographs of American Architecture V.)

In an early example of the role of general contractor in modern building practice, all the basic woodwork in the church and parish house, from scaffolding to finished architectural woodwork, was supplied by Norcross Brothers, which acted as general contractor for the project. In his description of Trinity Church published for the church's consecration, Richardson stated that "the contract was made with Messers. Norcross Brothers, of Worcester, Mass., for the masonry and carpenter work of the structure."[4] This "carpenter work" included all the interior architectural woodwork for the church and the parish house, which Richardson and Norcross Brothers repeatedly refer to in letters and other documents simply as "finish." For instance, on September 29, 1876, in a good example of practical material knowledge, Norcross Brothers again warned the building committee that they had better have the furnaces installed "as soon as possible" or the "the finish will be apt to swell and warp."[5]

The Gambrill & Richardson design specifications do not describe the church furniture or the pews, as they were not part of the original contract. Bids for their construction were solicited from local manufacturers while the church was being built, following design drawings furnished by Richardson's office. (The term "office" refers here to the collaborative design effort of Richardson and his assistants at his architectural firm.[6] Throughout his career, Richardson relied on talented assistants to realize his furniture designs, but there can be no doubt that the inspiration for the Romanesque-influenced designs for Trinity Church furniture originated with Richardson's intimate understanding of the style.) Although these bids were not solicited through Norcross, in some cases Norcross Brothers was one of the bidders, which is not surprising, as the firm is known to have had millworking facilities in Worcester which supplied the interior woodwork for the project. The bidding process was coordinated by T. M. Clark, an architect on Richardson's staff who worked at the building site to supervise construction. Guided by Richardson and Clark, the building committee reviewed letters of interest and proposals from at least five local woodworking manufacturers to construct, carve, and varnish the pews. Preliminary design sketches for the pews were provided by Richardson's office, possibly drawn by Stanford White. In a letter dated September 19, 1876, Charles H. Rutan of Gambrill & Richardson wrote Clark that "Mr. White wishes me to inform you that the details for pews of Trinity Church will be sent tomorrow night"—rather late, considering the looming deadline for completion of the church, but not unusually so, as other sometimes heated correspondence has shown.[7]

Despite the late date and the fact that he was by then working on new projects, Richardson was still intimately involved in the details of the furniture construction. When he wrote to Clark on September 24, 1876, Richardson was on his way to Albany but still took the time to declare that one local woodworker, "the creature who attempted to make a pew from my drawings—should be debarred from estimating further on any of the church furniture."[8] The individual in question was a Mr. McNutt who did business in Boston under the name J. J. McNutt Novelty Wood Works, a business name that does not exactly inspire confidence. Another and perhaps more reputable local manufacturer, D. Shales & Co. Parlor Furniture Manufactory, also expressed interest in the contract. Norcross Brothers submitted what seems to have been a rather cursory bid by telegram: "Will make and finish pews set up complete in church for thirty dollars per pew." Norcross Brothers did not receive the contract, for the firm was well underbid by T. B. Wentworth, director of Osborn's Mill on State Street in Cambridgeport, described on its printed business forms as a "Manufacturer of Pews, Pulpits, and all kinds of Church Furniture." Osborn's Mill was awarded the contract to construct the pews for $18.50 each, including installation but not the carving or varnishing. The carving was contracted separately to the firm of Roeth & May for an additional $450. Norcross Brothers then bid on and received the contract to "fill and finish the Blk Walnut Pews of the Trinity church for the sum of $875," bringing the final cost a little closer to their original bid. Meanwhile, Osborn's Mill billed for numerous additional details of the pew installation as construction progressed.[9]

The tight deadline for finishing the church required that all the furniture be completed while the building itself was still under construction. As the church was consecrated on February 9, 1877, construction of the furniture and pews must have been substantially complete before the end of 1876. Insurance records indicate that the church paid to insure the pew cushions against fire while they were stored offsite in a Boston warehouse until construction of the church was finished—a prudent choice, considering that the cushions alone cost more than half as much as the carved wooden pews.

In his description of the church Richardson stated, "As soon as the decoration [La Farge's] was finished, the scaffoldings were removed; and the pews and chancel furniture, which were already made and ready to set up, were rapidly put in place." Since the scaffolding wasn't removed until the first days of February, the Norcross Brothers carpenters and laborers must have proceeded quite rapidly to install the furniture, and the carpets too, in time for the consecration—with or without heat in the building. Even at this late date the craftsmen were not working in a well-heated building as La Farge also complained about the lack of heat and its effect on both his paint and his fingers. Presumably, the pews had already been "filled and finished" off-site.

It is obvious from numerous drawings that the pews and all the chancel furniture were designed by the office of H. H. Richardson. Although the hands vary, sheet numbers on the drawings for the chancel furniture are consecutive and consistent with those on many of the other architectural drawings. The costs of the furniture are recorded in the building committee's journals.[10] One entry dated October 5, 1876, includes the following:

| | |
|---|---|
| Pews 238 @ 18.50 | $4,218 |
| Carving on same | $450 |
| Walnut bases to Pews | $84 |
| Cushions | $2,500 |

On the following journal page the October 5 entry includes this expense:

| | |
|---|---|
| Pulpit & Desk & Stalls | |
| Chancel furniture | $3,000 |

While the pews were being constructed, Richardson and the rector, Phillips Brooks worked with the building committee to review bids for the chancel furniture, a process noted by Robert Treat Paine in his personal journal. Once again, Norcross Brothers submitted bids and were underbid by their local competitors, although this time by a lesser amount. The contract for the chancel furniture went to "Roeth & Co.," the carvers of the pews, and "D. Shales & Co.," another bidder for the pews, who were now working together, possibly at the same location in Cambridgeport. Paine reported visiting the Shales factory on First Street on November 18, 1876, and noted that the "Pew heads" and the furniture were "well along." Business arrangements between Shales and Roeth are still unclear, but this sort of competition and cooperation was not unusual in the woodworking business and has been found in period documents as early as the 1750s. Interestingly, Paine later noted payment for the pew carving as going to Shales rather than to Roeth, who had been awarded the original contract.[11]

Richardson met frequently with the building committee during the years that the church was planned and built, and minutes of the meetings dryly note lengthy and often indecisive discussion of the furnishing designs. Debate on the number and placement of pews, in one trying example, continued for well over a year, and further changes were recommended and discussed long after a plan had been approved. The final design for the pews, though, is very close to that in the preliminary sketches.

For the chancel, Richardson's designs often depict pieces of furniture that were more elaborate than those actually built. These changes can be traced in part to the building committee's well-documented concerns to manage costs; many details of the building itself were also scaled back from the architect's designs. For the furniture, however, the issue may have been that some of Richardson's designs were simply too ornate for Bostonians in the 1870s. Although he had spent time in New England while attending Harvard, Richardson's southern heritage remained a source of personal pride, and when he returned to Boston, it was by way of an architectural practice in New York City after years of study in Paris. Early in the 1870s, his Beaux Arts–influenced decorative tastes might not yet have been in sympathy with Boston's tradition of proud Yankee austerity. Even his close friend John La Farge recollected not too kindly in later years that early on, Richardson "knew almost nothing of Gothic, being fresh from Beaux Arts of the worst possible kind."[12] Then again, knowing or, perhaps more likely, caring for "almost nothing of Gothic" may have been a blessing of sorts in the development of Richardson's career and his signature style.

The evolution of Richardson's mature vocabulary on a more modest scale seems to have been reflected in the design process for Trinity Church's furniture. For many pieces of the chancel furniture, more than one version of the design drawings were prepared. Drawings for the pair of freestanding chairs, for example, include compositions with considerably more carved decoration than those that were actually commissioned. Some proposed pieces of furniture, such as an elaborate "Bishops Chair" with a small roof (fig. 5-3), were not built at all, although the committee did receive one bid for it. Like the church tower, the roof over this chair seems to have been inspired by a feature of the cathedral in Salamanca—one of its cupolas. Apparently these more elaborate designs, as well as their cost, did not impress the building committee or Phillips Brooks, who was known to have had strong feelings about the kind of decoration appropriate for Episcopal churches. All the chancel furniture that was commissioned was constructed as shown in at least one of the sets of drawings supplied by Richardson, but the designs not approved for the chancel are generally more ornate than the furniture that was constructed.

As early as 1875, Richardson submitted plans to the building committee for the placement and design of the chancel furniture. Minutes of the December 10 meeting of that year state, "The Architect Mr. Richardson then presented a pewing plan, and proposed arrangement of the Chancel, and the same was fully discussed, but no definitive action was taken thereon." This last, and similar phrases, appear repeatedly in the committee's minutes. Four months later, at the meeting of April 15, 1876, the building committee finally "voted that Mr. Richardson be requested to consult with the Rector as to the Chancel furniture, pulpit and reading desk."[13]

Richardson honored this request and presumably resolved the final designs in cooperation with Phillips Brooks. In his personal journal, Robert Treat Paine, chairman of the building committee, noted this cooperation with such entries as, "PB & HHR arrange about Chancel furniture, pulpits, etc."[14] Their collaboration may have had a lasting influence on Richardson's furniture designs, as many of the drawings for Trinity Church's chancel furniture are more ornate than any other furniture attributed to his office. Judging from the character of the designs that were not approved, however, it is possible that it was the discrimination of the Reverend Mr. Brooks that guided Richardson's Beaux Arts–influenced southern taste toward a slightly more austere New England sensibility.

Having studied at Harvard, Phillips Brooks was a reasonably knowledgeable critic of architecture, and he quite naturally demonstrated a strong interest in church architecture. On his trips to Europe, in 1865, 1872, and again in 1874, the churches he toured included Byzantine and Russian examples, some of which he described none too reticently as "barbarous in taste, but very gorgeous."[15] From the start, Brooks took an active part in the design of the new church, and church historians tend to view the finished product as a material expression of his theological views, repeatedly referring to his disapproval of ostentatious ecclesiastical decoration. One history stated that even in 1902 the Trinity Church vestry was "sensitive to the residual distaste evinced by Brooks for elaborate, remote, and high church decoration."[16] Brooks's judgment of church furnishings also reflected broader ecclesiastical issues in the Episcopal Church in America. Within the Trinity congregation too, differences in preference between adherents of a high-church" style and church members who favored a simpler approach to worship seem to have been an ongoing dynamic well into the twentieth century as the church interior was built and remodeled.

In form and in decoration, Trinity Church's furniture is designed in a robust, somewhat masculine style. The furniture shows some influence of Aesthetic movement furniture designs, often referred to as the Eastlake style, but both the overall proportions and the relatively thickly proportioned structural members are decidedly characteristic of Romanesque furniture, of which many surviving examples were executed in stone rather than wood. The chairs in the chancel, for example, were almost certainly inspired by an early twelfth-century Italian bishop's throne built in white marble. Trinity's furniture also subtly exhibits a wonderful unity with the building itself: quite a few of the carved and molded shapes on the furniture relate to details in the church's architectural woodwork, stonework, and stained glass, including the use of the trefoils that represent the Trinity in Episcopal and Roman Catholic iconography. Quatrefoils and chamfered edges are also characteristic, elements that Richardson used on both earlier and later furniture for his churches and libraries. On thick table and chair legs for instance, the wide chamfered edges of square legs lend the profiles an aspect close

5-3. Working drawing for "Bishop's Chair" (never built), office of H. H. Richardson.
(H. H. Richardson Papers, TC E17, Department of Printing and Graphic Arts,
Houghton Library, Harvard College Library.)

to that of the octagonal stone columns that Richardson used so well for the exterior of the parish house. Notwithstanding the elaborately carved decoration, the solid and simple character of Trinity Church's furniture offers a marked contrast to the Gothic-inspired forms that were pretty much de rigeur for church furniture of the period. Indeed, the stolid nature of these designs is a critical element in their success. On a certain, perhaps unconscious, level the forms themselves impart an air of security and calmness appropriate for what was intended to be a more simple place of worship.

But above all, it is the philosophical and perhaps romantic significance of the Romanesque style that was and still is especially compelling for the congregation of Trinity Church. Richardson's mastery of the Romanesque was particularly sympathetic to the desires of Phillips Brooks for a simpler church. For the rector and much of his congregation, the style evoked a time in European history when the Roman Catholic Church was thought to have been more spiritually pure, as opposed to the corruption that later became associated with the Gothic style. By combining his knowledge and understanding of the Romanesque with the philosophy of the emerging English Arts and Crafts movement, Richardson and his assistants succeeded in designing furnishings for Trinity that met the need of the congregation to express its theological beliefs in a tangible form. Richardson accomplished this romantic feat not by simply applying Romanesque decorative elements to contemporary forms but by understanding and adapting the solid forms of Romanesque furniture to fit more modern expectations. This combination of form and philosophy is one of the elements that enabled Trinity Church to capture so definitively the spirit of the Reverend Phillips Brooks's ministry in Boston at the end of the nineteenth century.

In form, this stylistic expression seems to signal the emergence of what later became a significant influence in American furniture design. By the time Trinity Church was being built, furniture manufacturers in Great Britain and America were well into the revival period of design. Most of this so-called revival furniture, however, consisted of what were essentially the same old northern European forms with various applied decorations. Richardson's adoption of the more massive Mediterranean Romanesque furniture form, rather than just the decorative elements, expressed a design sensibility that became increasingly significant toward the turn of the century with the popularity of what is loosely called Arts and Crafts furniture in America. Philosophically, the Arts and Crafts movement, which had developed much earlier in England, represented a rebellion against the fanciful but uninspired manufactured furniture of the period. In England, furniture makers influenced by this philosophy most often turned to Gothic and Gothic Revival examples for design inspiration. The earliest furniture designers working in what was only later named the Arts and Crafts style often collaborated with architects who at the time were quite enamored of the Gothic as a romantic expression of British nationalism. In France however, the Romanesque style was a far more powerful source of inspiration for students at the Ecole des Beaux Arts when Richardson studied there in the 1860s. At one point, students including Richardson rebelled when the Gothicist E. E. Viollet-le-Duc, was appointed to the faculty.

By the mid-1870s, Boston was proving to be an early and welcome market for the Arts and Crafts philosophy in the United States. Richardson and his assistants seem to have been both influenced by and a part of this developing stylistic expression. His affinity for the style in furniture design, particularly in the 1880s, has been well described elsewhere, but this influence has not been explored in connection with his earlier work, when the style was just reaching America.[17] The overall style and many of the details of the furniture at Trinity Church are consistent with the philosophy of the Arts and Crafts movement, for the most part eschewing elaborate applied decoration and overly fanciful carving for what was considered to be honesty of form and function. But a true appreciation of the Romanesque sources at their disposal permitted Richardson and his assistants to design furniture that was quite unlike either the mass-produced or the so-called art furniture of their day.

Considering the chancel furniture in its historic setting may be helpful. The original chancel decoration was somewhat simpler than the present marble-covered walls and stone altar would suggest, and the space was a little more sparsely furnished as well. The focal point, of course, was the communion table (fig. 5-4), an essential symbol of the celebration of the Last Supper. From the earliest floor plans onward, and in all the nineteenth-century photographs, the communion table was positioned at the center of the chancel on a wide raised platform, bringing it closer to the celebrants than if it had been placed against the rear wall of the apse, as in the Roman Catholic tradition. The raised platform, surrounded by a carved wooden altar rail, served both to elevate slightly the communion table and the celebration and to place the cushions of the altar rail kneelers at the floor level of the minister as he offered communion to the faithful. There is also some ecclesiastical significance to the use of the term "communion table" rather than "altar," a distinction that was theologically significant to Phillips Brooks and his congregation at the time the table was commissioned.

The communion table was not built en suite with the rest of the chancel furniture. Oral history suggests that Richardson designed it for Brooks's use during services held across the square at MIT's Huntington Hall while the new church was still under construction; then the table was used at Trinity until around 1914. It does not appear in photographs taken after that time and may have been removed for installation of the "temporary baldachino" in that year. In 1938 it was donated to Emmanuel Church in Braintree, Massachusetts, and is still in use there today, albeit with modifications, some of which may have taken place before the table was donated.

Trinity Church's original communion table was an ornate but tastefully carved walnut table that still somehow retained a certain air of simplicity. It is noticeably different from the rest of the chancel furniture, its design being more in the Classical style. There is a definite Renaissance influence in the carving on the tapered columns and the apron rail, but it is certainly not an example of Renaissance Re-

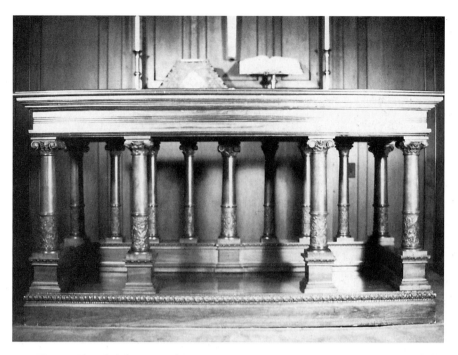

5-4. Trinity Church. The original communion table with twentieth-century alterations, now located at Emmanuel Church, Braintree, Massachusetts.
(Photo by Maggie Redfern.)

vival furniture, a style whose connection to the Renaissance was tenuous at best. In this case, Richardson's Beaux Arts training certainly brought him closer to genuine Renaissance sources. Although it is a large table, its proportions are not as massive as those of the distinctly Romanesque-inspired furniture in the chancel suite. The design drawing, labeled "Sketch for Communion Table Trinity Church" (fig. 5-5), is in a hand quite different from that of the rest of the chancel furniture drawings, and it does not share their numbering sequence, facts further supporting the oral history that it was designed earlier than the other pieces.

The communion table was originally flanked by the elegant pair of carved walnut chairs (fig. 5-6) inspired by an Italian Romanesque marble bishop's throne, that of Bishop Elia at the church of San Nicole in Bari. Dating to the late eleventh or early twelfth century, this early marble throne seems to have provided the inspiration for the overall form of the chairs and especially for the chair backs, with

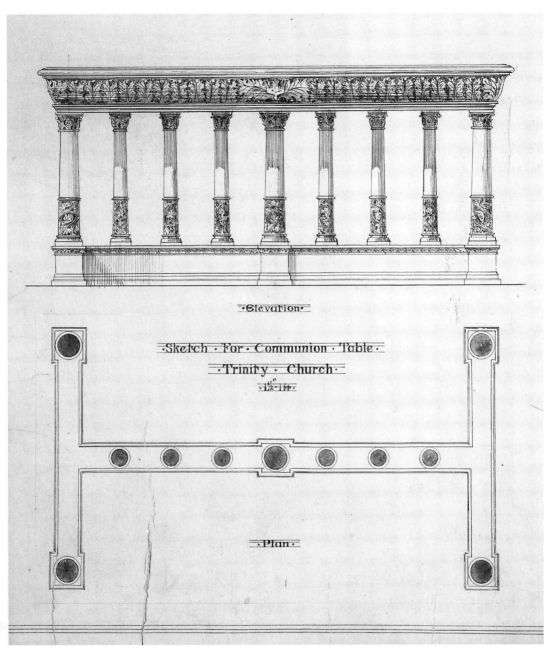

·Elevation·

·Sketch·For·Communion·Table·

·Trinity·Church·

·1½ In·

·Plan·

5-5. Sketch for communion table, office of H. H. Richardson. (H. H. Richardson Papers, TC E27, Department of Printing and Graphic Arts, Houghton Library, Harvard College Library.)

5-6. Trinity Church. One of a pair of chairs for the chancel. (Photo by Maggie Redfern.)

5-7. Working drawing for chancel chairs, office of H. H. Richardson. (H. H. Richardson Papers, TC G21, Department of Printing and Graphic Arts, Houghton Library, Harvard College Library.)

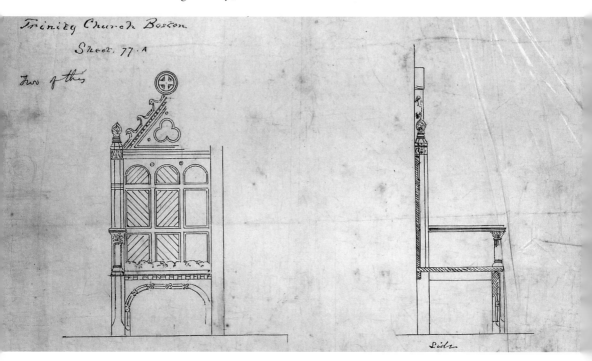

their angled crest rails and carved finials. The Trinity Church chairs have flat open arms and thick square legs shaped with wide stopped chamfers ending in square feet. Richardson used this leg profile again on some of the benches built for the Oliver Ames Memorial Library in North Easton, Massachusetts, 1877–83. The chairs match one of the simpler Richardson drawings, which includes a tufted seat cushion (fig. 5-7); other drawings for them show considerably more carved decoration. These chairs were also donated to Emmanuel Church, Braintree, with the communion table, in 1938.

The beautifully carved altar rail that originally surrounded the communion table and other pieces of chancel furniture (fig. 5-8) was supported by quadruple sets of turned columns with carved capitals, each set connected by carved arches. One of the altar rail drawings (fig. 5-9) is a very close match, whereas another is considerably more elaborate, with floral carvings along the arches instead of the simpler triangular shapes. The altar rail was probably removed when the chancel was remodeled in 1938, as it still appears in earlier twentieth-century photographs, but the church still retains some intact sections of it (in storage).

Behind the altar rail a continuous row of thirty-four attached, built-in chairs, apparently no longer extant, was originally installed against the back wall of the apse (fig. 5-2). Referred to on the original drawings as "Sedilla," the chairs had large round arms between the seats and smaller circular dividers above the arms, both molded with concentric astragals. The same high seat back used on the free-standing chairs was repeated along the row, the only difference being pinecone finials in place of the Maltese crosses used on the other chairs. Bishop Elia's throne also has a pinecone finial, and, and as with the freestanding chairs, the other carved shapes on the crest rails flanking the finial are quite similar to those on the crest rail of the early marble throne. The same shape also appears in the copper decorative elements on the ridge caps of the central tower of Trinity Church, and again on the ridge caps of the Winn Memorial Library in Woburn, 1876–79. Drawings for the sedilla include a preliminary sketch, very loosely drawn (fig. 5-10), and a number of working drawings that are close in detail to the final form (fig. 5-11). This row of chairs was probably removed for the 1938 renovation, when the walls of the chancel were faced with Italian marble. They are presently unac-counted for. Since no one section would have formed a complete chair after re-moval, it is probable that the parts were discarded.

Placement and number of the chancel suite's two carved benches or stalls with three or four matching reading desks and kneelers (fig. 5-12) vary among the early photographs. Most still survive intact, and two stalls and one reading desk are still in use in the chancel today. The stalls have lower backs than the other chairs and are of two different designs, but both designs match drawings in the chancel fur-niture sequence, and both are visible in photographs from 1877 (see fig. 4-5) and

5-8. Trinity Church. Detail of the altar rail. (Photo by author.)

5-9. Working drawing of the altar rail, office of H. H. Richardson. (H. H. Richardson Papers, TC E21, Department of Printing and Graphic Arts, Houghton Library, Harvard College Library.)

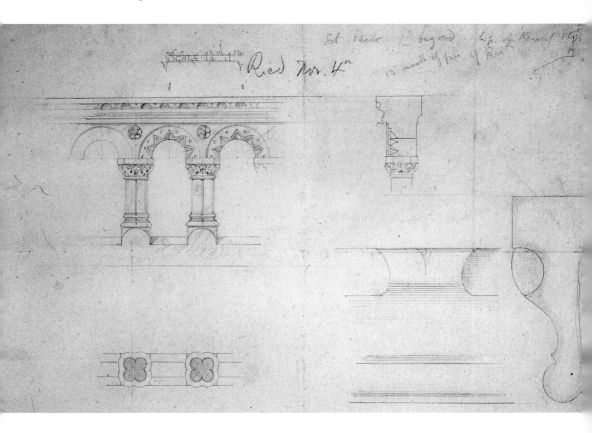

5-10.  Sketch for the "Sedilla," office of H. H. Richardson. (H. H. Richardson Papers, TC E25, Department of Printing and Graphic Arts, Houghton Library, Harvard College Library.)

5-11.  Working drawing for the "Sedilla," office of H. H. Richardson. (H. H. Richardson Papers, TC E26, Department of Printing and Graphic Arts, Houghton Library, Harvard College Library.)

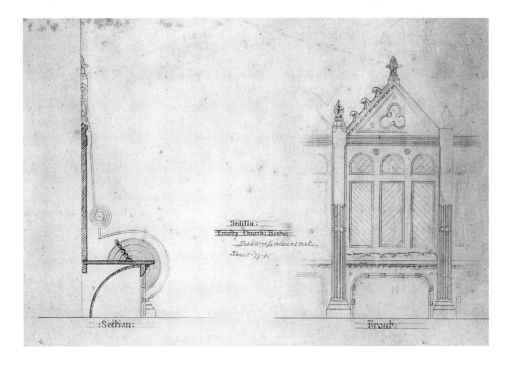

5-12. Trinity Church. Stall, kneeler, and reading desk. (Photo by Maggie Redfern.)

5-13. Trinity Church. Detail of a pew. (Photo by author.)

1888 (fig. 5-1). On some drawings they too are referred to as Sedilla but on other drawings are simply called stalls. The stalls have large circular ends, their flat surfaces decorated with low-relief, spiraling carved foliage. In the 1888 photographs a single-seat stall is placed at the right front corner of the chancel with a matching reading desk and kneeler, and a triple-seat stall with matching desk and kneelers can be seen within the altar rail. Only one of the carved kneelers remains in use in the chancel, its top supported by short, turned columns that relate to the columns on the altar rail. The top is now covered in needlepoint, but the original may have been a tufted red velvet like that now found on the bench cushions.

One more reading desk is now referred to at Trinity Church as "the Phillips Brooks lectern." It is similar to the other reading desks but more elaborately carved and constructed of finely figured solid walnut. In 1877 it was placed at the front of the chancel, but it is not present in any of the 1888 photographs and is not currently used in the chancel. Richardson's office prepared three or four designs for this reading desk, all with more carved decoration than was actually employed.

According to the building committee's expense report, 238 pews were built for the nave (fig. 5-13). This number probably included the pews in the chancel alcove, which have since been removed. The ends of the pews in the nave are carved; those in the galleries are not. Both designs match preliminary sketches or working drawings from Richardson's office (fig. 5-14). All the pews have flat seats with tufted cushions, possibly covered originally in red silk. In 1888 there was also a tall wooden screen installed across the backs of the pews in the last row of the nave. It seems to have been designed to block drafts from the doors to the narthex and may have been removed when radiators were installed in the nave.

Additional pieces of furniture at Trinity Church that may have been designed by Richardson's office include a set of simple benches with spindled backs, a large library table, and a small walnut table. It is not clear whether they were designed and executed during his lifetime, but all exhibit stylistic details found on attributed examples of Richardson furniture. The benches can be seen in the chancel, the nave, and the original choirloft in many of the 1888 photographs. Those in the chancel do not appear in the 1877 photographs; they may have been installed as a result of ongoing debate within the congregation and the vestry regarding pew proprietorship. The spindles on the benches are similar to those on benches designed by Richardson for some of his libraries, especially the Winn Memorial Library, and on chairs in both the Oliver Ames Memorial Library and the Winn Memorial Library. The legs on the library table are similar to the legs on the chairs in the chancel, and the simple carved capitals on the smaller table match the capitals on stone balustrades on the porch of the Trinity Church rectory, also designed by Richardson. None of the objects in this group have been conclusively

5-14. Sketch detail of a pew, office of
H. H. Richardson. (H. H. Richardson
Papers, TC E41, Department of Printing
and Graphic Arts, Houghton Library,
Harvard College Library.)

attributed by design drawings or written records, but all display numerous details
characteristic of Richardson's early furniture design vocabulary.

Richardson continued to employ this Romanesque vocabulary throughout the
decade and into the early 1880s. Although many of the details were creatively
reused for furniture at his libraries, the later furniture of this form does not develop any new design ideas. As some of his early assistants, such as Charles
McKim and Stanford White, went on to popularize the Beaux Arts style, they
were replaced by furniture designers such as Francis Bacon, who turned to other
forms to capture the Arts and Crafts aesthetic, which was becoming increasingly
popular in the United States. Some of the models that they looked to for this expression, particularly the English Windsor chair, were much lighter in form.
Thus, Richardson's later furniture—which is the furniture most often publicized
in connection with his architecture—abandons the Romanesque mass and solid-
ity that characterize Trinity's furniture. In retrospect, it seems that the most lasting influence of the Trinity Church collaboration may have been to help guide
Richardson away from the Beaux Arts influence of his student years toward a
simpler expression of the Arts and Crafts aesthetic in furniture design.

# NOTES

1. Mariana Griswold Van Rensselaer, *Henry Hobson Richardson and His Works* (Boston: Houghton Mifflin, 1888; reprint, New York: Dover, 1969), 133.

2. *Trinity Church, Boston, Mass.,* Monographs of American Architecture V, issued in connection with *American Architect and Building News* (Boston: Ticknor, 1888).

3. Charles D. Gambrill and H. H. Richardson, "Specifications for the Construction of Trinity Church," 16–17, Trinity Church Archives.

4. "Description of the Church by H. H. Richardson, Architect," in *Consecration Services of Trinity Church, Boston, February 9, 1877* (Boston: Trinity Church, 1877), 55–70.

5. Trinity Church records at the Massachusetts Historical Society, entries in a bound journal titled "Trinity Church Copies of contracts, agreements and orders with memoranda referred to relating to the new Trinity Church 1813–1877," MHS #H39.

6. Although Trinity Church was nominally the work of Gambrill & Richardson, Architects, Richardson moved from New York to the Boston suburb of Brookline in 1874, and the designs for furniture presumably came from that office. The cooperative nature of the design process and the division of labor between architect and draughtsmen in the firm is well explained by James F. O'Gorman in *H. H. Richardson and His Office: Selected Drawings* (Cambridge, Mass.: Department of Printing and Graphic Arts, Harvard College Library, 1974).

7. Trinity Church records at the Massachusetts Historical Society, numerous letters and other loose documents filed under "Pew plans and documents," MHS, folder 1 in folder H33/N1.

8. Ibid., and James F. O'Gorman, *Accomplished in all Departments of Art: Hammatt Billings of Boston, 1818–1874* (Amherst: University of Massachusetts Press, 1998), 221–22.

9. "Pew plans and documents," and "Trinity Church Copies of contracts, agreements and orders."

10. "Trinity Church Copies of contracts, agreements and orders."

11. Robert Treat Paine Diary, December 7, 1876, Archives of Stonehurst, Waltham, Mass., owned by city of Waltham and Robert Treat Paine Historical Trust, Inc.

12. Quoted in H. Barbara Weinberg, *The Decorative Work of John La Farge* (New York: Garland, 1977), 75.

13. "Records [of the building committee], meeting minutes relating to the second sanctuary, and records relating to the third sanctuary, 1828–1830, 1870–1877," in Trinity Church records at the Massachusetts Historical Society, MHS #H31.

14. Paine Diary, August 9, 1876.

15. Quoted in Weinberg, *Decorative Work,* 87–88.

16. Bettina A. Norton, ed., *Trinity Church: The Story of an Episcopal Parish in the City of Boston* (Boston: Wardens and Vestry of Trinity Church in the City of Boston, 1978), 53.

17. Marian Page, *Furniture Designed by Architects* (New York: Whitney Library of Design, 1983), 62–69; and Ann Farnam, "H. H. Richardson and A. H. Davenport: Architecture and Furniture as Big Business in America's Gilded Age," in *Tools and Technologies: America's Wooden Age,* ed. Paul B. Kebabian and William C. Lipke (Burlington, Vt.: Robert Hull Fleming Museum, University of Vermont, 1979).

6-1. Orlando Whitney Norcross (1839–1920). (*Worcester: Its Past and Present*, 1888.)

# 6

## *Builder: Orlando Whitney Norcross (Norcross Brothers)*

JAMES F. O'GORMAN

THE ORIGINAL EDITION of the *Kidder-Parker Architects' and Builders' Handbook,* a pocket-sized compilation of useful technical information first published in 1884 and updated at various times until the mid-twentieth century, contains a dedication that reads in part as follows: "This Book," wrote Frank E. Kidder, the sole author of the original edition, "is respectfully dedicated to those whose kindness has enabled me to produce it." And, after some personal references, he continued: "To Orlando W. Norcross of Worcester, Mass. [fig. 6-1], whose superior practical knowledge of all that pertains to building has given me a more intelligent and practical view of the science of construction than I should have otherwise obtained."[1]

This dedication provides a glimpse of O. W. Norcross's reputation during his lifetime. It was written by an architect who practiced in Boston during the 1880s, while O. W.'s firm was building several of H. H. Richardson's most characteristic designs. It is remarkable because it stemmed from a graduate of MIT and praised a man with almost no formal education. Norcross, according to this testimonial by an expert witness, possessed "superior practical knowledge" of "all that pertains to building," and imparted to others an "intelligent and practical view of the science of construction." Kidder repeats the word "practical," and Norcross was at bottom a practical man whose many contributions to the building industry grew out of his firsthand knowledge of men, materials, and methods of construction. He was a perfect balance to the artistic Richardson.

His firm, Norcross Brothers of Worcester, Massachusetts, pioneered general contracting in this country, but O. W. was a builder first of all, one who over the course of a long career proved himself to be among the best in the business. He was also an entrepreneur who dealt in building supplies ranging from millwork to stonework, a cost estimator of storied accuracy, a consultant to the major architects of his day, and an imaginative, if conservative, technical innovator. That he was a conservative builder especially endeared him to Richardson.

At the end of his life the city of Worcester honored Orlando Whitney Norcross with a memorial to the "master builder," mounted on a public wall of its city hall. He had long been the more important principal of Norcross Brothers. His older sibling, James Atkinson Norcross (1831–1903), oversaw the office, while O. W. (1839–1920) ran the construction sites, quarries, milling shops, and other parts of the multifarious operation. They were born in Maine, the sons of a carpenter who vanished in the California Gold Rush, but they early moved through Salem and North Adams, Massachusetts, to Worcester. O. W. served in the Union army during the Civil War and considered his most notable military achievement, ironically enough, the demolition of a bridge while under enemy fire. He was discharged in 1864 and joined his brother in the construction business.[2]

Their firm grew rapidly as the building industry expanded in the 1860s, a decade during which new construction in the United States rose 260 percent.[3] The brothers' first significant commission came in 1866 from the Congregational Church in Leicester, just west of Worcester. Between 1868 and 1872 they built the Compton Block, the First Universalist Church, and the high school in Worcester. The school was designed by Richardson, and this contract marked the first known meeting of builder and architect. An advertisement in the *Worcester Directory* of 1872 announced the arrival of the firm with a cut showing the school, one of the last of Richardson's awkward juvenilia. The two men worked hand in glove for the remainder of Richardson's life. Through his collaboration with the architect, Norcross rose to prominence in his field, and conversely, Richardson's reputation rests in significant part on the superior organizational skills of Norcross and the careful craftsmanship of Norcross's workmen.

Norcross Brothers lasted sixty years. Between 1869 and 1886 the firm built the majority of Richardson's buildings. At his death it moved on to work for Shepley, Rutan & Coolidge (Richardson's successors), McKim, Mead & White, Carrère & Hastings, Ernest Flagg, Bertram Grosvenor Goodhue, Peabody & Stearns—in all, some three dozen of the major design firms in America at the end of the nineteenth and the beginning of the twentieth century (fig. 6-2). Norcross built over a dozen buildings at Harvard, five at Columbia, and four at Princeton—just three examples of the firm's campus work. It also erected the New York Stock Exchange and South Station in Boston, did the stonework of the Pennsylvania Station in New York and the remodeling of the White House, and built the State House of Rhode Island, to name just a few of the more than 340 buildings on a preliminary list of Norcross achievements.[4]

Norcross Brothers was more than a construction company, however. It was

6-2. Buildings erected by Norcross Brothers. (*Tribute to the Columbian Year by the City of Worcester*, 1893.)

founded in an era when an owner would hire independent craftsmen to work on parts of a building, as did Henry Fowle Durant in the early 1870s when he oversaw the erection of College Hall at his new endowment at Wellesley College.[5] The Boston architect Robert Andrews recalled that until Norcross Brothers arrived on the scene, it was usual for the construction of even a dwelling to require up to twenty different contractors.[6] Norcross was among the first to offer a general contracting package, and he ran a full-service enterprise. The firm was what we would now call vertically integrated; that is, it not only directed the building process, using its own workmen, but supplied the materials that went into the work. Over the course of O. W.'s long career the firm and its subsidiaries owned, by one count, fifteen quarries (with their attendant stoneworking shops) spread out from Massachusetts to Connecticut, Rhode Island, Maine, New York, Vermont, and Georgia, as well as nine companies that supplied stone to other contractors.[7]

Norcross Brothers' quarrying operations reflected the firm's work in construction. Red sandstone came from its site at East Longmeadow, Massachusetts; pink and gray granite came out of the ground at Milford, Massachusetts; quarries in Pickens County, Georgia, shipped white marble; slate came from North Monson, Maine; green granite, from Windsor, Vermont. As architectural fashion shifted from the polychromatic picturesque work that coincided with the founding of the firm to the bleached classicism of the turn of the century and beyond—a shift evident on Copley Square in Boston, for example, in the contrast between Cummings & Sears's New Old South Meeting House and McKim, Mead & White's adjacent Boston Public Library—Norcross kept up with the times. His shipments changed from colorful sandstone and granite, destined to be worked into highly textured surfaces, to varieties of light-hued marble polished to a smooth finish.

But stone was not the firm's only material contribution to a building. It was said that Norcross Brothers "were the first-hand producers of more lines of work entering into building construction than any other organization doing a general building business."[8] The stonework usually faced brick walls, and Norcross owned at least two brick companies. Iron was necessary for some construction details, and Norcross Brothers fabricated these members in its Worcester shops (although at Trinity, at least, the iron was rolled elsewhere). Interiors required millwork, and this too came from woodworking sheds in Worcester. When an architect and his client chose Norcross as their builder, they knew they were hiring the most proficient contractor and supplier of quality materials and workmanship. If that architect was H. H. Richardson, he called O. W. in at the beginning of the design process to take full advantage of the builder's practical skills in estimating the cost of the job and of his ability to produce solid, conservative work.

Witnesses from the period make it clear that Norcross carried on all the traditional aspects of building at the highest professional level. Let me emphasize "the traditional aspects of building." The list of structures erected by Norcross includes the Custom House Tower in Boston but very few other skyscrapers, *the major building type of his era.* Norcross was a master of time-honored, load-bearing masonry construction, and an inventive and innovative craftsman within that tradition, but he was not one to embrace technologically cutting-edge projects with structural steel frames and curtain walls. Stone, brick, wood, concrete: these were his primary structural materials. Even when Richardson and Norcross needed to incorporate structural iron into their buildings, they almost never gave it visual expression. Norcross brick walls faced with Norcross stonework exhibit load-bearing stereotomy of the highest quality. This suited Richardson, whose works were closer to the conservative ideals of William Morris and the English Arts and Crafts movement than to the industrialized aesthetic of his Philadelphia contemporary, Frank Furness, or the technically advanced works of the commercial Chicago School.[9]

Norcross not only oversaw the construction of the finest conservatively built buildings of his time; he invented improvements in the production and detailing of those buildings. In 1889 he was awarded the first of his eighteen patents for a method of fastening roof slates to a metal frame. Others dealt with improved ways to cut and polish stone and to fabricate fireproof flooring. The last led eventually to his most important contribution, a system of flat-slab, reinforced concrete construction. Only recently has his place in the history of reinforced concrete technology been recognized. Since this hybrid is the child of the twentieth century, it might seem that I have overstressed Norcross's conservatism, but his innovation grew out of his desire to adapt load-bearing masonry to the erection of the large fireproof buildings that modern society needed.

O. W. developed into an innovator, at least in masonry materials, after Richardson's death. During the decade and a half they worked together, they built superbly but traditionally. H. H. and O. W. not only became "great business associates" but "strong personal friends," although in person and personality they were an ill-matched pair. O. W. was a "short, sturdy, dark complexioned man, with snapping brown eyes," a big nose, and a walrus moustache. A strict temperance man, and a Union army veteran, he was described by one of Richardson's clients, J. J. Glessner (whose Chicago house he built), as "quick thinking, quick speaking, determined."[10] Louisiana-born Richardson, on the other hand, sat out the war in France as an enemy of the North. Although he was slender at the beginning of their association, he developed into a gargantuan and colorful figure remembered for his halting, orotund speech, infectious enthusiasm, and thirst for the bibulous glass. In Richardson's office at the beginning of a project, however, or at a building site, the two met on common ground. And they met often: Norcross Brothers erected the bulk of Richardson's executed designs after 1869.

Although we often think of Richardson as an independent form-giver, Norcross was in fact his collaborator, one who contributed to the final building on an equal footing with the architect. We know this from many sources. The memoirs of Glenn Brown, for example, who worked as a carpenter at Trinity and later became the influential secretary of the American Institute of Architects and chronicler of the United States Capitol, give us a glimpse of the relationship between the architect's office and that of the building firm. During the mid-1870s—as Trinity neared completion—Brown worked for Norcross as clerk of the works at Richardson's Cheney Brothers building in Hartford. "Richardson," he remembered, "relied without ever regretting it upon him [Norcross] for construction and practical details." Brown, who himself translated drawings from Richardson's drafting room into construction documents at the site, emphasized the practicality of Norcross's services and contrasted them with Richardson's visionary designs: "While enlarging the scale details to full size," he noted, "making the shop drawings and patterns, I became very familiar with the drawings from Richardson's office—was much impressed with their artistic qualities and wondered at his ability in ignoring practical considerations when attaining artistic effects." He summed up his experience at the Cheney Building by writing that "Richardson placed great confidence in . . . [Norcross's] integrity and good, clean craftsmanship and . . . I could see that he was justified in that confidence."[11]

The degree of cooperation between architect and builder that this suggests is revealing, and this during the period when Trinity too was under construction. Richardson knew he had in his builder a practical extension of his own intentions. No wonder the architect mistrusted the lure of drawings, and, whenever he could, whenever he had a pliable client, altered buildings in progress. With the help of Norcross he tested his paper creations in the light of the actual work. The builder's traditional methods reinforced Richardson's preindustrial vocabulary, and both expressed an innate New England upper-crust conservatism.

Richardson first engaged Norcross Brothers' services in late 1869 for the Worcester High School, and the years during and following work on this building were crucial ones in the architect's search for a formal language of his own. The vacillation between French academic classicism and picturesque English sources that had marked his earlier efforts began to shift toward the identifiably Richardsonian works of the early 1870s.[12] The change is made evident in part by a shift in materials, resulting in a shift in scale. The high school, a gawky red-brick building of ham-fisted details and scrawny proportions, was one of the last structures of his immature phase. At the Hampden County Courthouse in Springfield, Massachusetts, commissioned in mid-1871 and also built by Norcross, Richardson leaned toward the large-scale arcuated stonework that marks the designs of his maturity. Knowing that Norcross controlled stone quarries, we are led to ask if he influenced the architect's shift. It could be argued that the drawings for the high school were complete before Norcross bid the job, and therefore, he could not influence Richardson's choice of material, whereas the builder *was* available as the architect's office detailed the courthouse in rough-faced Monson granite. But there is no evidence that Norcross owned quarries at Monson or elsewhere as early as 1871, so we must attribute this fundamental shift in the architect's work to him alone.

Still, the superb execution of the arches and ashlar walls of the courthouse may have given Richardson confidence to pursue, with Norcross's help, the stony Romanesque in subsequent works. Just as a composer must rely on the artistry of the performer to bring out the quality of the music in public performance, so the value of the architect's graphic creations remains in doubt until it has been realized among the lights and shadows of reality by the work of skilled fabricators. I side with Geoffrey Scott, who in his celebrated *Architecture of Humanism* defined architecture as "the art of organizing a mob of craftsmen" and later added that "the conceptions of an architect must be worked out by other hands and other minds than his own."[13] From this point of view, Norcross stands on equal terms with Richardson among the Makers of Trinity Church.

Trinity was the cornerstone of Richardson's career and of Norcross's as well. The builder signed the contract for all material and labor necessary for the erection of the building in early October 1873, at a time when there were still many decisions to be made about the final design. As is well known, the winning drawings of June 1872 were very different from what was eventually erected. Many minds and hands contributed to the process of modification, but the partnership of architect and builder was at the core of realizing those decisions. It was Trinity that sealed the collaboration between the two that lasted until Richardson's death, and it was the design *and* execution of that great work which launched their national—and, in Richardson's case, international—reputations.

Trinity remains the most important of Richardson's buildings, and it was a proving ground for Norcross. Both were effectively at the beginning of their careers when work began. Neither had yet attempted anything so large and so difficult, or so highly visible. Construction was problematic because of the soil conditions of the Back Bay, a former brackish pool that had been filled in recent years. Norcross was self-taught as an engineer. He perused the works of E. E. Viollet-le-Duc, John C. Trautwine's *Civil Engineer's Pocketbook,* and who knows what other standard works. According to his daughter's memoir, he also studied existing load-bearing masonry. She tells us that he "had gained his knowledge through practical work and reading . . . but at that time [the early 1870s] this country had little to offer in . . . completed [large-scale masonry structural] work, and he felt the need of actual contact with well-tried construction. . . . At great expense to himself he went to Montreal to make observation of some of the old stone churches there."[14] So Trinity afforded Norcross the opportunity to further his education as a builder, and the skills he developed at the church carried over into the remainder of his career.

During the summer and fall of 1873, spruce piles were driven into the blue clay stratum beneath the church and the foundations prepared for the massive superstructure of the walls and central tower.[15] It was then that Norcross came aboard. According to the architect, "Choice had been made of the Dedham granite for the ashlar [facing the brickwork of the aboveground walls], and of [East] Longmeadow freestone for the trimmings and cut stone work, and the contractors hired land and opened quarries of their own, both at Dedham and Longmeadow." When it proved difficult to extract stones from the Dedham quarry large enough for some sections of the wall, such as the basement, "the contractors," again according to the architect, "with praiseworthy enterprise, secured land . . . [at Westerly, Rhode Island] and opened a third quarry."[16] So far as we know, these were the first of Norcross Brothers' quarrying operations, the first of what grew into a major addition to the firm's contracting business. In this, Norcross seems to have been reacting to Richardson's needs.

A successful general contractor must possess exceptional organizational skills, and Norcross must have developed his keen logistical abilities during work on Trinity. As remembered by the engineer Ernest Bowditch—who, among other important contributions to the erection of the church, oversaw the driving of the foundation piles—"his great forte then and since has been in systemizing of his work so that there might be no lost time. . . . He made very good money just by that one element."[17] Norcross also made good money out of the historical circumstances in which his firm contracted for building Trinity in October 1873. The failure of Jay Cooke & Company in the previous month precipitated a major financial panic, and building prices fell sharply for the next few years. Having estimated the job at pre-panic prices, we are told, the Norcross firm profited from these reduced costs.[18] This financial windfall gave Norcross a leg up, although Bowditch also remembered him as a man "ingenious and resourceful and while desirous of making money . . . ready to subordinate the financial profit to excellence of results." Bowditch's positive characterization of O. W.'s personality is noteworthy, for as a critic of men he was no panegyrist.

Such a man as he describes would naturally work to Richardson's exacting standards, and rising from Trinity's auditorium plan is a building that reflects those high standards. It is also a work largely of traditional technology and traditional

Pl. 1. Trinity Church. Exterior from the west. Porch by Shepley, Rutan & Coolidge, Architects, with carving by John Evans Company, 1894–97. (Photo copyright Cervin Robinson.)

Pl. 2. Trinity Church. Exterior from the east. (Photo copyright Peter Vanderwarker; Courtesy of Trinity Church.)

Pl. 3. Trinity Church and Parish House from the east. (Photo copyright Cervin Robinson.)

Pl. 4.  Trinity Church. Detail of the exterior. Granite ashlar stonework by Norcross Brothers, Builders, 1874–76. (Photo copyright Cervin Robinson.)

Pl. 5. Trinity Church. Interior looking into the north transept. Murals in tower (*Isaiah* and *Jeremiah*) and nave (*Christ with the Woman of Samaria*) by John La Farge and assistants, 1876–77. Clerestory windows in nave by Henry Holland of London, 1878. Windows above the gallery in the transept designed by Edward Burne-Jones and made by William Morris & Company of England, 1880. Robert Treat Paine memorial pulpit designed by Charles A. Coolidge, with carving by John D. Evans, 1914–16. Lower windows in nave, *Eight Apostles,* by Margaret Redmond, ca. 1927. (Photo copyright Cervin Robinson.)

Pl. 6. Trinity Church. *The Resurrection,* stained glass in the north transept by John La Farge, 1902. (Photo copyright Peter Vanderwarker; Courtesy of Trinity Church.)

Pl. 7. Trinity Church. Interior looking toward the chancel. Tower murals *St. Peter* and *St. Paul* by John La Farge and assistants, 1876–77. Chancel glass by Clayton & Bell of London, 1877–78. Chancel remodeling by Maginnis & Walsh, Architects, 1937–38. (Photo copyright Cervin Robinson.)

Pl. 8. Trinity Church. Detail of the east wall of the tower with mural decoration by John La Farge and assistants, 1876–77. (Photo copyright Peter Vanderwarker; Courtesy of Trinity Church.)

Pl. 9.  Trinity Church. Detail of mural decoration by John La Farge and assistants, 1876–77. (Photo by Virginia Chieffo Raguin.)

Pl. 10. Trinity Church. *Presentation of Mary in the Temple,* stained glass in the nave by John La Farge, 1888. (Photo by Virginia Chieffo Raguin.)

Pl. 11. Trinity Church. Chancel as remodeled by Maginnis & Walsh, Architects, 1937–38. (Photo copyright Peter Vanderwarker; Courtesy of Trinity Church.)

Pl. 12. Trinity Church. Baptistry font by Forsyth of London, 1876; portrait of Phillips Brooks by Daniel Chester French, 1898. (Photo copyright Peter Vanderwarker; Courtesy of Trinity Church.)

Pl. 13. Trinity Church. *Christ in Majesty,* stained glass above the west entrance by John La Farge, 1883. (Photo copyright Peter Vanderwarker; Courtesy of Trinity Church.)

Pl. 14. Trinity Church. *The Apostles James, Matthias, Thomas, and Bartholomew,* stained glass in the nave by Margaret Redmond, 1927. (Photo courtesy of Trinity Church.)

Pl. 15.  Trinity Church. *The Evangelists St. Luke and St. John,* stained glass in the nave by Margaret Redmond, 1927. (Photo courtesy of Trinity Church.)

Pl. 16. Trinity Church. Interior looking toward the west. *The Transfiguration,* stained glass in the south transept by Henry Holiday, ca. 1878. *Christ in Majesty,* stained glass above the main entrance by John La Farge, 1883. (Photo copyright Cervin Robinson.)

materials. The stylistic keynote is Romanesque mass rather than Gothic line, but a Romanesque adapted to existing tectonic possibilities. Trinity has wall arches but no structural stone vaults. The large-scale masonry vaulting that characterizes the twelfth-century Romanesque did not occur in this building or anywhere else in the country at this time. The "vaults" covering nave, transepts, and chancel at Trinity are composed of lath and plaster hung from wooden arches tied to the wooden roof rafters with scantling. These exert little or no diagonal thrust, so there are no working external buttresses (those outside the chancel are there of stylistic preference). The structural and spatial core of the church rises from massive granite foundations through the four crossing piers tied together at the top by the thick brick arches that hold up the crowning tower. The visibly wooden ties spanning between the imposts of the arches in fact conceal iron tension rods counteracting the outward thrust of these planar arches.

This concealment of structural metal corresponded with Richardson's conservative design program. It is probable that he would rather have avoided it altogether. Since he proudly declared in his 1877 description of the church that "no masonry . . . is dependent on metal for support," either he chose to ignore the occasional iron members supporting masonry around the base of the tower, or Norcross kept him in the dark.[19] (These ancillary supporting members are "signed" by the Phoenix Iron Company of Philadelphia, the largest rolling mill in the country and one that shipped its products broadly.)[20] He did admit that iron beams were necessary in the chapel, where "one or two of the stone lintels are reinforced by concealed [iron] girders." This was a structural section repeated at the Marshall Field Wholesale Store in Chicago, and probably elsewhere in Richardson-Norcross work.[21] Traditional load-bearing masonry construction—or, on occasion, at least the appearance of such traditional technology—informed the essential characteristic of a Richardson-Norcross building.

Once the pyramidal pier foundations were laid, Norcross stone began to accumulate at the Trinity building site. The chapel neared completion by the end of 1874, and the main walls of the church began to rise (figs. 6-3, 6-4). They are of rock-faced Dedham granite backed by brick, the stone laid in a random ashlar pattern set in red mortar. Belt courses, the frames of openings, and carved details are of sandstone from East Longmeadow. The contractor's masons characteristically laid up stonework of the highest degree of craftsmanship. The dance of light and shadow over the surfaces of these walls animates the exterior. When we admire Richardson's design, we are at the same time admiring Norcross's realization of that design.

In calling this building a collaboration, I do not mean to suggest that construction proceeded without friction. The archives of the church hold many a let-

6-3. Trinity Church under construction looking west, early 1875. (Author's collection.)

6-4. Trinity Church under construction looking east, June 1875. (Author's collection.)

ter from one or another of the principals in this large and complex undertaking: Paine, Brooks, Norcross, or Richardson complaining about delays, lack of information, cost overruns, and even personal grievances. Ernest Bowditch tells us that Paine got into the habit of giving directions to workmen without consulting Norcross. Eventually, the contractor "lost his temper, and told him plainly that if he ever opened his mouth again on his work he would have him put off the job." According to the same source, "the rebuke was effectual."[22] In June 1874, Norcross wrote the building committee to complain about the many changes in the design and the lack of definitive drawings. "If eight months is not time enough to find out what you are to build how long will it take? We want to know, now, at once, this day, what we are to do. . . . [W]e have had more bother, trouble, and delay on this building than in all the works we ever did.[23] Richardson early on in his career had written that "architects should not be made the convenience of contractors" and should not be pressed for drawings.[24] He complained to Henry Parker of the building committee in January 1875 that Norcross had refused to give him figures concerning the difference in the cost of materials between the old and the new tower designs; on the other hand, Paine complained to his diary at a later date that the committee had "been waiting & telegraphing HHR for a drawing . . . till we are in despair."[25]

Anyone who has ever watched a building operation, even one as small as a kitchen remodeling, understands that such an endeavor will cause strains among client, architect, and builder. A large public project, built under difficult conditions and budgetary stress by relatively inexperienced men, magnifies the problems. But these were all capable men of good will, and since each of them had a special reason for successfully carrying off the project, conflict seems to have brought out the best in each one. Despite the battles of the moment, Trinity Church emerged as a masterpiece; Paine later had Richardson design the large addition to his summer house in Waltham (see fig. 3-8);[26] and Norcross went on to collaborate on the finest of Richardson's remaining works.

An engraved stone tablet mounted in the cloister on the exterior wall of the chancel, put there by the architects of Boston in 1913, declares Trinity Church to be Richardson's "noblest work." But Trinity is more than that, and it is an achievement he shared. One of Richardson's finest gifts was his ability to collaborate with men of his own stature in their different fields: Phillips Brooks, Robert Treat Paine, O. W. Norcross, the artist John La Farge. At Trinity they came together under his direction to create one of the noblest monuments in American or, rather, Western architecture.

# NOTES

1. Frank E. Kidder and Harry Parker, *Kidder-Parker Architects' and Builders' Handbook* (New York: John Wiley & Sons, 1944).

2. The only recent publication on Norcross is James F. O'Gorman, "O. W. Norcross, Richardson's 'Master Builder': A Preliminary Report," *Journal of the Society of Architectural Historians* 32, no. 2 (May 1973): 104–13. Two later, unpublished studies are Diana Evelyn Prideaux-Brune, "Builder as Technical Innovator: Orlando Whitney Norcross and the Beamless Flat Slab" (M.A. thesis, Cornell University, 1988); and Christopher F. Girr, "Mastery in Masonry: Norcross Brothers, Contractors and Builders, 1864–1924" (M.S. thesis, Columbia University, 1996). All three sources contain extensive references to earlier literature.

3. Prideaux-Brune, "Builder as Technical Innovator," 12, citing Miles Colean and Robinson Newcomb, *Stabilizing Construction* (New York, 1952), 54–57.

4. Girr, "Mastery in Masonry," 61–67.

5. Peter Fergusson, James F. O'Gorman, and John Rhodes, *The Landscape and Architecture of Wellesley College* (Wellesley, Mass.: Wellesley College, 2000), 39.

6. Robert D. Andrews, "Conditions of Architectural Practice Thirty Years and More Ago," *Architectural Review* (Boston) 5 (November 1917): 1.

7. Girr, "Master of Masonry," 24–38.

8. Edward F. Miner, "Memoir of Orlando Whitney Norcross," *Transactions of the American Society of Civil Engineers* 84 (1921): 896–98.

9. See James F. O'Gorman, "Then and Now: A Note on the Contrasting Architectures of H. H. Richardson and Frank Furness," in *H. H. Richardson: The Architect, His Peers, and Their Era*, ed. Maureen Meister (Cambridge, Mass.: MIT Press, 1999), 76–101.

10. Mary Alice Molloy, "Richardson's Web: A Client's Assessment of the Architect's Home and Studio," *Journal of the Society of Architectural Historians* 54 (March 1995): 8–23.

11. Glenn Brown, *Memories, 1860–1930* (Washington, D.C.: n.p., 1931), 23 ff.

12. For a brief overview of Richardson's career, see James F. O'Gorman, *H. H. Richardson: Architectural Forms for an American Society* (Chicago: University of Chicago Press, 1987), 29–53.

13. Geoffrey Scott, *The Architecture of Humanism* (1914, 1924; reprint Garden City, N.Y.: Doubleday Anchor Books, n.d.), 42.

14. Edith Norcross Morgan, "Memorial to Orlando Whitney Norcross," in the typescript "Proceedings of the Worcester Historical Society" (comp. William Woodward) 27 (1931): 197–203 (Worcester, Mass., Historical Society).

15. My thanks to Director of Facilities John Clift for correcting several erroneous details of the structure of Trinity that I have, unfortunately, published in previous works.

16. H. H. Richardson, *A Description of Trinity Church*, talk given at the dedication in 1877 and reprinted as a pamphlet handed out at the church.

17. Ernest Bowditch Papers, vol. 2, "Orlando Norcross" (copy in author's files.)

18. Robert K. Shaw, "Norcross, Orlando Whitney," in *The Dictionary of National Biography*, vol. 13 (1934), 545–46.

19. Richardson, "Description of Trinity Church."

20. Phoenix was at nearly the same date supplying the exposed ironwork of Furness & Hewitt's Pennsylvania Academy of the Fine Arts in Philadelphia. My thanks to George E. Thomas for information about the company, whose shops were in fact located in Phoenixville, Pennsylvania. See also Carl W. Condit, *American Building Art: The Nineteenth Century* (New York: Oxford University Press, 1960), 71.

21. See O'Gorman, "Then and Now," fig. 4.3.

22. Bowditch Papers, "Orlando Norcross."

23. Norcross to Henry Parker, June 2, 1874, Archives of Trinity Church.

24. Quoted in James F. O'Gorman, *H. H. Richardson and His Office: Selected Drawings* (Cambridge, Mass.: Department of Printing and Graphic Arts, Harvard College Library, 1974), 212, a note from Richardson's sketchbook dated 1870.

25. Robert Treat Paine Diary, 25 July 1876, Archives of Stonehurst, Waltham, Mass.

26. But, as Ann Clifford (director and curator of Stonehurst) reminds me, he did not have Norcross build it.

7-1.  John La Farge (1835–1910). (Photo by Marian Hooper "Clover" Adams, n.d.; Courtesy of the Massachusetts Historical Society.)

# 7

## *Decorator: John La Farge*

VIRGINIA CHIEFFO RAGUIN

THE PICTORIAL DECORATION of Trinity Church stands as a landmark in nineteenth-century American art at a time when places of worship attracted the most progressive architectural and artistic expression. All the images in glass, in sculpture, and on the walls are the product of a community articulating links between the past, present, and future. The murals and the stained glass present a program that influenced the progress of ecclesiastic work for a generation. Appropriately, we start with John La Farge's murals from 1876 through 1877.

La Farge (fig. 7-1) was uniquely qualified to accept the commission. Multilingual, with strong European ties, he possessed a sweeping intellectual and cultural erudition. He was born March 31, 1835, in New York, the son of John Frederick La Farge and Louisa Binsse de Saint-Victor, French émigrés. His early education was bilingual and emphasized literature and art. His Roman Catholic background encouraged a Catholic-affiliated schooling, and he matriculated at Mount Saint Mary's College, Maryland, receiving a master's degree in 1855. Thereafter, he studied law in New York while continuing to mingle in artistic circles. From April 1856 to the fall of 1857, La Farge traveled in Europe, predominantly France and Belgium. He broadened his literary and artistic horizons by contact with his mother's cousin Paul de Saint-Victor, a well-known Parisian literary critic, and the study of the paintings of Eugène Delacroix (1798–1863) and Théodore Chassériau (1819–1856), among others. La Farge had studied briefly in the studio of the French academic painter Thomas Couture (1815–1879) as had the Boston painter William Morris Hunt (1824–1879) in 1847.[1] He also associated with the painter and muralist Puvis de Chavannes (1824–1898), later responsible for the Boston Public Library's great cycle of the arts and sciences in its main entrance stairwell.

Upon his return from Europe, La Farge established studio space in New York and continued to broaden his circle of artistic and cultural acquaintances. These included the architects of Harvard's Memorial Hall, William Robert Ware (1832–1915) and Henry Van Brunt (1832–1903); the philosopher William James (1842–1910) and the novelist Henry James (1843–1916); and the muralist William Morris Hunt, with whom he studied in Newport, Rhode Island. From 1860 through 1876, La Farge was engaged in painting and illustration work. In 1874, Ware and Van Brunt, representing the Harvard class of 1844, offered him the commission for a *Chevalier Bayard* stained glass window for Harvard's Memorial Hall, never brought to fruition. From 1876 through 1877 he was involved in stages of the mural decoration of Trinity Church, and from this time until his death in 1910, he designed extensively in the applied arts of murals and stained glass.

La Farge's first foray into the monumental arts was his work on the murals of Trinity. He was the personal choice of the architect, H. H. Richardson. Not only did La Farge develop the schema for the murals, but one version of the story credits him with suggesting the design of the tower and providing the architect with photographs of the tower of Salamanca's cathedral in Spain as a model for Trinity's crossing. La Farge's mural design, besides providing powerful thematic content, reinforced the architectural elements in Trinity—most evidently in the structure of the decoration in the tower, where the geometric elements of the rectangle bases of the wall shafts are augmented by contrasting turquoise molding and square decorative insets. Early writers on La Farge have suggested his training in architecture as a contributing factor to such sensitivity. La Farge's advice on building had been sought for the planning of the Church of St. Paul the Apostle, New York City, through his longtime association with the pastor and founder of the Paulist Fathers, Isaac Thomas Hecker.[2] For both St. Paul and Trinity, it sufficed for La Farge to be aware of architecture as sculpting space in the same way that color and form sculpture space in painting. In addition, La Farge's unusually cultivated European culture would argue for his awareness of buildings as vital elements of culture. In the heady atmosphere of Parisian artistic criticism, where his cousin Paul de Saint-Victor was an important voice, vigorous debates were waged over appropriate building styles.[3]

La Farge agreed to undertake the Trinity work within the time frame required by the architect in order to make use of the existing staging that had been erected by the contractors. The entire program was executed in a little more than four months. The Romanesque style of the architecture afforded excellent mural expanses to receive decoration, and it is clear that both the rector, Phillips Brooks, and Richardson wanted a color-drenched interior. Richardson was specific about the overall ground of Pompeian (La Farge's "Persian") red. Murals, as La Farge knew well, were the decoration of choice for the twelfth-century buildings from which Richardson had drawn his inspiration. Evidence of the architect's intent is found in the report of the building committee, where, despite its expectation of the "simplest" program, Richardson urged the adoption of the extensive system of murals.

A brilliant schema emerged wherein La Farge was able to apportion the work of the decorators and the painters. The curving shape of the vaults of the transept arms is accented by successive bands of variegated circular and square motifs (pl. 5). The supporting piers are lightened by the contrast of green and red so that they almost achieve an open texture. The tower ceiling shows a consistent pattern of lacy circles within a square, emphasizing its flat form. Over the tower windows, as on the exterior stonework of the church, polychrome defines the different segments of the arch (pl. 8). The tower wall's rectangular divisions are reinforced by molding within which symbols of the evangelists appear in panels on the north and south walls; on the west and east are two panels with a jeweled cross and two with inscriptions. Above the arches of the crossing, bust-length images of angels with scrolls gesture toward six monumental figures of apostles and prophets, which stand in the spandrel areas above the crossing piers (pl. 7). The nave painting was accomplished slightly later, giving La Farge more time to execute it. Two majestic compositions, *Christ Visiting Nicodemus* on the south wall and *Christ with the Woman of Samaria* on the north, have been widely praised (pl. 5).[4] The original decoration of the chancel included six rectangular panels with gold background set between the windows. They bore Latin crosses, similar to those in the tower, and texts: the Apostles Creed and the Lord's Prayer in the center, passages from the communion service at the sides (see fig. 4-5). Upper and lower sections of the church were thus unified in an apportioning of symbol, figure, and inscription placed within geometric units tied to the structure of the architecture.

La Farge subcontracted the general painting of the walls and ceilings to the New York firm of Hill & Treharne.[5] He recounted later that he knew their limitations, confiding, "I left large spaces bare, with no indication of my intention, which places I proposed decoration through men whom I was training for the purpose." In a discussion with the foreman, he characterized the difference between a creative and a mechanical approach to the execution of large-scale decorative work. The foreman had advocated starting at the top and finishing at the bottom to avoid paint drips. La Farge reflected that such thinking was an indication of "many methods which are used because they are convenient and not because they are the best."[6] His goal was the creation of an artistic interior, one that would rival the medieval as well as the contemporary work he knew from France. The men whom La Farge "trained" included the artists John de Fais, George

Willoughby Maynard (1843–1923), Francis Lathrop (1849–1909), Augustus Saint-Gaudens (1848–1907), Francis David Millet (1846–1912), Sidney Lawton Smith (1845–?), George L. Rose (1861–?), and Edwin G. Champney (1842–1899). The first seven—along with Richardson, La Farge, and T. M. Clark, the architect's superintendent—are named in the inscription in the lower border of the decorative panel above the arch of the chancel. Like La Farge, Millet and Lathrop would later design stained glass.

The expressive figures were painted using encaustic, a wax-based paint melted with turpentine and alcohol (pl. 9). Weinberg traces La Farge's use of this technique to a meeting in Brussels with Henry Le Strange in 1856 or 1857. Le Strange had used encaustic in decorating the ceiling of the west tower at Ely Cathedral in 1855. The possibility of swift execution without using wet plaster must have been attractive, as well as the ability of pigment to retain its freshness within the wax medium. Color was clearly a major concern. La Farge's plans for the decoration are known from sketches that are now a part of various museum and private collections.[7] The black-and-white images give little understanding of the painterly execution and the gestural energy of the brush strokes, but detailed views show the use of a variegated palette for the blue and green of the shadows of the faces, as well as many hues in the garments and wings of the angels. As he did with so much of his art, La Farge made historic precedent live as a practical modus vivendi. Despite the variety of his collaborators, some of whom would go on to highly distinguished careers, he managed to achieve a common expression. In this he saw a direct parallel to Raphael's workshop, executing murals for the Vatican in the early sixteenth century. He stated later of Raphael's example that "the habit of the day was to do work in common. . . . [T]he point of view of that day was the moral one—lost by us—that the result was everything and that the aim was the work itself, and not who did this or that part. It is to the changes of the past century that we owe the departure from that holy and only true ideal."[8]

What needs to be made clear here is that La Farge was a believer—in art and in established religion. In her preface to his posthumously published *The Gospel Story in Art* his editor, Mary Cadwalader Jones, writes that La Farge had long reverenced the subject of the book. Having been "born and educated in the older faith of Christendom," as she phrased it, explained the author's reverence for the subject, to which he brought a lifelong study of the history of works of art and "classical writings of the Western and the older Eastern world." In this text, as in all his writings, La Farge stressed the content of the image. With the ease of long familiarity, he quoted an author such as St. Bonaventure on the *Meditations of the Life of Christ* (now attributed to an anonymous Franciscan) as he discussed images of the Deposition. In a continued analysis of the theme, he presented Eugène

Delacroix with deepest affection: "With this modern painter, whom many of us have known, passes the last ray of the expression of religious feeling."[9]

Religious feeling was, indeed, a goal of La Farge. Henry Adams characterized his art as one of "intellectuality" and "deep immersion in culture."[10] La Farge saw himself representing something much broader than his own talent. In *Considerations on Painting,* he explained that differences in national schools occur because the artist represents his entire culture in his painting, which bears "the marks of the places where the works of art were born. Climate, quality of light, specific landscape," as well as "manners, laws, religious and national ideals" will be part of the art. For the artists, "the fact that they used their eyes more or less is only a small factor in this enormous aggregation of influences received by them and transmitted to us."[11] La Farge saw himself in the same way, absolutely a part of his time and bringing to a house of worship his exposure to a long heritage of religious expression.

The conviction that the artist is a crystallization of his society was also articulated by Martin Brimmer, a member of Trinity Church and founding director of Boston's Museum of Fine Arts. Art for Brimmer was an indicator of the moral fiber of a nation, for great art, he believed, cannot be produced by an ignoble society: "It demands a high national pride, a past that is cherished with pride, a future bright with hope." Brimmer dedicated Wellesley College's museum of art by evoking three civilizations embodied through art: classical Athens through the sculpture of Phidias, seventeenth-century Holland through Rembrandt, and the period from the Restoration to the Second Empire in France through the art of Delacroix, Rousseau, and Millet.[12] Significantly, the painting the Museum of Fine Arts acquired in 1896 by subscription in Brimmer's memory is Delacroix's *Entombment of Christ.*[13]

La Farge was bolstered in his convictions by his French heritage. In France, religious mural painting was the most prestigious and the most contested artistic commission. His bilingual culture allowed him full access not only to view but to acquire what was distinctive about the Paris of his time. He knew the status of painting, admiring Théodore Chassériau's mural work, especially that depicting St. Mary the Egyptian in the church of Saint-Merri, and of course, the widely influential work of Couture, with whom he had studied.[14] Thus he approached Trinity with a sense of familiarity and confidence that few Americans could bring. La Farge's expression, which he managed to share with his team of partners, involved rich broken strokes of paint; as he explained, for a great and skilful painter "the very surface of the paint [will] literally embody his feeling."[15]

Although in all of La Farge's figural work one sees how deeply he was influenced by the example of Couture, his deepest inspiration was Delacroix. His admiration for the *Expulsion of Heliodoros,* one of the murals of Delacroix in the church of Saint-Sulpice, Paris, prompted him to commence his *Gospel Story in Art* with a discourse on that painting.[19] In the fervor of description he compared the work favorably with Raphael's on the same subject, stating that Delacroix "saw further than the outside of beautiful objects; he saw men themselves with their anxieties and their delights and to each one he gave a colour and shape."[16] La Farge's *Three Wise Men,* painted 1878–79, is unabashedly modeled after Delacroix's compositions, including the vagueness of anatomical structure, the concomitant emphasis on surface, and atmosphere.[17] It was the imprecision in the handling of the large standing figures on the corners of the crossing where this "want of good drawing" drew criticism even from his fervent admirers of the program as a whole.[18]

La Farge had hopes for a muted, grisaille (neutral color) glazing to better illuminate his murals. He commissioned from Samuel West of Boston the fish-scale patterned windows in the tower, after concern about the jarring effect that an inappropriate color selection might impose on the interior (pl. 8). Apparently, he intervened even after the windows were installed placing a neutral cold paint over the glass to mitigate the light further. (I only recently discovered this by close inspection from the scaffold erected by Goody, Clancy, Architects, Boston, as part of the restoration project.) The artist also commissioned the grisaille window that West installed in the north nave to the right of *Christ with the Woman of Samaria.*[19] A wood engraving of the north nave showing the grisaille panel designed by La Farge appears in Roger Riordan's 1881 article in *American Art Review.* Riordan's opinion, which undoubtedly echoes La Farge's sentiments, castigates the European windows in the church: "The failure of the other windows, in the modern English style, to harmonize with the mural decorations, was what caused Mr. La Farge seriously to turn his attention to the making of stained glass, and the first fruit of this was the strikingly successful window in question (the rejected grisaille), the only one in the church which is in keeping with the general scheme."[20]

The vestry had determined from the outset, however, to seek donors for major figural windows. Those installed by spring of 1879 were by the French and English firms of Cottier & Co. (Daniel Cottier, 1838–1891); Clayton & Bell (John Richard Clayton, 1927–1913, and Alfred Bell, 1832–1895); Burlison & Grylls (John Burlison, 1843–1891, and Thomas John Grylls, 1845–1913); Henry Holiday (1839–1927); then designing for Powell & Sons; and Eugène Oudinot (1827–89).[21] The grisaille window was replaced in April 1879 with figural glass designed by Henry Holiday of London, who also supplied the similar window to the west. The donors of these windows that visually overpower La Farge's painting represented two of the most powerful social forces of the congregation: the head of the building committee and the rector. To the west, *Scenes from the Life of St. Paul* honors the Reverend Frederick Brooks, the brother of Phillips Brooks. To the east, *Christ and the Children* was given by Robert Treat Paine in honor of his great-grandfather, Robert Treat Paine, a signer of the Declaration of Independence. Paine mentions that Brooks had personally selected the artist and discussed the design during a visit to England in the summer of 1877. Holiday was one of the most prestigious designers in England, and the windows, especially that of St. Paul, do show some of the most exquisite draftsmanship in the church.[22] More-over, the subject matter of St. Paul's conversion and preaching was entirely ap-propriate for a clergyman, and that of Christ with the children related to the loss of a child in the Paine family. Nonetheless, the choice of Holiday was a severe dis-appointment to La Farge, who felt that he had completed the murals at great fi-nancial and physical strain. His 1894 recollection of the context was that "the En-glish glass stainers were also convinced, and had persuaded the architects and persons of influence that I was incapable of making anything of value [in glass]."[23]

Donor identification, the primary association of memorial windows in nine-teenth- and twentieth-century churches, is a time-honored tradition operative since the Middle Ages.[24] American churches that have kept any kind of record of their windows invariably list the names of the donors, often with little indication of the subject matter of the window. In fact, windows appear to have become in the modern world the most prominent means of the laity's self-expression within the material church structure. It was this reason, far more than a disagreement with La Farge's aesthetics, that made plain grisaille windows absolutely unthink-able for Trinity.

La Farge, however, benefited equally from donor acumen and loyalty when he himself began to design figural windows for Trinity. One of the best known, the *Presentation of the Virgin in the Temple* in the south nave, is a memorial to Julia Appleton McKim, donated by her husband, Charles Follen McKim, and her sis-ter Alice (pl. 10). The donor was the key identification point, and one of the first citations of the window in print refers to the "McKim Window in Trinity Church, Boston."[25] McKim was a partner in the prestigious firm of McKim, Mead & White, the architects of the Boston Public Library. He selected the artist and also, apparently, the model to commemorate his wife's death at age twenty-eight.

The window's central image depends on the painting by Titian (1535–1538), now in the Accademia, Venice, and a Latin inscription cites this source.[26] In *The Gospel Story in Art,* La Farge would discuss several artists' versions of the subject, introducing "the great" Titian's painting "as the final representation, famous throughout the world."[27] The Renaissance painting is a huge canvas showing a long stairway, framed at the bottom by a crowd of onlookers and at the top by the high priest and two assistants. Only the segment showing the isolated figure of the Virgin on the stairs was transferred to the window composition, framed within the compositional design as if it were a relic from the past. At the bottom of the frame, set on another spatial plane and seeming to reflect on the image above, a seated figure plays a lute.[28]

This work harmonizes like no other of the nave windows with the architectural framing of the painting to its side, La Farge's *Christ Visiting Nicodemus*. The painted wall is divided into horizontal and vertical banding, those segments closest to the image overtly illusionistic as if they are architectural supports. The window continues to build an architectural system within the glass with fluted pilasters, triangular pediment, and a stepped base. In this format, La Farge expanded significantly on the architectural illusionism of the window of *The Infant Bacchus* of 1882–84, designed for the Washington B. Thomas house at Beverly, Massachusetts.[29] In the earlier work, three-dimensional fluted columns support an entablature restricted to a flat decorative plane.

In its Renaissance sense of space, the *Presentation of the Virgin in the Temple* prefigures La Farge's Oakes Ames memorial window, *Wisdom Enthroned:* installed in 1901 in Unity Church, North Easton, Massachusetts, that window evokes a Renaissance *sacra conversazione,* a holy conversation among a standing group of saints and the divine presence, emulating models such as Veneziano's fifteenth-century *St. Lucy Altarpiece,* which La Farge surely must have known from his visits to the Uffizi in Florence in 1894.[30] Temporal as well as spatial illusion permeates the interchange. It is fruitful, I would argue, to see both the lute player and the image of the Virgin as experiential responses to the art of the past. Music-making figures appear frequently in Venetian art, particularly at the base of a throne or set within an architectural border to both frame and honor the subject.[31] Patron and artist were united by a common culture, both aware of Italian Renaissance models, as exemplified by McKim's work in Boston's library and at the Walker Art Building at Bowdoin College, Brunswick, Maine, for which McKim commissioned La Farge to execute a lunette on the theme of *Athens.*

In this respect, Trinity's memorial program speaks to a much longer tradition, one displayed in city churches of late medieval societies. A striking parallel is found in St. Lorenz, Nuremberg (fig. 7-2), like Trinity a product of a mercantile society where prominent families exercised civic and religious influence. St. Lorenz, spared the Reformation iconoclasm that destroyed so many monuments, preserves the quintessence of the late medieval sacral ambiance. A wide circle of affluent citizens from various levels of society had competed to furnish the structure within and without, and—as generally during the late Middle Ages—the

7-2. St. Lorenz, Nuremburg, early sixteenth century. View of the choir.
(Author's collection.)

7-3. "Beau Dieu," 1220–30. Central portal of Amiens Cathedral. (Author's collection.)

themes and the placement of monuments reflect the donors' deep conviction of the importance of sacred space. Donors were thought to accrue special merit via the images with which they were associated. Corine Schleif observes that the continued use of the church after the Protestant Reformation enhanced the association with the donors. The altar of St. Bartholomew became known as the Krell altar, after the donor, and the chapel dedicated to St. Anne was at times referred to as the Horn Chapel because Kunz Horn had funded it.[32]

Trinity Church demonstrates the same collaboration of donor, artist, and community that produced such great churches of the past. La Farge's greatly admired west window, *Christ in Majesty,* testifies to the ideas of the rector, Phillips Brooks, the hand of the artist, John La Farge, and a shared cultural and historic awareness of the cultural tastemakers of late nineteenth-century Boston (pl. 13). The result has been described as the finest window in America. In 1893, Siegfried Bing, visiting America to survey for France the state of the arts at Chicago's Columbian Exposition, observed that in Boston, "all marveled at the large stained glass window whose astonishing brilliance surpassed in its magic, anything of its kind created in modern times."[33]

La Farge had been awarded Trinity's west window commission in 1880. The long process of his experiments with his opalescent style (discussed below) so occupied his energies that he appears to have begun planning the window seriously only in 1883, producing a small sketch that incorporated early Christian architectural motifs. His original multilevel design included two narrow Gothic arches that housed figures, but his pencil note next to the image, "Perhaps better empty without figures," suggests that he wanted them removed.[34] Phillips Brooks, Trinity's charismatic rector, presumably did not. Biographers of the artist have assumed that Brooks suggested the sculpture of the Christ of Amiens as the basis for the window (fig. 7-3); La Farge then replaced the multilevel design and set the "Beau Dieu" image of Christ in the central lancet and sections of an arcade at the sides. Whether Brooks or La Farge initiated the use of the image is less important than the reality that an accepted model was known to both patron and artist. In fact, I would suggest that this image of the central portal figure from the thirteenth-century facade of Amiens Cathedral had become one of the near-universal references for its late nineteenth-century audience. Its status reflects the context of the nineteenth century's canon of great works of art, communicated through photograph, engraving, and literary description.

In Boston, these judgments were propagated through a small but passionate and cultivated group that included the patrons of the windows at Harvard and Trinity Church. One of the chief figures at this intersection of art, culture, and religion was Charles Eliot Norton, from 1874 through 1899 the first professor of the history of art at Harvard. In 1855 he had begun a long and productive friendship with John Ruskin, the extraordinarily prolific English writer on Romantic painting, architecture, and religious feeling.[35] Ruskin did not invent the importance of the Amiens Christ but made it an ineluctable part of any cultivated Christian's awareness; his *Bible of Amiens* described the sculpture as the true keystone of both art and faith. He published the book in stages and the description of the cathedral's sculptures separately in 1881 to facilitate its use as a guidebook.[36] Ruskin harks back to another authority, citing Viollet-le-Duc's analysis of the Beau Dieu of Amiens.[37] Few have come close to the eloquence of Ruskin's description of the sculpture as the center of the portal, the center of the building, and the center of religion itself. A small indication of the impact of these thoughts may be seen twenty years later upon opening Frederic W. Farrar's popular book *The Life of Christ as Represented in Art.* Its frontispiece is the Christ of Amiens, and Farrar's description within the text repeats Ruskin's evaluation: "Mr. Ruskin selects as the noblest ideal of Christ known to him a sculptured figure of the thirteenth century on the west front of Amiens Cathedral. . . . Into this figure the artist has put a world of true and noble thought. Christ is standing at the central point of all History, and of all Revelation: the Christ, or Prophesied Messiah of all Past, the King and Redeemer of Future Time."[38]

Norton knew Ruskin; Brooks knew Ruskin's writings; and certainly La Farge, of French heritage, knew the ideas of both Ruskin and Viollet-le-Duc, as well as the sculpture itself. La Farge owned a number of Ruskin's works, including *Lectures on Art*. Client and patron intermingled intellectually and socially; La Farge writes that he, Brooks, and Richardson had viewed Giotto's Arena Chapel in Padua together.[39] A telling connection between Norton and Trinity was Martin Brimmer's long friendship with Norton; among other joint activities, they had helped to found the Archaeological Institute of America in 1879, Norton serving as the first president and Brimmer as first vice president. The success of the *Christ in Majesty* at Trinity, then, came from widely shared cultural expectations, an increasingly unusual context in our present time. La Farge did not simply replicate his model; he assimilated its form and power and communicated it to an audience already receptive to the issues behind the selection of the image.

The new style that La Farge employed so well at Trinity, however, was developed through patronage at Harvard College, often related to Trinity through shared donors. Memorial Hall, dedicated to the Union soldiers who had fallen in the War between the States, was begun in 1871; Victorian Gothic as espoused by England's John Ruskin influenced Ware & Van Brunt, the architects. The dining hall was to receive double-light windows that would show historic figures honoring the sacrifice of young lives in the Union cause. The intent of the original plans would have seen most of the glass designed by La Farge and executed by a Boston stained glass studio, MacDonald & McPherson (Donald MacDonald, 1841–1916, and William J. McPherson, fl. 1845–88), which had glazed the transept windows and provided the temporary windows of Memorial Hall. La Farge began with a window showing Christopher Columbus and the Chevalier Bayard, a model of late medieval chivalry.[40] Not content, however, with traditional stained glass manufacture—pot-metal color modeled with the application of vitreous paint—he experimented on a test panel with techniques of plating (placing two or more panes of glass behind each other in a single leaded segment). These innovations pushed the projected price to more than twice the sum that the class of 1844 had assumed, and the project was abandoned. The class eventually chose Henry Holiday for the window it contributed—the same artist who designed the windows of Trinity's north nave, which compete with La Farge's murals.

Only in 1882, after success elsewhere, did La Farge succeed in creating the *Battle Window* for Harvard. The technique that he ultimately developed restructured the window as a kind of relief-mosaic. He also became entranced with using "opalescent," the milky, translucent glasses commonly used for commercial objects, as well as the traditional, clear, single-color glass. In 1879, La Farge had filed for a patent for the new system of constructing windows. He described color "enhanced by the great or less smoothness of one or both surfaces of the opalescent glass, and by its thickness. The glass may be waved, corrugated, or roughened in molds, or be hammered or rolled or be stamped or treated—to accord with the design." The shifting colors and value changes caused by different thicknesses of glass approximated what could be achieved with a brush manipulating oil-based pigments. Later, La Farge would explain that in this new style, "painting was almost wholly dispensed with, and the work became a form of translucent mosaic, held together by lead instead of cement. Only the heads, hands, faces—what the trade calls flesh—still continued to be painted, especially because with them, expression, an element of design and not of colour, would always be the principle aim."[41]

A closer look at La Farge's material reveals an extremely broad variety of types of glass, much of it emulating ancient techniques of inlay and mosaic. Dumping ladles of different colors together and putting them through a roller before mixing produced marbled patterns. The addition of multiple chips resulted in what is known as confetti glass. Sections of a window could actually be molded: for example, for flowers, the varying thickness of the glass defined the petals.[42] The effect of relief is also achieved by setting nuggets of glass in a pattern that resembles ancient pebble mosaics. Installed in 1883, a year after the successful *Battle Window,* Harvard's window of *Homer and Virgil* shows a pebble border and segments of opalescent and cathedral glass that evokes classical inlay in architectural niches, as in the Pantheon in Rome. These design choices for Memorial Hall confirm the pervasive use of the past by artists of the late nineteenth century. Such decisions were predicated on the broad reverence for a canon of great art of the antique and the Renaissance world available in image and—for the elite traveler—in memory. In *Homer and Virgil,* for example, the recessed space framed by slender columns and projecting overhang, and the lower border of vertically thin leafy fronts and intertwining meanders are typical of wall painting from Pompeii. Not only would the traveler to Italy have seen these forms, but schematized renderings were available at the time in meticulously illustrated publications of historic ornament such as Owen Jones, *Grammar of Ornament* (1856) or Auguste Racinet, *L'Ornament polychrome* (1875).

Antique references conditioned the techniques of windows as well as their imagery. Distinctive in La Farge's work is his employment of unusually complex narrow segments of glass, unlike the predominant use by his contemporary Louis Comfort Tiffany of drapery glass. Drapery glass was created by manipulating cooling puddles of glass with tongs so that the material set in folds and ridges; the glass cutter then selected a section of the puddle to correspond with a determined area in the window design. (Drapery glass can be seen in Boston's Back Bay in Arlington Street Church, where a series of windows by the Tiffany Studios were installed, beginning in 1898.) La Farge's draperies, however, were modeled primarily through multiple, irregular flat segments, invariably in more than one layer. In Trinity Church the technique appears in the garments of the figures in the window of the *Resurrection* in the north transept (pl. 6). At Harvard, one of the clearest examples is found in the graceful flow of deep rose drapery of the *Mourning Athena* in Sander's Theater, in Memorial Hall. These small, almost segmented folds can be linked to La Farge's admiration for early Christian ivories. He actually owned a plaster replica of the early sixth-century leaf of a diptych showing an angel carrying an orb and staff, often called the Archangel Michael, from the British Museum (fig. 7-4).[43] Rippling over the angel's monumental body are scoops and indentations that La Farge translated into specific segments of glass. Ivories, popular as collectibles, also served as thematic models for La Farge. In a window commissioned for the Crane Memorial Library in Quincy, also with Richardson as architect, he based the seated man called *Old Philosopher* on a late-antique ivory from Monza, Italy.[44]

The window of St. John's vision of the Apocalypse at Trinity likewise demonstrates an assimilation of traditions of Renaissance and medieval pictorial language. Titled *Heavenly Jerusalem,* it commemorates George Nixon Black and his daughter Marianne Black. Commissioned in April 1882, it had been placed in the west wall of the north transept by April 1884. The theme refers to the biblical text "And I John saw the holy city, new Jerusalem, coming down from God out of heaven, prepared as a bride adorned for her husband" (Revelation 21:2). The window is of extraordinary complexity, perhaps one of La Farge's most transcendent works.

H. Barbara Weinberg believed that his "narrative realism . . . integrated with decorative flatness" most successfully with supernatural themes, as in this Trinity window. La Farge designed an image that was both an anthropomorphic representation—a heritage of the Renaissance—and traditional architectural allegory. Medieval representations in stained glass, manuscripts, and wheel lights depicted the heavenly Jerusalem as a city. Accustomed to a more abstract rendition of theoretical concepts, the Middle Ages could see the concept of a spiritual home and a physical place manifest in the precise allegories of the biblical text. Undoubtedly familiar with this tradition, La Farge created an image of descent shifting from the abstraction of architecture to the fully realist image of the bride herself. Weinberg comments: "However realistically modeled, their flesh in paint and their draperies in modulated opalescent glass, the figures are restricted to a narrow plane. . . . An admirable synthesis of the necessities of realism and decoration is effected."[45] This ability to bridge the three-dimensional realism of the prevalent figure style of the nineteenth century and the abstracted heritage of early Christian and medieval art distinguished La Farge among his contemporaries.

7-4. Archangel Michael, early sixth century. Leaf of a diptych. (Author's collection.)

An extraordinary tour de force, the window incorporates the technique of rough-hewn and smooth nuggets of glass. La Farge had used large circles of brilliant blue glass in the background of *Christ in Majesty* of the west facade and a pebble border in Memorial Hall's *Homer and Virgil* of 1883. The prismatic effect in the upper portion of this window, however, is more complex. La Farge's glass suggests an effulgence of the divinity itself, calling to mind the description of the Heavenly City: the walls of jasper, the city itself pure gold "like unto clear glass," the foundations adorned with precious stones and the gates with pearls (Revelations 21:18–21). La Farge would again use this technique in 1887 to evoke the spiritual realm in the Helen Angier Ames window at Unity Church, North Easton, Massachusetts: in that memorial window an antique sarcophagus is lifted to heaven, flanked by angels and surrounded by prismatic light.

In La Farge's work we see the intersection of the artist with the donors of the windows, the spiritual leadership of the church, the architect, and a deep tradition of imagery and form. This calls us to reassess our present evaluation of the creative process. Much current discussion of art focuses on the artist's differences, the things that distance him or her from the community. Creative artists are characterized as expressing personal vision. Such thoughts show a bias toward defining art as that which is produced self-consciously by an "artist" in a society valorizing this function but essentially seeing fine art as separate from patron or purpose. At best, the patron becomes a passive purveyor of funds; at worst, an interfering impediment. The evidence of the stained glass of Trinity Church contradicts this attitude. With La Farge we see the tradition of art meeting the deep and broad needs of a society. These great works in glass, lead, iron, and paint, set within the noble frame of the architecture, are far more important than singular or personal statements; they have been produced by an artist responding to the collective desires of a generation. That spiritual complexity, as well as their beauty, resonates even today.

## NOTES

The most exhaustive and insightful references to the mural painting and stained glass of John La Farge remain the work of H. Barbara Weinberg, *The Decorative Work of John La Farge* (New York: Garland, 1977), and her "John La Farge: Pioneer of the American Mural Movement," in *John La Farge,* ed. Henry Adams et al. (New York: Abbeville, 1987), 165–71.

For insight into La Farge, see his own publications: *Considerations on Painting: Lectures Given in the Year 1893 at the Metropolitan Museum of New York* (New York: Macmillan, 1895); *Great Masters:*

*Essays on Michelangelo, Raphael, Rembrandt, Rubens, Velasquez, Dürer, and Hokusai* (New York: McClure, Phillips, 1903); essays on eleven painters, including Chassériau, Delacroix, Géricault, Millet, and Corot, in *The Higher Life in Art: A Series of Lectures on the Barbizon School of France, Inaugurating the Scammon Course at the Art Institute of Chicago* (New York: McClure, 1908); "Minor Arts," *New England Magazine* 40 (May, 1909): 331; *One Hundred Masterpieces* (Garden City, N.Y.: Doubleday, Paige, 1913); *The Gospel Story in Art* (New York: Macmillan, 1913); "Window, Part II," in *A Dictionary of Architecture and Building,* ed. Russell Sturgis (New York: Macmillan, 1902) 3: cols. 1067–92.

1. Albert Boime, *Thomas Couture and the Eclectic Vision* (New Haven: Yale University Press, 1980); for Boime's comments on La Farge, see 571–72.

2. This was La Farge's only Roman Catholic commission of stained glass and mural decoration; he accomplished it in various stages from 1884 through 1899. See George Parson Lathrop, "John La Farge," *Scribner's Monthly* 21, no. 4 (February 1881): 513; and H. Barbara Weinberg, "The Work of John La Farge in the Church of St. Paul the Apostle," *American Art Journal* 6 (1974): 20–21.

3. Barry Bergdoll, "The Ideal of the Gothic Cathedral in 1852," in *A. W. N. Pugin: Master of Gothic Revival,* exhibition catalogue of the Bard Center for Studies in the Decorative Arts, ed. Paul Atterbury (New Haven: Yale University Press, 1995), 103–35; Michael Paul Driskel, *Representing Belief: Religion, Art, and Society in Nineteenth-Century France* (University Park: Pennsylvania State University Press, 1992).

4. *Christ with the Woman of Samaria* was completed by October 1877; *Christ Visiting Nicodemus* between February 1878 and May 1879. La Farge later used the design of the Visit for stained glass in the Church of the Ascension, New York City, between 1883 and 1885; see *The Quest for Unity, American Art between World's Fairs, 1876–1893,* exhibition catalogue of the Detroit Institute of Arts (Detroit, 1983), 116–17, no. 49.

5. Treharne withdrew before the tower was completed, and the firm of Daniel Cottier, which would also execute the stained glass windows below the south transept, was at work October 19, 1876. Weinberg, *Decorative Work,* 105.

6. La Farge, "What museums of art offer for study," in *Considerations on Painting,* 63-64.

7. Weinberg, *Decorative Work,* 101; Weinberg, "John La Farge," 165–71, figs. 117–25.

8. La Farge, *Great Masters,* 83–84.

9. La Farge, *Gospel Story,* (posthumous publication may explain why the cover came to be embossed with an image of Holman Hunt's *Light of the World*), 350, 359; *Meditations on the Life of Christ,* trans. Isa Ragusa (Princeton: Princeton University Press, 1950).

10. Adams, *John La Farge,* 18.

11. La Farge, *Considerations on Painting,* 14–15.

12. Martin Brimmer, *Address Delivered at Wellesley College upon the Opening of the Farnsworth Art School, October XXIII. MDCCCLXXXIX* (Boston: Houghton Mifflin, 1889), 9, 27.

13. Painted 1848; Museum of Fine Arts, Boston, 96.21.

14. Driskel, *Representing Belief,* 136–39, figs. 52–53.

15. La Farge, *Considerations on Painting,* 18.

16. Jack J. Spector, *The Murals of Eugene Delacroix at Saint-Sulpice* (New York: College Art Association of America, 1967), esp. 108–18, 148–53; La Farge, *Gospel Story,* 14.

17. Museum of Fine Arts, Boston, gift of Edward W. Hooper; see Weinberg, "John La Farge," 174, fig. 130.

18. Lathrop, "John La Farge," 514.

19. Weinberg, *Decorative Work,* 107–8, 343–44, fig. 253, which shows the interior north nave wall with a grisaille window. For a comparable situation of the architect's original plans partially controverted by the insistence of the congregation on figural designs, see the essays on decorative work in Christine Smith, *St. Bartholomew's Church in the City of New York* (New York: Oxford University Press, 1988), 142–52. There, the architect, Bertram Grosvenor Goodhue, had planned for geomet-

ric designs rather than figures in mosaics and windows, but in 1927, after the architect's death, the vestry altered the program. In 1917, however, there had already been demands by the parishioners for stained glass throughout the church.

20. Roger Riordan, "American Stained Glass," pt. 2, *American Art Review* 2, no. 2 (1881): 7–11, image opp. 7. See also Weinberg, *Decorative Work,* 343–45, fig. 253. One may contrast the 1877 disposition of the wall with the present one illustrated in Adams, *La Farge,* fig. 24. The modern color illustration of the north nave and west walls of Trinity distorts the visibility of the murals through massive illumination of the interior.

21. Weinberg, *Decorative Work,* 343–42; Bettina A. Norton, ed., *Trinity Church: The Story of an Episcopal Parish in the City of Boston* (Boston: Wardens and Vestry of Trinity Church in the City of Boston, 1978). For the English studios, see Martin Harrison, *Victorian Stained Glass* (London: Barrie and Jenkins, 1980), 76–77, 79–80; and Elizabeth Morris, *Stained and Decorative Glass* (New York, Exeter Books, 1988), 40–61.

22. Peter Cormack, *Henry Holiday, 1839–1927,* exhibition catalogue of William Morris Gallery (London, 1989).

23. La Farge wrote, "None of us is supposed to have been paid even our living expenses" (quoted in Weinberg, *Decorative Work,* 143–44). For comments on the English glass stainers, see manuscript report of 1894 by La Farge for Siegfried Bing, in La Farge Family Papers, Yale University Library.

24. In stained glass we recognize issues crucial to the medium in the Middle Ages: the commemoration of the dead and, through such remembrance, self-definition for the living. Many Christian confessions are explicit in embracing the ideology of a "communion of saints." This belief posits a real and affective bond linking the members of the community who "are asleep" in Christ with those who "are alive and remain unto the coming of the Lord." (1 Thessalonians 4:13–15). An individual's thoughts—or prayers, depending on one's confessional distinction—linked the living with the dead. For the more orthodox, such bonds even allowed the living to participate in the continuing redemption of those already departed. For both the general congregation and the specific family, these links were a vivid aspect of community self-identity. Peter Brown, *The Cult of the Saints: Its Rise and Function in Latin Christianity* (Chicago: University of Chicago Press, 1981), esp. 50–68.

25. Clara Erskin Clement, "Later Religious Painting in America," *New England Magazine* 12, no. 2 (April 1895): 132. The window, installed in 1888, is inscribed "PLACED IN LOVING MEMORY OF JULIA APPLETON/1859–1887/BY HER HUSBAND CHARLES F MCKIM AND HER SISTER ALICE."

26. "NITET VITRO VIRGINIS BEATAE FACES A TITIANO PRIVS DEPICTA CONIVCI DILECTA SIMILLIMA CVIVS HAEC RECORDATIO LVCET."

27. La Farge, *Gospel Story,* 88.

28. The cartoon for the *Suonatore* (Luteplayer) is now in the collection of the Worcester, Mass., Art Museum (1907.4). See *Half a Century of American Art,* exhibition catalogue of the Art Institute of Chicago (Chicago, 1940), 29, pl. 8. The painting had been exhibited in 1890 with the title *Child Playing upon a Guitar, Italian Motive.*

29. Museum of Fine Arts, Boston, gift of W. B. Thomas; Henry A. La Farge, "Painting with Colored Light: The Stained Glass of John La Farge," in Adams et al., *John La Farge,* 211, pl. 25.

30. Weinberg, *Decorative Work,* 404–6, figs. 299–300.

31. It is possible that the juxtaposition of Titian's painting and paintings such as Giovanni Bellini's *San Giobbe Altarpiece* or a similar composition by Vittore Carpaccio, *The Presentation of Jesus in the Temple with Minstrel Angels,* in the Gallerie dell'Academia in Venice, encouraged the association of architectural frame, detail of the Virgin, and luteplayer in La Farge's composition. At this time, La Farge would have known these images from publications.

32. Corine Schleif, *Donatio et Memoria, Stiftung, Stifter, und Motivationen an Beispiele aus der*

*Lorenzkirche in Nürnberg* (Berlin: Deutscher Kunstverlag, 1990). Schleif has remarked (College Art Association, 1989) that for most art historians, yet another spatial ambient would be in force in St. Lorenz: "We would sense little of the sacral topography and perceive less of the Nuremberg social structure. Our perceptions, formed by our shared experiences mediated by books and reproductions, would place us in the presence of Albrecht Dürer, Veit Stoss, Peter Vischer, and Adam Kraft."

33. This is one of the rare, if not singular, instances when Bing referred to a specific installation. Siegfied Bing, *La Culture artistique en Amérique,* trans. Benita Eisler as "Artistic America," in *Artistic America, Tiffany Glass and Art Nouveau* (1895; Cambridge, Mass.: MIT Press, 1970), 132.

34. Sketch for west windows of nave, Trinity Church, Boston 1883, private collection; Henry La Farge, "Painting with Colored Light," 208–10, figs. 153–54.

35. For Norton's influence, see Kathryn McClintock, "The Classroom and the Courtyard: Medievalism in American Highbrow Culture," in *Medieval Art in America: Patterns of Collecting 1800– 1940,* exhibition catalogue of Palmer Museum of Art, Pennsylvania State University, ed. Elizabeth Bradford Smith, Kathryn McClintock, R. Aaron Rottner, et al. (University Park: Pennsylvania State University, 1996), 41–54; Martin Green, *The Problem of Boston: Some Readings in Cultural History* (New York: W. W. Norton, 1966), 122–41. See also *Letters of Charles Eliot Norton,* 2 vols. (Boston: Houghton Mifflin, 1913). Norton was literary executor for Ruskin, probably best known today as the author of *The Stones of Venice,* 3 vols. (London: Smith, Elder, 1851–53), and *The Seven Lamps of Architecture* (London: Smith, Elder, 1849).

36. John Ruskin, *Bible of Amiens* (1880–84; Paris, 1904). Ruskin sent the first part of the book, "By the River of Waters," to Norton in January 1880: see *Letters of John Ruskin to Charles Eliot Norton* (Boston: Houghton Mifflin, 1904), 2:162. The book was projected as the first part of a long essay series to be titled "*Our Fathers Have Told Us": Sketches of the History of Christendom for Boys and Girls Who Have Been Held at Its Fonts.* The text was reprinted many times and in 1903 translated into French with long introductory comments by Marcel Proust.

37. Eugène Viollet-le-Duc, *Dictionnaire raisonné de l'architecture française* (Paris: A. Morel, 1869), 3:216–18. With the article on the subject "Christ," the sculpture at Amiens is illustrated in full and in a detail of the head. The author compares the head to Greek statuary, describing the High Gothic image as the supreme accomplishment of the type from the eleventh through sixteenth centuries.

38. Frederic W. Farrar, *The Life of Christ as Represented in Art* (London: Macmillan, 1901), esp. 488–90.

39. La Farge, *Gospel Story,* 279. John Ruskin, *Lectures on Art* (Oxford: Clarendon, 1875), is listed in *Catalogue of a Portion of the Library of John La Farge,* sale catalogue #740, Anderson Auction Company (New York, 1909), nos. 393–95.

40. Weinberg, *Decorative Work,* 339–43. Julie L. Sloan and James L. Yarnell, "Art of an Opaline Mind: The Stained Glass of John La Farge," *American Art Journal* 24, nos. 1–2 (1994): 4–43, concentrates on the artistic impetus of La Farge.

41. La Farge, "Window, Part II," col. 1080.

42. See, e.g., *Peacocks and Peonies,* commissioned in 1882 by Frederick Lothrop Ames for his townhouse in Boston (now in the National Museum of American Art, Smithsonian Institution, Washington, D.C.), in Adams et al., *John La Farge,* 200–206, figs. 146–50.

43. Kurt Weitzmann, *Age of Spirituality,* exhibition catalogue for the Metropolitan Museum of Art (New York, 1979), no. 481, 536–37.

44. Diptych of Muse and Writer, Cathedral Treasury, Monza, Italy; see Weinberg, *Decorative Work,* 372–73, fig. 277. The ivory was well known at the turn of the century and included in the 1901 edition of Walter Lowrie's *Monuments of the Early Church* (New York, 1901), reissued as *Art in the Early Church* (New York: Pantheon, 1947; reprint 1969), 170, pl. 105a. For museum copies of ivories, see R. Aaron Rotter in *Medieval Art in America,* 102–5, nos. 20–25.

45. Weinberg, *Decorative Work,* 394, 397.

8-1.  Henry Adams (1838–1918). (Photo by Marian Hooper "Clover" Adams, 1883; Courtesy of the Massachusetts Historical Society.)

# 8

## *User: Henry Adams and* Esther

CHARLES VANDERSEE

BOSTON IN EARLY 1877 was host to a major religious event: the great revival conducted by the most famous evangelist of the day, Dwight Moody, with music by Ira Sankey. It overshadowed another Boston religious event, the formal consecration on February 9 of Trinity Church, a few blocks north of the revival site. The *Boston Globe* on the day after Trinity's consecration devoted one column to "Boston's New Basilica," whereas the Moody-Sankey revival spread over seven columns. The *Globe* did run a favorable, if also a bit condescending, editorial: "The Episcopal Church is evidently to have a future in Boston, and has now, at least, one house of worship to which all can point with local pride."[1]

At that time a Harvard history professor named Henry Adams, thirty-eight years old, lived up the street—Clarendon Street—from both the Moody Tabernacle and Trinity Church, with his wife Marian Hooper "Clover" Adams (fig. 8-1). Today a plaque on the Clarendon Street side of their house, at 91 Marlborough, commemorates their brief occupancy. Already having gained fame at Harvard as a stimulating teacher, Adams would receive national acclaim for his quirky autobiography, *The Education of Henry Adams,* awarded a posthumous Pulitzer Prize in 1919. In the second chapter, titled "Boston," Adams would recall that as a boy in the 1840s he had been taken to the Unitarian church "twice every Sunday," but "neither to him nor to his brothers or sisters was religion real. Even the mild discipline of the Unitarian church was so irksome that they all threw it off at the first possible moment, and never afterwards entered a church" (751).[2]

This statement may not be literally true. Henry Adams famously cultivated his friendships, and friends he admired had built Trinity Church. Its architect, Henry Hobson Richardson, had been Adams's Harvard college classmate; in the *Education,* Adams said that he made "no acquaintance there [at Harvard] that he valued in after life so much" as Richardson (778). Within a few years Richardson would design a distinctive house for Henry and Marian Adams in Washington.[3] Adams had met John La Farge, artist for Trinity's acclaimed murals and windows, as early as 1871, and had instantly fallen under his sway aesthetically and intellectually: "The question of how much he owed to La Farge could be answered only by admitting that he had no standard to measure it by" (1057).[4] The rector of Trinity Church, Phillips Brooks, was Henry Brooks Adams's second cousin.

"For months and years we have watched the rise and spread of [Trinity's] massive proportions," said Dr. A. H. Vinton, rector of nearby Emmanuel Church, in his consecration sermon, and "have marked each new decoration as it revealed a fresh beauty of light or shadow or color, until we saw the structure complete, and the aesthetic sense was satisfied." Biographers have assumed that Henry and Clover sometimes walked the three short blocks down Clarendon Street to watch work in progress, possibly on occasion inviting La Farge and Richardson to join them in their Marlborough Street house, being proud of its "fashionable" location in Boston's new Back Bay (2:180).

When the Adamses moved to Washington nine months after Trinity's consecration, they kept in touch with La Farge and Richardson; Clover, an accomplished photographer, made portraits of both men. So it was understandable that Trinity Church would make its way into Henry's second novel, *Esther,* published in March 1884 under the feminine pseudonym of Frances Snow Compton.[5] The action of the book centers on a large and fashionable church named St. John's (in New York, not in Boston); it examines the character of the congregation's impressive rector, Stephen Hazard, and the process of decorating the interior walls of the new building. During that process the rector falls in love with the protagonist of the novel, an accomplished young artist named Esther Dudley, and she with him. For her first "professional" (221) assignment she is at work high on the scaffold in the nave of St. John's, painting a figure of St. Cecilia, the patron saint of music.

The opening sentence of the novel draws attention to the building rather than the characters: "The new church of St. John's, on Fifth Avenue, was thronged the morning of the last Sunday of October, in the year 1880." With the second sentence we are in the "gallery, beneath the unfinished frescoes," and in the fourth sentence, "The sun came in through the figure of St. John in his crimson and green garments of glass, and scattered more color where colors already rivaled the flowers of a prize show; while huge prophets and evangelists in flowing robes looked down from the red walls." Those red walls and frescoes are internal clues that St. John's in the novel is based on Trinity Church, Boston. Richardson famously had wanted a red church, and he got it. "The walls throughout the edifice are all finished in red," reported the *Boston Evening Transcript* on the day of Trinity's consecration, "with the exception of the chancel, which is in dark green." As for the frescoes, Trinity Church was among the first and certainly the most prominent of American sanctuaries to have this kind of decoration, as Kathleen Curran ably delineates.[6]

The Manhattan location of St. John's is thus something of a diversionary tactic, along with the unknown "Frances Snow Compton" on the title page, to keep the novel from being read as a roman à clef. The artist Esther Dudley, whose spiritual and artistic struggles are the heart of the book, was capable of being seen all too quickly and all too fully as the thwarted and unfulfilled Clover Adams, should the secret of her husband's authorship be discovered. And very little prompting was required to see in the vigorous mind and personality of Stephen Hazard the rector of Trinity, Phillips Brooks.[7]

For external confirmation that Adams was thinking of Trinity Church in Boston, we need to jump to Christmas Day of 1911, on board the great ocean liner *Olympic,* sister ship of the *Titanic.* On this day, bound from France to the United States, seventy-three-year-old Henry Adams made a startling revelation to his traveling companion, Clover's niece Louisa Hooper. She became on that day apparently only the fifth person besides Clover and Adams's publisher who knew he had written the novel *Esther,* the first and only person in her generation.

"I was electrified at being told," Louisa Hooper later wrote. "I could not look at him because of emotion. I was on his bed in the big stateroom looking at the ceiling, he was on the sofa between the port-holes, . . . books on books piled up near the sofa"—these books being "fourteen fierce novels," as we know from one of Adams's letters (6:486). Adams was not only revealing himself as author; he wanted Louisa Hooper to know also that the heroine, Esther Dudley, was "composite," "two or 3 in one, and he left me with the impression that it was 3 rather than 2." He did not name any names, she recalled, though she would have thought instinctively of her aunt, Clover Hooper, as a later reader may wonder if Henry James's adored cousin Minny Temple also had entered Adams's mind.[8] There was one other fact Adams wanted Louisa Hooper to know: "Definitely he said he took the theme from the building of Trinity Church & placed it in New York." Louisa Hooper Thoron had earlier written to Louis Bancel La Farge, her nephew and a grandson of John La Farge: "H. A. told me in 1912 [*sic*] that he'd taken the building of Trinity Church as the inspiration for his theme (& his plot worked about it). . . . You can see H. A. incorporated great sections of real conversations that went on with the real characters."[9]

For a tragic and unforeseeable reason, *Esther* was to become a book uniquely precious to Henry Adams. Esther Dudley, a witty, passionate, artistic woman with a mind of her own, and a bedrock skeptic in religious matters, was to a considerable degree modeled after Henry Adams's wife—who committed suicide in Washington two and a half years after the book's publication. A few months after Clover's death, Adams made one of his very few utterances concerning *Esther,* writing to his closest male friend, John Hay: "To admit the public to it would be almost unendurable to me. . . . [I]ts value has nothing to do with the public who could never understand that such a book might be written in one's heart's blood" (3:34, August 23, 1886).[10] In 1891, seven years after publication, Adams wrote to his closest woman friend, the wife of Pennsylvania Senator J. Donald Cameron: "I care more for one chapter, or any dozen pages of Esther than for the whole history, including maps and indexes; so much more, indeed, that I would not let anyone read the story for fear the reader should profane it" (3:409, February 13, 1891).[11] By "the whole history" he meant all nine volumes of his magisterial *History of the United States during the Administrations of Thomas Jefferson and James Madison,* just published and destined to be still admired more than a century later.

"*Written* in one's heart's blood"—this is a different thing from revisiting one's novel later (Clover dead barely eight months) and only then feeling the heart bleed. Any reader of this short novel must be struck by how dark a book it is, despite passages of banter and repartee. It is as dark as the human figures painted high on the walls of Trinity Church, almost lost beside the light coming through La Farge's windows. It is as dark as the figure of St. Cecilia being painted by Esther Dudley on the north transept wall of St. John's Church: "Except in certain unusual lights, it could hardly be seen at all" (222).[12]

The darkness is double. It has to do with a frustrated soul and a thwarted calling in life. Esther Dudley, a prominent Manhattan heiress as well as an artist, is intellectually and temperamentally unable to make herself believe in the God of the Bible and the Episcopal Church. Despite the eloquent sermons of her fiancé, Stephen Hazard, and his private efforts to reason her into faith, and despite studying theology, she cannot accept the Christianity of this man she loves. Because of Henry Adams's "heart's blood" outcry, we suspect that something of the same ordeal had beset Clover Adams during the years before her death. It was not that her husband was, like Hazard, a believer and that she therefore wanted to conform. But did she herself, quite independent of her agnostic spouse, engage in one of those spiritual struggles in the age of Darwin? What is it like to watch such a struggle? To gaze upon spiritual desire unrequited is to feel one's heart's blood churning.

"Written in *one's* heart's blood." Adams meant, of course, his own, but we should not assume that he means only his. Adams expressed himself with uncommon and even fastidious care; with that indeterminate "one's," we ought to suppose that Clover Adams herself had a hand in writing the novel, was responsible for some of the wittier passages and possibly some in which Esther Dudley expresses her post-Christian exasperation: "It must be that we are in a new world now, for I can see nothing spiritual about the church. It is all personal and selfish. What difference does it make to me whether I worship one person, or three persons [the Trinity], or three hundred, or three thousand. I can't understand how you [Stephen Hazard] worship any person at all" (332).[13]

Though they become engaged, Esther decides she must not marry Stephen Hazard unless she can carry off with sincerity the role of a Christian pastor's wife. Gossip about her paganism would cripple her husband's effectiveness (280, 288–90). But despite the heroic effort that constitutes the last half of the novel, she cannot find a path toward belief. That effort is so strenuous that her aunt expects she will take to her bed "with a sick headache on account of the Athanasian creed" (281). The Athanasian Creed is of course the early church's heroic effort to demystify the Trinity, the doctrine for which the church in Copley Square is named. Two more times in the novel this prickly concept assaults poor Esther (284, 321).

Like a painter whose bold strokes quicken a figure to fullness of representation, Adams in his novel becomes incautiously expressive and poignant on occasion— incautious in the sense of revealing to casual readers more than he might have wanted to, concerning the barren reality of women in realms other than spirituality. Consider three such bold strokes.

First, early in the novel, Esther Dudley's invalid father makes a prophecy concerning his talented daughter, as he considers her marriage prospects: "Poor Esther! She has been brought up among men, and is not used to harness. If things go wrong she will rebel, and a woman who rebels is lost" (206). This is a painful gender observation. The novel is set in New York City in 1880 (187), but even in such an urbane milieu the situation of the uncommon woman is—as novelists William Dean Howells, Henry James, and Edith Wharton have shown—nearly hopeless. A selection of Clover's letters published in 1936 indicated that she too, like Esther, had been brought up among men and had a mind tending toward irreverence and rebellion.[14] Her father, Dr. Robert William Hooper of Beacon Street, "reared the children after his wife's death," when Clover was only five.[15] That early companionship led Clover every Sunday morning, even as a married adult in Washington, to write him in Boston in a quasi-confessional ritual, confiding pungent views concerning her week in Washington society. It was on a

8-2. "L. S." (otherwise unidentified woman). (Photo by Marian Hooper "Clover" Adams, n.d.; Courtesy of the Massachusetts Historical Society.)

Sunday morning, eight months after this father/confessor died, that Clover Adams killed herself.

Here is the second bold brush stroke. Henry Adams imagines Esther Dudley on the scaffold in St. John's Church in the middle of winter, painting the figure of St. Cecilia: "Esther, like most women, was timid, and wanted to be told when she could be bold with perfect safety. . . . To be steadily strong was not in Esther's nature. She was audacious only by starts, and recoiled from her own audacity" (218). Again a gender distinction: timid "like most women." Those who know Adams's later writing still register a shiver of wonder when in the *Education* he insists that throughout his life "he owed more to the American woman than to all the American men he ever heard of" (1124). But this tribute acknowledges his uncommon good fortune in knowing uncommon women. What is the consequence of timidity? Timidity does not lead to sustained public achievement, to active and visible expression of talent. The thwarting of potential is, in the human condition, one of the darkest of stories, particularly when talent has been enhanced by earnest study and effort, like that of Esther Dudley as painter—or Clover Adams as photographer (fig. 8-2). Wharton, the figure in the novel modeled on John La Farge, admires Esther's dedication: "The way she takes my brutal criticisms of her painting makes my heart bleed" (200).

As for Clover, the one time that her photographs had a chance to attain national attention, through reproduction of one of them in the popular *Century* magazine, her husband exercised the veto. "We have declined [editor Richard Watson] Gilder's pleasing offer," to publish Clover's study of the aged and distinguished historian George Bancroft, their H Street neighbor in Washington (fig. 8-3), wrote Henry Adams to John Hay. The reason? Publication would amount to "flaunting our photographs in the 'Century,'" and thus "unphotographed friends" would launch their curses (2:527, January 6, 1884). This was the "editorial we," as Eugenia Kaledin has noted, citing Clover's letter to her father the same day: "I've just written [Gilder] to decline & telling him Mr. Adams [her husband Henry] does not fancy the prevailing literary vivisection," meaning living writers and scholars commenting critically on each other.[16] Such an objection seems evasive; the stunning photograph in question could hardly have provoked disparagement and might have generated real acclaim. Was Henry therefore saying something else, insinuating that Clover was (like Esther Dudley) not capable of being "steadily strong"—that magazine publicity might weigh her down with acclaim, even reveal her as a serious competitor against male artists? Would she then, expected to produce and publish more, "recoil from her own audacity"?[17]

Here is the last of the three alarming brushstrokes that move us toward, if not actually into, the "heart's blood" that Adams felt to be the medium in which he had worked. Clover too had a need for projects and achievement, having become a considerable artist in the difficult new medium of photography. But what could be her next step, if she was too good for just her local circle but denied access to the wider public? That further touch of Adams's brush we encounter as the figures being painted at St. John's Church are "nearly finished" (244). Work takes place in "the last days of January" (243), precisely the time of year that John La Farge and his assistants on the Trinity scaffolding were trying to finish. Esther Dudley, now that her work on St. Cecilia is completed, "became a little depressed. This church life, like a bit of religious Bohemianism and acted poetry, had amused her so greatly that she found her own small studio dull. She could no longer work there without missing the space, the echoes, the company, and above all, the sense of purpose, which she felt on her scaffolding. She complained to Wharton [the character based on La Farge] of her feminine want of motive in life" (244).

8-3. George Bancroft (1800–1891), historian. (Photo by Marian Hooper "Clover" Adams, 1883; Courtesy of the Massachusetts Historical Society.)

Review these brush strokes: rebellion, timidity, lack of purpose. These are the authentic expression of an intelligent and talented upper-class woman in the late nineteenth century in the United States.[18] These, one might say, are the dark spaces high on the walls of Trinity Church, not illuminated by light through stained glass windows, emblematic of needs not ministered to by the traditional theology of church fathers. *Esther* is both a love story with religion as a hopeless obstacle and a religious story in which the God of love turns out to be inapproachable. It is also the story of a woman with an artistic calling who is not granted a vocation. The mere will to believe (270, 329) can no more induce genuine belief than a figure may be painted high on a wall without a scaffold. And possessing talent but lacking motive and purpose is like being an architect without a client.

Meanwhile, in the last half of the novel, readers have to face the idea darkest of all in its implications for the rich decoration of a church like Boston's Trinity or New York's fictional St. John's. On these walls and in these windows are figures of saints and symbols of teachings. Do they work? Is it true, as Dr. Vinton poetically asserted in his Trinity consecration sermon, that in such a church "all its beauties [are] subdued as if self-subdued by their consciousness of their consecration to a diviner use than the aesthetic"?[19] Esther has a cousin watching her struggle, the geologist George Strong (based on the real-life Clarence King), who suggests to Esther a new strategy. Try what the Roman Catholic church prescribes: "Millions of men and women have gone through the same struggle [toward desired belief], and the church tells them to fix their eyes on a symbol of faith." As he talks, he takes up "the little carved ivory crucifix which stood on the mantelpiece" in Esther's house and holds it up before her: "There! How many people do you think, have come to this Christ of yours that has no meaning to you, and in their struggle with doubt, have pressed it against their hearts till it drew blood? Ask it!" (286–87). She does press this ivory against her heart, with such fervor that Strong catches her hand "in alarm" and pulls it away. But this brief experiment has no more effect than her other efforts.

Without the building of Trinity Church, and the involvement of his friends in the project, Henry Adams quite clearly could not have written the disturbing novel *Esther* as it exists. He might, however, have written some similar novel on the issue it raises, an issue of permanent importance to Christianity among world religions: what—to use an artist's metaphor—is the basic palette of approaches to God? In this novel the opulence of Trinity Church and the charisma of its rector enable Adams to paint pathways to God using five colors: reason, worship, submission of the will, art, and imagination. Red is Trinity's defining color, and reason is Rector Hazard's most vigorous strategem.[20]

But there exists a sixth primary color, which Adams curiously leaves undeployed, though blatantly signaled, and it is with this color that Dwight Moody and Ira Sankey triumphed at the Tabernacle, their unadorned new hall on the northeast corner of Clarendon and Tremont. Sankey was a soloist whose rich voice at each service put people in the mood for salvation. The revival further flourished because of a massed choir, drawn from churches all over Boston. The *Globe* reveled in printing a full list of individual participants in this choir, giving their names and their home parishes—overwhelmingly Congregational, Methodist, Presbyterian, and Baptist, with only a few token Episcopalians.[21] So the sixth color on the palette of approaches to God is, of course, music, expressed in the novel *Esther* by the nearly silent organ in Stephen Hazard's church and more conspicuously by the figure Esther Dudley is assigned to paint high on its north transept wall. When Wharton, who is Esther's art teacher as well as the decorator of St. John's Church, invites her to "come and help me finish St. John's," he specifies only that he wants "a large female figure on the transept wall." The rector claims the right to choose that figure and announces, "It must be St. Cecilia, of course" (221), the patron saint of music.[22]

With that unexplained "of course," we may wonder whether this is yet another bit of Boston in the novel. It happens that the winter of Trinity Church's completion, 1876–77, was also the first independent season of the still-flourishing

Boston chorus called the Cecilia Society, dating from 1874, when it was the choral auxiliary of the Harvard Musical Association. Another historical fact: in Boston's Roman Catholic Holy Cross Cathedral, on Washington Street in the South End, dedicated fourteen months before Trinity (December 8, 1875), there is a window in the south nave showing St. Cecilia playing the organ. The window dates to "around 1880," according to the Holy Cross website.

But Henry Adams in Washington was likely not paying attention to Boston's Irish Catholic architecture, or to fledgling choirs in his native city. A careful reader of *Esther* notices hardly any music except for incidental mention of the organ (191, 193, 271) and of one Sunday service in which "the music" produces "sympathetic" feelings in Esther (271): no choirs, no hymns, no instruments. No wonder, lacking such inspiration, Esther Dudley views her completed St. Cecilia with embarrassment, as a blandly secular representation: "My St. Cecilia looks like a nursery governess playing a waltz for white-cravated saints to dance by" (247).

Clover Hooper herself had at least a trace of susceptibility to music. Like Emily Dickinson in rural Amherst—who stayed away from village worship on Sunday but had a bobolink as chorister[23]—Clover heard sacred music emanating from tree branches. In one of her Sunday letters to her father she mentions putting aside her pen to listen to the birds "sing Sunday hymns in their new furnished choirs."[24] Her vaguely Shakespearean allusion brings forth an important point, which is not that music might help one *reason* one's way into belief—not that the human making of hymns, masses, oratorios, and spirituals must somehow be proof of God's existence and goodness. Instead, for a person like Esther Dudley, truly wanting to believe, music might simply elasticize the rigidly modernized mind.

In the novel *Esther*, Stephen Hazard's disheveled library, in need of a wife's attention (295), does hold "a shelf of music" (196), and "in case of necessity [he] could sing fairly well" (235), but like those of Phillips Brooks, his main interests are elsewhere. Brooks does, though, remind us of that sixth color missing from Adams's palette and of its transformative power. When Brooks spent a year in Europe at age thirty, mass at the Frankfurt Cathedral supplied "the most superb congregational singing I ever heard. . . . Those full German voices, every one singing the sonorous German words, produced a wonderful effect"—which, for Esther, will power and theology and visual art could not do: "I almost trembled when I saw and felt the power of pure emotion in religious things, and thought I could understand how so many have yielded to the impulse to bow as that splendid procession of the host went by with its thrilling incense and thrilling music, and then by and by bowed to the system of the church that it belongs to."[25]

# NOTES

1. The *Boston Evening Transcript* (February 9, 1877, 4), a newspaper more in harmony with the spirit of Boston's elite, editorialized in a less chary vein: "The consecration of Trinity Church, to-day, is elaborately described elsewhere [in the paper], as are the impressive ceremonies, and the ed-ifice itself, with its massive, commanding exterior, as well as beautifully and artistically decorated interior. The erection of such a church is not only an era for Episcopalianism in Boston, but an era for Boston, which can now boast of a structure for worship built in accordance with a design the marked originality of which strikes every competent observer."

2. Throughout, Henry Adams is cited in the text by page number from Henry Adams, *Novels,* ed. Ernest Samuels and Jayne S. Samuels (New York: Library of America, 1983), and by volume and page from *The Letters of Henry Adams,* ed. J. C. Levenson, Ernest Samuels, Charles Vandersee, and Viola Hopkins Winner, 6 vols. (Cambridge: Harvard University Press, 1982–88).

3. Richardson was further connected to the Adamses by living and working, from 1874 to 1886 (the year of his premature death), in a house in Brookline, Massachusetts, rented from Clover Hooper's brother Edward. See James F. O'Gorman, *Living Architecture: A Biography of H. H. Richardson* (New York: Simon & Schuster, 1997), 113–19. For a fuller account, with floor plans and photographs of this Cottage Street house-studio (and site for musical events), see O'Gorman, "The Making of a 'Richardson Building,'" in *H. H. Richardson and His Office: Selected Drawings* (Cambridge, Mass.: Department of Printing and Graphic Arts, Harvard College Library, 1974), 2–10.

4. Edward Chalfant, *Better in Darkness: A Biography of Henry Adams—His Second Life, 1862–1891* (Hamden, Conn.: Archon, 1994), 737.

5. Robert E. Spiller, introduction and bibliographical note to *Esther: A Novel* by Henry Adams (New York: Scholars' Facsimiles & Reprints, 1938), iii.

6. Kathleen Curran, "The Romanesque Revival, Mural Painting, and Protestant Patronage in America," *Art Bulletin* 81 (1999): 693–722.

7. Anne J. Fannin, in her pioneering and briskly informative study "*Esther* as Art History" (un-published seminar paper, University of Pennsylvania, 1970), considers parallels and discrepancies between the novel and the real-life drama of decorating Trinity Church (Trinity has, for example, no St. Cecilia figure). The chief similarities between Hazard and Brooks: same age, thirty-five, in taking up their respective posts; a preaching style that begins quietly and increases in fervor; fond-ness for European travel and visits to galleries and museums; serious acquaintance with literary clas-sics; cultivated family background; tall of stature, with black hair and penetrating eyes (19–27). The two chief differences: theology and girth. Theologically, as Fannin observes, "Hazard, the young rector of St. John's, holds the strictest orthodox beliefs" (2), whereas the latitudinarian Brooks con-spicuously permitted three Unitarian clergymen to take communion at the Trinity consecration ser-vice, one being the celebrated Boston orator Edward Everett Hale (*Boston Evening Transcript,* Feb-ruary 10, 1877, 4). As to girth, Brooks, like architect Richardson, weighed over three hundred pounds; the *Evening Transcript* (February 12, 1877, 4) observed that the new church was "one worthily devoted to the ministrations of one of the most symmetrically qualified clergymen the pul-pit of New England contains." Adams described Hazard, by contrast, as tall and "slender," with a "thin, long face" (189).

8. Mary ("Minny") Temple (1845–1870) is securely famous in American literary history as inspi-ration for certain of Henry James's major characters, notably Isabel Archer of *The Portrait of a Lady* and the doomed Milly Theale of *The Wings of the Dove.* Minny Temple's anxiety over Christian be-lief would much later (1914) be exposed at some length, through her own letters in James's autobi-ographical *Notes of a Son and Brother* (New York: Charles Scribner's Sons, 1914); reprinted as *Auto-biography,* ed. Frederick W. Dupee (Princeton: Princeton University Press, 1983), (522–44). For her

remarkable pilgrimage to Philadelphia, hoping that the preaching of Trinity's future rector, Phillips Brooks, would resolve her religious doubts, see note 18.

9. Chalfant, *Better in Darkness,* 846; and H. Barbara Weinberg, *The Decorative Work of John La Farge* (New York: Garland, 1977), 128, quoting an unpublished letter in the John La Farge Papers, Yale University.

10. Besides his publisher, Henry Holt, and Clover Adams, the only people within the first few years of its publication who knew that Henry Adams had written *Esther* were the geologist Clarence King (*Letters,* 3:34), on whom the character of George Strong is based, then John and Clara Hay (3:34) and Elizabeth Cameron (3:409). At some point, Professor Ephraim W. Gurney, husband of Clover's sister Ellen, acquired a copy, which eventually came to Harvard's Widener Library. Robert Spiller used it to produce the first reprint of the novel, in 1938 (xxv).

11. Elizabeth Cameron (1857–1944), twenty-four years younger than her husband and nineteen years younger than Henry Adams, became famously the love of Adams's life, perhaps beginning before Clover died, though throughout their long friendship they both carefully observed the proprieties of the day. When in summer 1887 Adams lent Mrs. Cameron the Beverly Farms house that he and Clover had built, while he worked on his *History* nearby in Boston, he suggested that Mrs. Cameron "come up to town" for a day "and we will do Boston." Prominent in his proposed itinerary was Richardson's masterwork, then ten years old: "You shall tell me whether New York or Philadelphia is the best place to buy table-clothes. I will show you the State House and Trinity Church, and we will lunch at Young's" (3:72).

12. Repeatedly in *Esther,* Adams makes the point that the figure of St. Cecilia is nearly invisible; Esther Dudley has chosen "the least conspicuous place" on the north transept wall for her work (222), which, "if it could be seen, which fortunately was not the case," would have seemed out of keeping with the surrounding work (233).

13. Cf. Minny Temple to John Chipman Gray, February 1870: "The doctrine of the vicarious suffering of Christ has been to me not only incomprehensible but also unconsoling" (James, *Autobiography,* 539).

14. Marian Hooper Adams, *The Letters of Mrs. Henry Adams, 1865–1883,* ed. Ward Thoron (Boston: Little, Brown, 1936).

15. Eugenia Kaledin, *The Education of Mrs. Henry Adams* (Philadelphia: Temple University Press, 1981), 32, 20.

16. Ibid., 191–92.

17. Seeing Clover declare explicitly that "Mr. Adams" is the one who disapproves, rather than concealing her apparent disagreement, biographer Otto Friedrich concludes that Clover "was not interested, in other words, in becoming a professional, or in turning her activities into a commercial career"; see his *Clover* (New York: Simon & Schuster, 1979), 292. But buying and selling are not the issue. Nor did Esther Dudley in the novel seek an income from her painting; the point in her case and Clover's is that serious and accomplished work in art deserves some public recognition. A penetrating discussion of the marital dynamics suggested by the two letters of January 6 appears in Laura Saltz, "Clover Adams's Dark Room: Photography and Writing, Exposure and Erasure," *Prospects: An Annual of American Cultural Studies* 24 (1999): 458–62.

18. Another upper-class New York woman, Edith Wharton, recalled that when publishing her first book of fiction, a collection of stories, the "whole business [of appearing before the public in book form] seemed too unreal to be anything but a practical joke." The year was 1899. She had already been "astonished enough [just] to see the stories in print" as magazine pieces, according to her memoir, *A Backward Glance* (New York: Charles Scribner's Sons, 1934), 112–13.

19. *Boston Globe,* February 10, 1877, 5.

20. It was Phillips Brooks's famous capacity for buttressing faith through reason that drew Minny Temple from her home in Pelham, New York (north of New York City), to Philadelphia in April

1869. This was the last year of her life; she would die of tuberculosis on March 8, 1870. "The chief object I had in coming was to listen to Phillips Brooks," she wrote John Chipman Gray (1839–1915). "I believe I did have a secret hope that he was going to expound to me the old beliefs with a clearness that would convince me for ever and banish doubt. I had placed all my hopes in him as the one man I had heard of who, progressive in all other ways, had yet been able to keep his faith firm in the things that most earnest men have left far behind them. Yet in preaching to his congregation he doesn't, or didn't, touch the real difficulties at all." In a later letter, matters remained unsatisfactory: "As for Phillips Brooks, what you say of him is, no doubt, all true—he didn't touch the main point when I heard him, at all events, and that satisfaction you so kindly wish me is, I am afraid, not to be got from any man." Later still, recalling the failure of her pilgrimage, she summarized Brooks's preaching as "all feeling and no reason; . . . he was good for those within the pale, but not good to convince outsiders that they should come in" (James, *Autobiography,* 517, 523, 537).

In an 1870 letter often quoted, Henry James fused Minny Temple and Clover Hooper in one sentence, both women embodying for him the admirable traits of "intellectual grace" and "moral spontaneity"; see, e.g., Leon Edel, *Henry James: The Untried Years, 1843–1870* (Philadelphia: J. B. Lippincott, 1953), 322. Clover, a few years before Trinity built its new church and a year before her marriage, had sat next to Phillips Brooks at a dinner party and enjoyed his jollity. Like Minny Temple, she responded less favorably to his sermons, rebelling against the prevailing adulation for Brooks as pulpiteer: "I've heard him preach twice," she wrote to her friend, Eleanor Whiteside [later Shattuck] on March 5, 1871, "but each time neither heart nor brain got any food" (quoted in Kaledin, *Education,* 98).

If Henry Adams had heard of Minny Temple's spiritual and intellectual struggles, one source other than his friends Henry and William James would have been John Chipman Gray himself, who years later provided Henry James with Minnie's agonizing letters. Adams had known Gray, a year younger, as early as 1868 when both were members of "The Club" in Boston; see Chalfant, *Better in Darkness,* 752, and Louis Menand, *The Metaphysical Club: A Story of Ideas in America* (New York: Farrar, Straus & Giroux, 2001), 216. Gray was then practicing law with the Boston firm Ropes & Gray; he joined the Harvard law faculty in 1875, while Adams was on the history faculty. In 1886, Adams designated Gray one of the three trustees of Clover Adams's estate (3:4 n.). On at least one occasion, in the early 1880s, Gray and his wife met Henry and Clover Adams in Washington (Marian Adams, *Letters,* 437). Clover had known Gray since at least 1870, mentioning his company at a "pleasant little dinner"; see Lyndall Gordon, *A Private Life of Henry James: Two Women and His Art* (New York: W. W. Norton, 1999), 84 (the two women being Minny Temple and the novelist Constance Fenimore Woolson).

21. *Boston Globe,* January 26, 1877, 8.

22. Here too is a correspondence between Brooks and Hazard: Brooks made suggestions to La Farge for the subjects of "several paintings" on the wall of Trinity's nave and also the tower, which La Farge followed (Weinberg, *Decorative Work,* 120).

23. Emily Dickinson, *The Complete Poems of Emily Dickinson,* ed. Thomas H. Johnson (Boston: Little, Brown, 1960), #755.

24. Marian Adams, *Letters,* 215.

25. Alexander V. G. Allen, *Life and Letters of Phillips Brooks,* 2 vols. (New York: E. P. Dutton, 1900), 2:38.

9-1. John White Alexander, *Portrait of Sarah Wyman Whitman* (1842–1904). Oil on canvas. (Neupert Collection; Photo courtesy of Childs Gallery, Boston.)

# 9

## *Women Artists at Trinity: Sarah Wyman Whitman and Margaret Redmond*

ERICA E. HIRSHLER

BOSTON'S TRINITY CHURCH has often been described as an imposing monument that grew out of the substantial brotherhood that created it. Embedded in the clay of Boston's Back Bay, solid and material, the church with its transcendent glimpses of pure beauty is characterized as a physical manifestation of the close-knit fraternity that brought it to life: Phillips Brooks, H. H. Richardson, O. W. Norcross, Robert Treat Paine, and John La Farge. But the church was not created by men alone. A number of women also made artistic offerings there, contributing their talent and expertise to enrich one of the city's most important aesthetic and spiritual sites. Among them were two specialists in stained glass, Sarah Wyman Whitman and Margaret Redmond. Neither is as well known as their male colleagues, but both helped to compose the visual symphony of Trinity Church.

Whitman (1842–1904), an active Trinity parishioner and friend of both Brooks and La Farge, was devoted to the concept of artistic unity that was made manifest at the church. The philosopher George Santayana fondly recalled her in the second volume of his memoirs. He wrote of Boston women in general that he "liked the elegance, the banter, the wit and intelligence that often appeared in them. I liked to sit next to them at dinner, when conversation flowed more easily and became more civilized in the midst of lights and flowers, good foods and good wines. The charm of the ladies was part of that luxurious scene." Santayana described two acquaintances in detail, both women without children, both married to men he called "invisible husbands." He characterized each man as "in his own world, an important person, esteemed as much or more than his wife in hers: but like royal spouses occupying opposite wings in a palace, they had their own exits and entrances, their own hours and their own friends."[1] One of these two women was Isabella Stewart Gardner, famous today for her talents as a collector, celebrity, and museum founder. The other was Sarah Whitman, now known only to a few historians interested in women artists or in the Arts and Crafts movement, and perhaps to the devotees of Trinity Church.

Whitman remains one of the most intriguing characters in late nineteenth-century Boston's art circles. Santayana described her, in comparison with Mrs. Gardner, as "more in the spirit of Boston, more conscientious and troubled." A Springfield reporter wrote of her as a "very distinguished looking woman, always elegantly gowned" (fig. 9-1) and added that with her wealth and social position "she might have chosen to live a far easier life" but, instead, gave herself to "real, valuable work."[2] Sarah Wyman Whitman found her calling through art, and she was devoted to the betterment of society through the spiritual benefit she found inherent in beauty and good work. Trinity Church represented all her ideals.

Born in Lowell, Massachusetts, Sarah Wyman spent her early years in Baltimore, returning with her family to Lowell in 1853. When she was twenty-four, she married Henry Whitman, a wool and dry goods merchant three years her senior. He provided his talented and affluent wife with a home on Beacon Hill and apparent support for her artistic activities (from which he excused himself entirely, as he apparently did from much of her life). Two years later, in 1868, she enrolled in the innovative classes offered to Boston women by William Morris Hunt, the city's leading painter. Whitman supplemented her art education with lessons from both William Rimmer (in Boston) and Thomas Couture (at Villiers-le-Bel, near Paris). She traveled to Europe several times, studying architecture and the old masters in Spain, France, Italy, and England, once in the company of fellow artist and Hunt student Elizabeth Bartol. With these credentials, typical for a woman of her class and talent, Whitman crafted a career that influenced almost every aspect of creative life in Boston.[3]

Whitman not only made art; she also collected it, wrote about it, and inspired it. The writer John Jay Chapman archly recalled that "the earliest reputation that Mrs. Whitman achieved was that of being an unknown lady from some savage town,—Baltimore, perhaps,—who had appeared in Boston. It was not many years, however, before she had become a center of social influence, and of that peculiar kind of social influence in which there are strands of art, idealism,—and intellect."[4] Like Santayana and the many other chroniclers of Boston who mention Whitman, including philosopher William James and historian Samuel Eliot Morison, Chapman admired Whitman's social skills and her ability to surround herself with "geniuses," a group in which he included himself. He barely mentioned Whitman's own artistic and philanthropic contributions, failing to recognize her as one of Boston's prodigies. "She was an intense woman," recalled her friend Henry Lee Higginson, a leading businessman, philanthropist, and collector. "She disliked ugly or unfit objects of daily use. . . . [S]he was fond of jewels and fine-bookbinding and, in general, of beautifying everyday life."[5]

Early in her career, Whitman devoted herself to painting. She used both oil and pastel, favoring floral studies (one of her enduring interests) and simple, rural landscapes of the type recommended by Hunt. Whitman began to show her work in the 1870s and held her first solo exhibition at the Doll & Richards Gallery in Boston in 1882. Whitman's landscapes are clearly indebted to Hunt in their diffuse tonal manner and often anonymous subject matter, but her interest in color is more pronounced than Hunt's and jewel-like in its delicacy. "Mrs. Whitman['s] . . . decorative color effects move all observers to comment," wrote "T" in the *Art Amateur* in 1885, "whether they approve the broadness of her methods or not."[6] In her images of Niagara Falls—an iconic subject which Hunt had explored in 1878 and which Whitman described as her "High Altar"—her rough scumbled pastel creates an opalescent richness that perfectly represents the watery rainbow effects of the thick mist surrounding the falls (fig. 9-2).[7] Her still lifes also display this radiance of color. In *Roses: Souvenir de Villiers-le-Bel* (fig. 9-3), Whitman's sensitive touch and ephemeral subject add poignancy to a composition that, with its multiple layers of work, came to serve as a personal tribute to the French realist painter Thomas Couture, who died in 1879.

Whitman painted landscapes in Rhode Island, Massachusetts, southern Maine, and New Hampshire. She often explored the mysterious effects created by fog, twilight, mist, or moonlight, using broad sweeps of color that favor atmospheric effects over specific detail. Whitman arranged her compositions with an eye to their decorative effects, often selecting a square format for paintings that emphasized two-dimensional design and arrangement. She also painted a number of portraits, including likenesses of Brooks and Higginson, in which she isolated her sitters against plain, dark backgrounds after the French manner of her teachers.

The Parisian writer S. C. de Soissons, who visited Boston in the 1890s, declared that Whitman's paintings "have all the marks of masculine art, and none of the feminine feeling we would desire to see." Such gender-based commentary is common in late nineteenth-century criticism, and a woman artist was most often faulted either way: if her work was described as masculine, displaying a direct and confident painting style, the painter had denied her "true" nature; if described as feminine, it was often dismissed as pretty, sensitive, and ultimately unimportant.[8] In Whitman's case, de Soisson's comments seem unusually harsh, for her subjects were well within the boundaries of acceptable topics for women. Her work consisted almost entirely of portraits, pastoral landscapes, and still lifes, not history

9-2. Sarah Wyman Whitman, *Niagara Falls,* 1891. Pastel on paper. (Courtesy of the Fogg Art Museum, Harvard University Art Museums, Gift of Mary C. Wheelwright; Photo by Katya Kallsen; © President and Fellows of Harvard College.)

paintings or action scenes. Instead of delicate glazes, however, Whitman achieved her iridescent color effects through the coarse application of paint or pastel built up in successive layers.

Whitman's paintings won many early admirers, among them Isabella Stewart Gardner; the moonlit landscape she purchased in 1878 was one of four works by Whitman that she would own. In 1880 the critic William C. Brownell credited Whitman with having "risen out of [Hunt's] crowd of aimless aspirants"; he had first noticed her work at the inaugural exhibition of the Society of American

9-3. Sarah Wyman Whitman, *Roses—Souvenir de Villiers-le-Bel,* 1877–79. Oil on panel. (Museum of Fine Arts, Boston, Bequest of the artist.)

Artists in New York.[9] Whitman was elected a member of that organization in 1880, and her desire to be affiliated with such a group clearly indicates her interest in modern art. The society had been established just two years earlier by young, European-trained painters who had found the juries of the important annual exhibitions at the National Academy of Design too conservative and too nationalist to promote their more cosmopolitan work. Whitman's tonal landscapes and broadly painted portraits would have been considered distinctly French in style, and although she also showed her pictures at the National Academy, she was more actively engaged with the Society of American Artists. In 1880 the *Art Journal* noted that "among the works by women" at the society's annual exhibition, "the two best, perhaps, are by Miss Bartol and Miss Whitman of

Boston." Their work was praised as "agreeable and sparkling . . . with charm and refinement," whereas the contributions by other women were dismissed as incomplete studies.[10]

Although several of the artists' groups that assembled in the late 1870s and early 1880s were hospitable to women, the Society of American Artists was not quite as open to them as it seemed. Despite the fact that women were encouraged to exhibit with the society and that one of the group's founders was Helena DeKay Gilder, a painter and tireless worker on behalf of other artists, only eight women were among its seventy-three initial exhibitors. Less than 5 percent of the membership was female, and when Whitman was listed in the roster of forty-five members published in 1881, the only other women painters included were Gilder and Mary Cassatt. Gilder may have blamed one of the most powerful members of the society, John La Farge, for this predicament. She noted in her diary La Farge's dismissal of her own work as "pretty" and his refusal to support the membership of her friend (and former Hunt student) Maria Oakey.[11] La Farge and Whitman, however, seem to have enjoyed an amicable relationship. No correspondence survives between them, but late nineteenth-century Boston's art and literary community was a small, insular dominion where each person knew everyone else, if indeed they were not related by blood or marriage. Whitman and La Farge could not have avoided each other even had they tried.

In the mid-1870s, one of the most important artistic undertakings in Boston was the construction of the new home for Trinity Church, the principal Episcopal congregation. It had already planned to move to the Back Bay when its crenellated Gothic building on Summer Street was destroyed in the great fire of 1872. H. H. Richardson, the architect, worked closely with the rector, Phillips Brooks, to create a sumptuous basilica decorated on the interior by a group headed by their friend John La Farge.

Following a course similar to that later taken by Whitman, La Farge had studied in France with Couture in the mid-1850s. In New York in 1858 he established his studio in the newly opened Tenth Street Studio Building, designed by architect Richard Morris Hunt (the painter's brother), who also had accommodations there. In 1858, La Farge moved to Newport, Rhode Island, to study painting with William Morris Hunt. Six years later he was living temporarily in Roxbury, studying with Rimmer and crafting decorations for the Freedland House on Beacon Street. Before Whitman's election to the Society of American Artists in 1880, La Farge had exhibited extensively in Boston and had sold many paintings and watercolors to local collectors, including Whitman. He had also lectured on art at Harvard, designed stained glass windows for Memorial Hall, and become a founder of the Museum of Fine Arts, where he lectured informally (as did Whitman) on art and decoration. La Farge's Boston connections and influence soon became comprehensive, and he would have intersected frequently with Whitman, who had studied with the same teachers, also had Rhode Island connections, and was involved in artistic activities in both Cambridge and Boston.

Whitman may have become acquainted with La Farge in Newport, where she painted before 1882, or in Boston, where she is said to have been part of the army of assistants who worked on the decorations at Trinity. Her portraits came to include a number of mutual friends, including William James, Martin Brimmer (founder and president of the Museum of Fine Arts), Henry Lee Higginson (one of La Farge's important patrons), and Phillips Brooks. Whitman's portrait of Brooks (now in the collection of Trinity Church) was complete by May 1881, when Brooks wrote to her that he "had no right to be painted as nobly as this."[12] That same year, Whitman and Brimmer corresponded about La Farge's stained glass window *Peonies in the Wind* (1879, Metropolitan Museum of Art), which was then on display at the Museum of Fine Arts.

Whitman admired La Farge's work and eventually owned four of his paintings; many others were held by her Boston friends and acquaintances. Whitman's *Roses: Souvenir de Villiers-le-Bel* (see fig. 9-3), with its gemlike blossoms isolated against a rough wall incised with text, recalls La Farge's floral still lifes such as *Agathon to Erosanthe* (private collection), then owned in Boston. The two artists also shared a delight in rich, suffused color, manifested not only in paintings but also in stained glass and architectural decoration, forms of artistic expression for which Whitman would become well known.

Whitman's first known assignment for decorative work was to ornament the interior of the Central Congregational Church in Worcester, Massachusetts. The pastor, Daniel Merriman, was the husband of Whitman's friend and fellow painter Helen Bigelow Merriman, who played a major role in the assignment of the commission. Merriman and Whitman had been friends since studying together in Hunt's class, and both were part of the close circle of talented women that surrounded the writers Annie Fields and Sarah Orne Jewett. Merriman later painted a portrait of Whitman for Radcliffe College (fig. 9-4), presenting her as a confident and competent painter, palette and brushes in hand, a lively sprig of greenery tucked into her plain tweed dress. In Merriman's vision, Whitman confronts the viewer directly, standing in a jaunty hand-on-hip pose that was most often reserved for images of men.

According to an unidentified newspaper clipping, La Farge had been invited to decorate the Worcester church but was "too busy to give the matter proper attention." Helen Merriman then suggested Whitman, "who went into the work with great fervor," designing not only the stained glass windows but also the wall

9-4. Helen Bigelow Merriman, *Portrait of Sarah Wyman Whitman,* ca. 1906. Oil on canvas. (Schlesinger Library, Radcliffe Institute, Harvard University.)

decorations and the gold leaf ceiling.[13] Thus began a second career for Whitman, who soon became more acclaimed for her glass than she ever had been for her easel paintings. She provided windows, and sometimes comprehensive design plans, for several churches in Massachusetts and Maine—including the parish house at Trinity Church—as well as for a number of private schools, among them Berwick Academy, Bowdoin College, Groton School, and Memorial Hall at Harvard. Whitman also created smaller compositions in glass: decorative panels meant to be hung in domestic interiors (fig. 9-5), small windows, and threefold firescreens.

To complete her designs, some of them monumental in scale, Whitman established a studio, called the Lily Glass Works, at 184 Boylston Street, near Park Square, an area of Boston that supported several women entrepreneurs. She employed a foreman, Alexander Walker, and a number of workmen. "Her studio was maintained in grand style," noted one writer. "They say it was an inspiring sight to see the cutters and glaziers going to work in their Prince Alberts and high hats."[14] The workshop was "high up," recalled another, "[with] an immense laurel wreath hang[ing] on the outer door, encircling the number of the studio." A newspaper described Whitman's working methods in detail in 1897:

9-5. Sarah Wyman Whitman, *Floral Medallion,* 1890s. Stained glass. (Museum of Fine Arts, Boston, Gift of Mary C. Wheelwright.)

Mrs. Whitman is the admiration and wonder of her friends, who stand aghast at the number of things she manages to do in a single day. . . . [She] is at her studio every day, coming early in the morning and sometimes working there into the night. In her glass room, she has several skilled workmen, but she personally oversees every bit of their work. The designs are all original with her, and are really as artistic and beautiful as it is possible to imagine. The design is first drawn onto heavy paper. Then every bit of the colored mosaic work is drawn in separately and pricked off with a pin. Then patterns are cut of every portion, even to the tiniest leaf, twig, or feature. . . . [T]he colored glass in every conceivable shade of coloring comes from the manufacturer. . . . [I]t is really a system of glass painting.[15]

Although several contemporary accounts describe Whitman as an acolyte of the English Pre-Raphaelites, she was adamant about the superiority of American glassmaking to that of the English. Writing in *The Nation* in 1892, she explained that American glassmakers (herself included) preferred to create their motifs by exploiting modulations in the colors and thickness of the stained glass itself rather than by applying paint to the surface of the glass or by depending upon the dark outlines of the leading, as did many English designers.[16] Her doctrine of truth to the nature of her materials was drawn from the principles of the Arts and Crafts movement, and Whitman would become a founding member of the oldest Society of Arts and Crafts in the United States, chartered in Boston in 1897.

Much of Whitman's work is representational, reminiscent of the work of La Farge and his competitor Louis Comfort Tiffany. Using many layers of material fused together to create rich, translucent color effects, Whitman created paintings in glass, often incorporating allegorical or religious subjects. For Memorial Hall at Harvard, for example, she designed a large window to commemorate the Harvard men killed in the Civil War (fig. 9-6). Commissioned by her friend Martin Brimmer in 1895, Whitman's window includes historical figures—among them the Chevalier Bayard and Sir Philip Sidney—of soldiers and poets to represent the dual roles of the dead. When Brimmer died the next year, Whitman memorialized him as well, using his features in her image of St. Martin. Above her five figurative lancets, a rose window surrounded by decorative angels was intended to communicate God's glory in color, said Whitman.[17] To achieve a particularly striking effect, she repeated juxtapositions of complementary tones throughout, setting in proximity blues and oranges, violet reds and greens, and so forth. La Farge also made use of color theory, but the scientific examination of color was common to many artists during the 1890s, including the Boston-based painter, color theorist, collector, and Whitman associate Denman Ross. Yet among her varied sources, La Farge's work was undeniably important to Whitman's style in pictorial glass.[18]

Whitman also became well known for another approach to stained glass, more

9-6. Sarah Wyman Whitman, South Transept ("Brimmer") Window, Memorial Hall, Harvard University, 1896–98. Stained glass. (*Harvard Library Bulletin* 11, no. 2, 2000; Courtesy of Harvard University Archives.)

9-7. Sarah Wyman Whitman, detail of the Phillips Brooks Memorial Window, 1895–96, in the Ferris Library, Trinity Church, Parish House. Stained and clear glass. (Photo courtesy of Museum of Fine Arts, Boston.)

IN MEMORY OF
PHILLIPS BROOKS

modern and innovative, in which clear panels work as windows; thus the format of the piece acknowledges its function. Charles Connick, later a leading glass manufacturer in Boston, recalled that Whitman was among the first artists to move toward designs "more clearly related to architecture."[19] One of the finest examples of Whitman's work in this manner is her window for the room in Trinity Church parish house dedicated to Phillips Brooks (fig. 9-7). The window, a gift of Whitman and her Sunday adult Bible class in honor of the church's late rector, was begun in 1895 and installed in March 1896, at Easter. Set low in the wall, it overlooks the small cloister garden that nestles between the church and parish house. It was not simply a decoration in a room that was, as Whitman explained, "used for many practical purposes" but was meant to be looked through, and Whitman adjusted her design accordingly. Her tripartite scheme is composed of clear glass set in square panes, enlivened by the subtle undulations of the lead cames. Each corner is decorated with small irregular chunks of colored glass nuggets that Whitman described as "jeweled flowers."[20] In the central panel a dark amethyst-colored cross is surmounted by an opalescent shield bearing a laurel wreath inscribed to Brooks. The decorative elements, simple and elegant, do not interfere with the practical function of the window. Here, Whitman's work points toward a much more modern aesthetic for stained glass, one that would be adopted early in the twentieth century by such artists as Frank Lloyd Wright.

During the 1890s, in addition to her work in glass, Sarah Whitman also became one of the most celebrated book cover designers in the United States. Boston, with its many publishing houses, played a leading role in the art of the book in the late nineteenth century. Whitman began creating covers in about 1884, and by 1887 she was a principal designer for Houghton Mifflin, who valued her work enough to feature it in their advertisements.[21] Whitman helped to establish the medium, long the domain of die-cutters and binders, as a suitable specialty for artists, thus ushering in a new era in American design. She worked almost exclusively for Houghton Mifflin, which (along with Copeland & Day) offered some of the most avant-garde book designs in the United States. Whitman produced about three hundred decorations, including almost all the covers for the novels of her close friend Sarah Orne Jewett.

Elegant simplicity and grace characterize Whitman's cover designs. She most often crafted stylized flowers or sinuous linear patterns on a monochromatic cloth or leather background. Her best-known book cover, for *An Island Garden* by her friend Celia Thaxter, employs ornamental poppies whose attenuated stems end in hearts, Whitman's signature (fig. 9-8). *An Island Garden* was available in either white or leaf green cloth, both stamped with gold. While publishers often enjoyed the financial rewards of producing limited, deluxe editions, Whitman was com-

9-8. Sarah Wyman Whitman, cover design for Celia Thaxter, *An Island Garden*, 1894.
(Courtesy of William Morris Hunt Library, Museum of Fine Arts, Boston.)

mitted to creating appropriate designs for mass-market books. In an address to the Boston Art Students' Association, Whitman advised her audience "to think how to apply elements of design to these cheaply sold books; to put the touch of art on this thing that is going to be produced at a level price."[22]

That refrain applied as well to Whitman's involvement with the Arts and Crafts movement. As early as 1849 the English critic John Ruskin had declared in his *Seven Lamps of Architecture* that ornament should be derived from nature and be consistent with the character of the materials from which it was made. By the 1870s, in the hands of William Morris and others, these ideas were being transferred from architecture to the decorative arts. There was a widespread movement to improve the quality of industrial design, to bring good art into everyday life, and many of the art classes that were offered in America after the Civil War were intended to train workers for practical careers in industry. The first president of the Society of Arts and Crafts, Boston, was Charles Eliot Norton, the distinguished professor of fine arts at Harvard, who was a friend and devotee of Ruskin. "The Society of Arts and Crafts," Norton wrote, "endeavors to stimulate in workmen an appreciation of the dignity and value of good design. . . . It will insist upon the necessity of sobriety and restraint, of ordered arrangement, of due regard for the relation between the form of an object and its use and of harmony and fitness in the decoration put upon it." Fifteen years earlier, in an article calling for art education in America, Sarah Whitman had declared the need for "the student who sees that in all beauty, fitness is a prime condition."[23] Whitman was not only a founder but also a craftsman member of the society. She exhibited there regularly and was an altruistic champion for its cause.

Three days before the opening of the society's inaugural exhibition in 1897, the *Springfield News* published a lengthy article titled "Women of Talent: Their Work in Industrial Art." The author noted that women had "devoted their talent and taste to greater and more remunerative lines of art work, and they have now not only a footing, but are recognized as leaders." The article declared, "It is the fact that such women as Mrs. Whitman are doing real, valuable work in the world today that gives intrinsic value to women's work everywhere and stimulates and inspires others who must and do work."[24] "Women's work" was here clearly defined as art, and particularly as decorative art. Within the Arts and Crafts movement, women would find unprecedented opportunity to fulfill their creativity.

Sarah Whitman did not only practice; she preached. She published numerous articles about the benefit of art to American culture, and she lectured frequently in Boston on similar topics. She offered her expertise in decorative design to students at the School of the Museum of Fine Arts and served on its governing council (the first woman to do so), beginning in 1885. Whitman was an early and dedicated advocate of Radcliffe College, sitting on a variety of the school's boards and committees, but she also "devoted herself," in the words of Santayana, "to instilling the higher spirit of the arts and crafts into the minds of working-girls."[25] She believed in equal education for African Americans, and she left a considerable sum of money to Tuskegee Institute in Alabama, founded by Booker T. Washington, and to Berea College in Kentucky, which admitted students of both sexes, black and white.

Sarah Wyman Whitman had remarked of her teacher Hunt in 1880 that "he planted a very fruitful seed," and many of the women who had studied with him took a major role in the fine arts in Boston.[26] Their contributions did not end with the new century; Hunt's students provided inspiration and support for the many women who flourished in Boston after 1900 as painters, sculptors, and decorative artists. One of them was Margaret Redmond, who would succeed Whitman as the city's best-known woman artist in stained glass. Like Whitman, Redmond designed windows for both religious and secular buildings and crafted firescreens and other decorations. She too was involved with Trinity Church.

Redmond (1867–1948) had also begun her career as a painter, specializing in floral subjects and landscapes, although she seems always to have been interested in stained glass, and she admired La Farge, with whom she was acquainted.[27] Born in Philadelphia and resident in that city until 1905, Redmond (like many women artists) trained at the Pennsylvania Academy of the Fine Arts. She exhibited watercolors there, most often landscapes, from 1895 to 1904. She also studied in New York with J. Alden Weir and John Twachtman, two leading painters of the American Impressionist movement, and later in Boston with Denman Ross, once an associate of Whitman. Redmond spent two years in Europe after 1908, taking art classes at the Académie Colarossi in Paris and studying medieval glass in Gothic cathedrals in France and Spain. It was this intensely colored narrative stained glass that most captured her attention and would serve as a model for her own mature work.

Redmond had joined the Society of Arts and Crafts, Boston, as a craftsman member, and she displayed stained glass panels and firescreens in its inaugural exhibition in 1897, even before making the city her permanent home. At some point, she apparently worked with fellow Pennsylvanian Charles Connick, under whose guidance she was said to have made her first glass medallion.[28] Connick, who had worked in Pittsburgh and New York before establishing himself in Boston, became one of the most important neo-Gothic glassmakers in the United States during the first half of the twentieth century. He was also perhaps the most prolific, with fifteen thousand stained glass windows to his firm's credit in buildings across the United States. Beginning his business in Boston in 1912, he founded a large studio the following year on Harcourt Street in the Back Bay, enlisting a number of assistants. By the 1930s, he was employing some forty men and women to help him "rescue [stained glass] from the abysmal depth of opalescent picture windows."[29] Connick frequently collaborated with Ralph Adams Cram, an influential professor at the Massachusetts Institute of Technology, a prolific architect and designer, and then a key member of Boston's Society of Arts and Crafts. Connick contributed windows to a number of Cram's most important buildings, including All Saint's Church in Ashmont, Massachusetts, the Cathedral of St. John the Divine in New York City, and the American Church in Paris. Like Denman Ross, he would have been an influential ally for Redmond.[30]

Redmond settled in Boston in 1906, taking a large corner room in the newly opened Fenway Studio Building. Along with her companion, miniature-painter Annie Jordan, she moved to 45 Newbury Street in 1925 and changed her descriptive listing in the city directory from "artist" to "stained glass." Redmond also worked at her summer home near Chesham, New Hampshire, just northwest of the artists' colony at Dublin. Among her first important commissions was a series of six windows, each devoted to a single saint, for St. Paul's Episcopal Church in Englewood, New Jersey, an 1899 Gothic structure that also housed windows by La Farge and Tiffany. Redmond's windows, made in the 1920s, are distinctly medieval in inspiration, for as one writer noted, "she transferred her allegiance from the modern pictorial treatment of Mr. La Farge to the methods of the French craftsmen of the middle ages."[31]

Redmond painted and fired her glass in a traditional manner, piecing together bright mosaics of glass and lead and eschewing the opalescent plated glass favored by artisans such as La Farge and Whitman. The two methods, which had been described and debated in the art press for many years, were still defined as "English" and "American," and Redmond, unlike Whitman, stood staunchly with the English.[32] Although she was not a purist in her technique, making limited use of plating and etched glass in some of her windows, she used a distinctly medieval aesthetic, one allied visually with the historicism promoted by such leading figures as Connick and Cram.

Redmond was the only woman artist whose glass was installed in the main part of the Trinity Church (pls. 5, 14, 15). Her first windows, located in the northwest vestibule and in the nave, served as memorials to the Cary and Lovering families. Installed in the late 1920s, they were described as having been composed to "glow and sing."[33] The vestibule windows represent scenes from the Old Testament; the four in the nave depict the evangelists and the apostles. Redmond modeled her figures after Gothic examples and employed rich, deep colors, variegated patterns, and stylized script throughout her designs. She was faithful to her medieval prototypes, drawing inspiration both from stained glass and from manuscript illuminations to create flat, ornamental compositions.

In 1930, Redmond received another order for a window at Trinity: the Bradley family commissioned her to design a memorial for Susan Hinckley Bradley (1851–1929), a painter whom Redmond likely knew. The Bradleys had lived in Philadelphia when Redmond was a student there, and Susan Bradley actively promoted the establishment in Philadelphia of independent exhibitions devoted to watercolor painting. She had returned to Boston by 1907 and continued to paint for the rest of her life. Like Redmond, she had specialized in watercolor landscapes, which she made during her extensive travels around the world. One of the first women to enroll in life drawing classes at the School of the Museum of Fine Arts in Boston, Bradley also studied in Italy with watercolorist Edward Boit and along with her brother, also an artist, was acquainted with a cosmopolitan artistic group. Her husband, Leverett Bradley, was assistant to Phillips Brooks at Trinity, and she undoubtedly knew Whitman's circle of friends. For her memorial, Redmond created a tree of life, combining jewel tones with large areas of white glass well suited to a woman described as a "seeker after light in every direction."[34] The window was installed in the parish house and dedicated in 1931.

Redmond's style was characteristic of the modern medievalism employed by Ralph Adams Cram, but she did not enter his neo-Gothic brotherhood. Cram's world was a masculine one, and Redmond never worked on window designs for his numerous architectural projects. Indeed, "one mention of Cram's name would set Miss Redmond sputtering," later recalled one of her friends. She added, whether accurately or not, that in Redmond's view, Cram "would not use her work because she was a woman and he did not believe in encouraging any woman in doing anything except housework."[35] If those memories were accurate, one of Redmond's most satisfactory commissions may have come from a female parishioner in Peterborough, New Hampshire, in 1937: a large window depicting the prophet Isaiah for All Saint's Episcopal Church, a building designed twenty years earlier by Cram.

In Henry Adams's 1884 novel *Esther,* his protagonist is a woman artist whom he describes as unable to become more than "a second-rate amateur." Esther explains her shortcomings by declaring that "men could do so many things that women can't." Within his account of the conflict between the intellect and the spirit in his thinly disguised fictive portrait of the circle involved with the decoration of Trinity Church, Adams tells another story: a cautionary tale about men, women, and the aesthetic enterprise. He published *Esther* under a pseudonym, using a woman's name, and later admitted that few people seemed familiar with the book.[36] That was just as well, for at the real Trinity Church, women did find a place for their artistic ambition.

# NOTES

This essay expands upon a chapter previously published in Erica E. Hirshler, *A Studio of Her Own: Women Artists in Boston, 1870–1940* (Boston: MFA Publications, 2001).

1. George Santayana, *The Middle Span* (New York: Charles Scribner's Sons, 1945), 123.

2. Ibid., 126; "Women of Talent: Their Work in Industrial Art," *Springfield (Mass.) News,* April 2, 1897, in Society of Arts and Crafts Papers, Archives of American Art, Smithsonian Institution, Washington, D.C., roll 322, frame 198.

3. For more on Whitman, see *Letters of Sarah Wyman Whitman* (Cambridge, Mass.: Riverside Press, 1907); Virginia C. Raguin et al., "Sarah Wyman Whitman, 1842–1904: The Cultural Climate in Boston" (typescript, Art History Department, College of the Holy Cross, 1993); and Betty S. Smith, "Sarah de St. Prix Wyman Whitman," *Old-Time New England* 77 (spring/summer 1999): 46–64. Both Betty Smith and Virginia Raguin have been tireless champions of Whitman's career. I am deeply grateful to Betty Smith for the information on Whitman that she has so generously shared with me over many years.

4. John Jay Chapman, *Memories and Milestones* (New York: Moffat, Yard, 1915), 103, 106.

5. Bliss Perry, *Life and Letters of Henry Lee Higginson* (Boston: Atlantic Monthly Press, 1921), 372. Whitman's decorative interests also included metalwork, and she may have proposed to the Phi Beta Kappa Society at Harvard the design for an elegant silver pitcher (I am grateful to Jeannine Falino for this information; the pitcher is marked Shreve, Crump, & Low). Whitman did design the college seal for Radcliffe upon its incorporation in 1894, the crest for Isabella Stewart Gardner's Fenway Court, and a few other such devices. There is also inconclusive evidence suggesting that she designed the original carpet for Trinity Church. A chalice and paten, medieval in style and bearing the hallmark of Arthur Stone, were given to Trinity in Whitman's honor by her Bible study class, but her role, if any, in their design is unknown.

6. T., "The Disciples of William Morris Hunt," *Art Amateur* 13 (July 1885): 41.

7. Whitman to Sarah Orne Jewett, 17 July 1898, in Whitman, *Letters*, 101.

8. S. C. de Soissons, *Boston Artists: A Parisian Critic's Notes* (Boston: Carl Schoenhof, 1894), 37. See the related discussion in Sarah Burns, "The 'Earnest, Untiring Worker' and the Magician of the Brush: Gender Politics in the Criticism of Cecilia Beaux and John Singer Sargent," *Oxford Art Journal* 15 (1992): 36–53.

9. William C. Brownell, "The Younger Painters of America, Part III," *Scribner's Monthly* 22 (July 1881), 329. Whitman showed a now unlocated painting, *Girl and Cat.* See also Jennifer A. Martin Bienenstock, "The Formation and Early Years of the Society of American Artists: 1877–1884" (Ph.D. diss., City University of New York, 1983).

10. S. N. Carter, "The Society of American Artists," *Art Journal* 6 (1880): 156.

11. See Bienenstock, "Formation and Early Years"; the Society of American Artists' catalogues; and the discussion in Kirsten Swinth, *Painting Professionals: Women Artists and the Development of Modern American Art, 1870–1930* (Chapel Hill: University of North Carolina Press, 2001), 67–68. La Farge's extramarital affair with Maria Oakey, which ended in the late 1870s, may have had more to do with his reluctance to support her than did consistent antifeminism on his part. I am grateful to James L. Yarnall for his insights and information on La Farge. Oakey became engaged to the painter Thomas Dewing in December 1880.

12. Phillips Brooks to Sarah Wyman Whitman, 24 May 1881, Archives of American Art, Smithsonian Institution, Washington, D.C., roll D32.

13. This clipping is cited by Betty Smith in her "Biographical Outline: Sarah Wyman Whitman (1842–1904)," typescript, curatorial files, Museum of Fine Arts, Boston. Whitman added a mural to the chancel of Worcester's Central Congregational Church in 1889; most of her work has since been renovated out of existence.

14. Orin E. Skinner, "Women in Stained Glass," *Stained Glass* 35 (Winter 1940): 114–15.

15. "Women of Talent." Whitman later established a larger studio in a former stable across the street from her home on Mount Vernon Street.

16. S.W.W., "Stained Glass Windows," *The Nation* 55 (December 8, 1892): 431. See also Skinner, "Women in Stained Glass," 113–15.

17. Quoted in Mason Hammond, "The Stained Glass Windows in Memorial Hall, Harvard University," 1978, typescript in Harvard University Archives, 282. See also Virginia Raguin, "Memorial Hall Windows Designed by Sarah Wyman Whitman," *Harvard Library Bulletin,* n.s., 11 (spring 2000), 29–53.

18. In 1890, Sarah Whitman had purchased a La Farge watercolor of a knight in armor holding a banner, a design for the Goddard Family memorial windows at Christ Church in Lonsdale, Rhode Island (now in the Museum of Fine Arts, Boston).

19. Charles J. Connick, *Adventures in Light and Color* (New York: Random House, 1937), 401.

20. Sarah Whitman to Mrs. Bigelow Lawrence, March 12, 1896, in Whitman, *Letters,* 40.

21. See Sue Allen and Charles Gullans, *Decorated Cloth in America* (Los Angeles: University of California, 1994); and Nancy Finlay, *Artists of the Book in Boston* (Cambridge, Mass.: Houghton Library, 1985). I am also indebted to Sue Allen's lecture "The Book Cover Art of Sarah Wyman Whitman," presented at the Houghton Library, Harvard University, May 6, 1999.

22. Sarah Wyman Whitman, *Notes of an Informal Talk on Book Illustration, Inside and Out, Given before the Boston Art Students Association, February 14, 1894* (Boston: Boston Art Students Association, 1894), 5.

23. Norton, quoted in Nancy Finlay, "A Millenium in Book-Making: The Book Arts in Boston," in *Inspiring Reform: Boston's Arts and Crafts Movement,* ed. Merilee Meyer et al. (Wellesley, Mass.: Davis Museum and Cultural Center, 1997), 129; Sarah Wyman Whitman, "The Pursuit of Art in America," *International Review* 12 (January 1882): 15.

24. "Women of Talent," 2 April 1897.

25. Santayana, *Middle Span,* 126.

26. Sarah Wyman Whitman, "William Morris Hunt," *International Review* 8 (April 1880): 397.

27. See Elizabeth B. Prudden, "History Written in Glass," *Christian Science Monitor,* June 30, 1931, 6. For Redmond, see also Elinor Morgan, "A Woman in Stained Glass: Against the Odds," *Stained Glass Quarterly* 85 (spring 1990): 45–50. Redmond's papers are held by the Archives of American Art, Smithsonian Institution, Washington, D.C. Her career is difficult to reconstruct. I am indebted to Kimberley Alexander for sharing her insights and for her two papers on Redmond: "Margaret Redmond and the Society of Arts and Crafts, Boston," delivered at the Deerfield-Wellesley Symposium on American Culture, Historic Deerfield, November 9, 1996; and "Margaret Redmond," presented at Trinity Church, December 3, 2002. I also thank Elizabeth Simmons for her careful corrections to my text and for her generosity in sharing her research for a master's thesis on Redmond for Boston University.

28. Prudden, "History Written in Glass."

29. Connick's obituary, *Boston Herald,* December 29, 1945, quoted in *"The Art That Is Life": The Arts and Crafts Movement in America, 1875–1920,* ed. Wendy Kaplan et al. (Boston: Museum of Fine Arts, 1987), 144. The dates of Redmond's work with Connick are unknown.

30. Sarah Whitman's foreman, Alexander Walker, also worked with Cram and perhaps with Connick, but no clear links between Whitman (who died in 1904, before Redmond moved to Boston) and Redmond have yet emerged.

31. Prudden, "History Written in Glass," 6.

32. For a contemporary technical description of the two styles of glassmaking, see Henry C. Tilden, "Pictorial Art in Glass," *Brush and Pencil* 18 (October 1906), 154–66.

33. Prudden, "History Written in Glass."

34. Laura E. Richards, "Susan H. Bradley," *American Magazine of Art* 15 (July 1924): 374.

35. Morgan, "A Woman in Stained Glass," 48, 50. Cram was connected to many women intellectuals and artists in Boston, however. For Cram, see Douglass Shand-Tucci, *Boston Bohemia, 1881–1900: Ralph Adams Cram: Life and Architecture* (Amherst: University of Massachusetts Press, 1995).

36. Henry Adams [Frances Snow Compton, pseud.], *Esther,* in Henry Adams, *Novels,* ed. Ernest Samuels and Jayne S. Samuels (New York: Library of America, 1983), 199–200, 244; Patricia O'Toole, *The Five of Hearts* (New York: Ballantine Books, 1990), 133–41.

10-1. Charles Donagh Maginnis (1867–1955), ca. 1920. (Author's collection.)

# 10

## Chancel Remodeling:
## Charles D. Maginnis (Maginnis & Walsh)

MILDA B. RICHARDSON

AT THE DECEMBER 18, 1938, dedication service of the new chancel at Trinity Church (pls. 7 and 11), redecorated by Boston architect Charles Donagh Maginnis (1867–1955), the Reverend Dr. Arthur Lee Kinsolving (1899–1977) declared: "We have found the power of great art dedicated in the spirit of worship. In the details as well as in the grand designs there has been lavished upon this chancel by architect, artists, and builders alike far more than the contract called for, that fine excess that makes of craftsmanship a very act of worship. It has been an act of devotion to Him whom we would serve."[1] Kinsolving, rector of Trinity from 1930 to 1940, reinforced Maginnis's own thoughts on an appropriate architecture for Christian worship: "Art history no longer has perspective. The glories of the past have been magically visualized to us, revealing the glamour of the days when Art was the handmaid of Religion, when the hands and imaginations of genius were busy in God's service."[2] Clearly, Kinsolving and Maginnis shared a keen sensitivity for the important role of architecture in imbuing spirituality with prerequisite dignity and repose.

The distinguished Boston firm of Maginnis & Walsh had been established in 1898 as Maginnis, Walsh & Sullivan. The partners were Timothy Francis Walsh (1868–1934), formerly of Peabody & Stearns, and Matthew Sullivan (1868–1938) of the Edmund M. Wheelwright office.[3] The senior partner was Charles D. Maginnis (fig. 10-1), a well-educated and ambitious immigrant to Boston from Londonderry, Ireland, by way of Canada. A prizewinning student of mathematics, he was educated at the South Kensington Museum School of Art in London, where his talent for drawing was recognized early on. In 1886 he secured a job as draftsman for William Wentworth in Boston. A year later he joined Edmund Wheelwright, head of the Boston City Architect's Office, and by 1891 he was chief draftsman. From the beginning, Maginnis was a prolific and gifted pen-and-ink illustrator, teaching as well at Cowles Art School, using his own textbook, *Pen Drawing: An Illustrated Treatise* (1889).

Under Maginnis's design leadership, his firm revolutionized the practice of Roman Catholic architecture in America and enhanced the prestige of Catholic culture. Associated primarily with ecclesiastical and collegiate commissions, the firm built a broad patronage network that included some of the highest-ranking leaders of the Roman Catholic Church at the turn of the twentieth century. By the time of the Trinity commission, Maginnis & Walsh had established itself as the leading Roman Catholic firm with prizewinning projects such as the Carmelite Convent, California (1925), and Trinity College Chapel, Washington, D.C. (1927)—both of which won the American Institute of Architects (AIA) Gold Medal—and the Boston College Science Building (today Devlin Hall), winner of the J. Harleston Parker Gold Medal in 1925. In 1909, Maginnis won the competition to design a master plan for Boston College, one of the earliest Collegiate Gothic campuses in the United States. Its four original buildings, completed by 1938, were universally praised as masterpieces in the English Gothic style.[4] With the patronage of the Jesuit, Maryknoll, Carmelite, Sisters of Notre Dame, and other religious orders, the firm executed nearly a thousand commissions in a wide variety of styles over the span of its existence. These included more than sixty parish churches and significant contributions to building programs on more than twenty college campuses, including the College of the Holy Cross and the University of Notre Dame. With his spirited intellect and reserved charm, Maginnis broke down many barriers and was honored by the church and the profession: the Laetare Medal in 1924, which carries the papal blessing, and in 1948 the AIA Gold Medal for Achievement.

An articulate and engaging writer and speaker, Charles Maginnis was an outspoken traditionalist who criticized the modern movement in architecture from several points of view. His response to the international modernist trend was that it made for a universal monotony, was impermanent, and had no bridge with the past and no link with the future. "My entire grievance with the modern postulate" he summed up, "could be disposed of in a single word. It proclaims that architecture is the expression of function. I hold instead that it is the felicitous expression of function, and as such must involve the principles of beauty and creative imagination." In an even stronger statement, Maginnis reinforced his position by pointing out that the modernists' reliance on new materials as a liberating force created an "architecture without memories."[5]

Maginnis was an enthusiastic participant in the Academic Eclecticism movement (1880s–1930s), which embraced historicity and inclusiveness as its guiding principles.[6] The basis for his eclecticism and traditionalism was a skepticism about the usefulness of modernism, but he added a creative dimension: historical forms and details are always modified and reintegrated through a process that adapts, not merely adopts. In his own terms, Maginnis referred to eclecticism as a valid element in traditional architectural practice: "And here, for the clarity of the matter, it should be emphasized that the traditionalist, sensitive to the stigma of archaeology, makes no claims for the literal relevance of European precedent, but holds to the view that, in the absence of a national vernacular, he is justified in an eclecticism that brings what is best in the past to modern correspondence."[7]

Since the re-creation of historical styles demands the highest level of craftsmanship, throughout his career Maginnis sought out master craftsmen of international reputation. His close collaboration with Irving & Casson was much like H. H. Richardson's relationship with A. H. Davenport, the firm of cabinetmakers that merged with Irving & Casson in 1914.[8] Maginnis's aesthetic philosophy came out of his belief in the totality of design. This was a major aspect of the Arts and Crafts movement, which he staunchly supported, becoming a founding member and president of the Society of Arts and Crafts, Boston, the Liturgical Arts Society, and the Federation of Catholic Art.[9] It was through these forums that he advocated Catholic architectural reform toward older, simpler Christian styles and complete integration of liturgical arts and architecture.

With his strong artistic credentials, effective diplomatic skills, and recent election to the presidency of the American Institute of Architects, Maginnis was a natural choice to be invited to submit a design for the redecoration of the chancel of Trinity Church. The 1937 competition was initiated primarily for three reasons: a fund had been established specifically for this purpose; Kinsolving was "desirous of having an Altar with more beauty and reverential appeal"; and, finally, the baldachino, always thought of as temporary, should be replaced.[10] The fund referred to was a legacy from James Arthur Beebe, a Boston merchant who had died in 1914.[11] By 1937 the original gift of $25,000 had more than doubled, and the attorney general of Massachusetts was concerned that the original terms of the will be implemented as soon as possible. A competition was launched in earnest with the active participation of Robert Treat Paine, senior warden of Trinity Parish. As previous senior warden, his father, also Robert Treat Paine, had worked very closely with Trinity's architect, H. H. Richardson, and its rector, Phillips Brooks. Following the completion of the chancel, the younger Paine received a letter saying, "It also seems to me most fitting that this should have been accomplished while you are Senior Warden for it completes the great work which your father began. Such things happen so rarely that they give an added thrill whenever they do occur."[12]

Professor William Emerson, dean of the Architectural School of MIT, was appointed professional adviser and convenor of the jury, the members of which were Robert P. Bellows, Ralph W. Gray, Andrew H. Hepburn, and Robert T. Paine, representing the church. All specifications were laid out in a formal and carefully organized "programme" written by Dean Emerson, expressing a strongly felt imperative that the winning architect should display a "consciousness of the inheritance and sentiment that has accumulated during the past two generations." Participation in the competition was limited to five Boston firms: Allen, Collens & Willis; Coolidge, Shepley, Bulfinch & Abbott; Cram & Ferguson; Frohman, Robb & Little; and Maginnis & Walsh. Maginnis & Walsh's agreement to submit a design was applauded in various circles, as exemplified by the text of a letter to Paine from the chairman of the committee on chancel decoration: "I quote from Maginnis & Walsh's letter of acceptance: 'We are very sensible of the compliment implied in this invitation, and shall be happy to enter on a study of the problem on receipt of the program.' I hope you will be as pleased as I am that we invited that firm."[13]

In preparation for the competition, H. H. Richardson's successor firm, Coolidge, Shepley, Bulfinch & Abbott, supplied the original Richardson drawings to all the competitors. Other recommendations included an invitation to attend a service: "Should competitors be uncertain as to the ritual followed at Trinity Church, in so far as this may affect their solutions, attendance at a typical Sunday Service will probably suffice to clarify this procedure." A relatively free hand was offered to the competitors in reworking the chancel (no budget constraints were imposed), but at least one issue was of particular concern—the lighting. The general feeling was that the great brass chandelier hanging in the central tower (fig. 5-1) should be removed because of its "blinding and shortening effect."[14] Ultimately, the chandelier was put into storage, and lighting thought to be more appropriate to the setting was installed.

At the dedication of Trinity Church in 1877, the chancel was relatively unornamented, reflecting the taste of Phillips Brooks (fig. 4-5). The focus had been on essential furnishings; the wooden communion table and semicircular rail, designed by the office of H. H. Richardson, were the central elements. The baptismal font stood on the left, and Brooks's simple lectern in the center. Although John La Farge may have suggested a processional frieze for the apse wall below the windows, it remained simply plastered.[15] A row of Gothic Revival oak chairs with triangular backs lined the apse wall (figs. 5-1, 5-2). Between the stained glass windows were six plaques containing prayers, extracts from the communion service, and two crosses on a gilt background. At the turn of the century, the Coolidge, Shepley, Bulfinch & Abbott firm had been engaged to make changes in the chancel, including the addition of a stone floor. The choir stalls of quarter-sawn oak, the light gray stone choir rail with Byzantine patterns and Christian symbols, and the pulpit were designed by Charles A. Coolidge and executed by A. H. Davenport's company. The carvings on the pulpit, completed in 1914 as a memorial to the elder Robert Treat Paine (a close friend of Brooks and parish warden from 1874 to 1910), depict figures of great preachers (including Brooks), between which are placed scenes from the life of Christ.

The chancel competition drawings were submitted in May 1937, and on June 1 the jury unanimously made its selection from among the blind entries. The winning envelope was opened in the presence of the wardens and vestry on June 8, revealing the firm of Maginnis & Walsh as the winner. Two of the nonwinning entries were criticized because of their proposal to install a larger baldachino that would have obstructed the view and reduced the scale of the church interior. In another entry, by Ralph Adams Cram, the problem of crowding and confused treatment was mentioned as unsatisfactory. The fourth was thought to be congested, with a questionable location for the altar; it would also have been the most expensive. In an eloquent letter, however, Kinsolving expressed to Cram his disappointment that Cram had not been chosen: "It is with real personal regret that I put away a hope long entertained that some day your touch might enhance and ennoble the chancel at Trinity Church. . . . It [the winning design] is indeed a splendid conception. The measure of unanimity preserved was interesting and curious. . . . [D]espite my agreement with the verdict . . . I am sorry not to have this prospect in common with you, because . . . it was you who inspired me to . . . know that something could be done."[16]

The prizewinning entry (fig. 10-2), described by the jury in the following terms, recognized Phillips Brooks's ecumenicalism but seemed to run counter to his demand for a simple communion table: "A simple, dignified, straight forward [sic] solution of the problem. Fine, both in scale and in detail. Expressive of the massive quality and originality of Richardson's work." Maginnis's statement accompanying his submission concentrated on four major points: (1) the radial system of truss cords and the trefoil vaulting was too complicated and not in proper scale with the square crossing; (2) the centrality of the altar should be defined by lateral enframement and sculpture in slight relief, including a cross suspended above; (3) it was imperative to sheath the apse walls with marble revetment; and (4) the overall lighting program needed to be modernized. In his acceptance letter, Maginnis referred to the importance of preserving the Trinity legacy: "I have already indicated in the thesis which accompanied the competitive design my sense of the intimidating architectural tradition which is associated with Trinity

THE CHANCEL OF TRINITY CHURCH

10-2. Prizewinning entry for Trinity chancel competition, May 1937, Maginnis &
Walsh, Architects. (Maginnis & Walsh Collection, Boston Public Library. Reproduced
courtesy of the Trustees of the Boston Public Library.)

Church, and I addressed myself to the study of the problem with very respectful attitude to the memory of Mr. Richardson."[17]

Despite the overwhelmingly recognized brilliance of Maginnis's skill in applying his expertise in the Byzantine style, the new chancel project was not without its detractors. The choice of a Roman Catholic architect for an Episcopal church was criticized by some, with references to the dominant suspended cross as too obviously papist. Maginnis was aware of these sentiments and intervened successfully with his skills of diplomacy and inclusiveness. As Emerson later recounted: "So sensitive was he [Maginnis] for the feelings of others that, after his firm had won the competition for the interior treatment of the apse of Trinity Church, Boston, he was fearful lest the Episcopalian congregation might not be in sympathy with the jury's selection of a design by a Catholic architect. So, in consultation with the then rector, . . . he appointed a time when he would answer all questions. As a result the congregation became fully as enthusiastic as the jury over the beauty and appropriateness of the Maginnis design."[18]

In June 1937, Maginnis submitted estimated expenditures of about $240,000. This budget was subject to numerous revisions, and the final amount the church approved for fund-raising was closer to $80,000, or $30,000 over and above the Beebe bequest. The smaller budget reflected changes in design and materials that Maginnis negotiated with Kinsolving, the committee, vestry, and wardens. That all decisions were made collaboratively is shown by the lively correspondence between principals, and the subsequent fund-raising campaign was highly successful.

What emerged over the course of the next eighteen months was the chancel as it is today (fig. 10-3). Maginnis's contribution revolved around significant alterations in five areas. First, the installation of book-matched marble sheathing on the lower section of the apsidal wall defines the chancel space and emphasizes the rectilinear geometry so characteristic of the Byzantine style.[19] Maginnis had used narrow panels of marble sheathing effectively to delineate the apse at the St. John Seminary Chapel (1905), Brighton, Massachusetts, which is an early example of a similar overall scheme. At Trinity the highly polished, shimmering quality of the marble panels concentrates visual attention on the wall surface (which until the renovation had been simply plastered), thereby deemphasizing the wall mass. Dark panels of Alps Green marble, framed in borders of Cosmati work,[20] provide a striking background for the white altar and also serve to pull together the green details in the ceiling coffers and the robes of the figures painted on the walls by La Farge.

One of the characteristics of nineteenth-century American Protestant religious practice was the emphasis on the Word, both written and preached, as part of the

10-3. Confirmation at Trinity Church, 1992. (Photo by Charles A. Meyer.)

liturgy and as an architectural feature.[21] The fact that American religious life was logocentric in character is corroborated by the original chancel's six plaques (eventually removed) with liturgical texts on gilt background, placed between the windows. To maintain the tradition, Maginnis designed a frieze of Red Levanto marble, installed above the new marble sheathing, which contains seven carved and gilded inscriptions chosen by Kinsolving, who expressed his priority "that the affirmations should be primarily spiritual rather than primarily ethical." Severe restrictions on the number of letters and the configuration of the typography made choosing the texts a demanding undertaking, and a number of combinations were offered. The final choices reflected the rector's own wish that the texts be "vital to the modern religious consciousness, in the spirit of the Trinity traditions."[22] An example of his selections is the first inscription on the Epistle side of the chancel, which reads, "One Lord, One Faith, One Baptism, One God and Father of All." The images in the small panel beside it are emblems of the unity of Christian doctrine: the ship is the Church; the fish in the water represents the sacrament of baptism; the triangle signifies the Trinity.

Above the frieze with its lettered affirmations are seven bas-reliefs modeled by Ernest Pellegrini of Irving & Casson, each with a thematic relationship to the text below.[23] Maginnis's original design called for a mosaic frieze of the twelve apostles at the base of the dome, accentuating the curvature of the apse. As finalized, the bas-reliefs punctuate the apse wall in a slow rhythm, and their placement directly under each of the stained glass windows slows the circular flow of the inscription frieze. Each relief contains a scene of two to four figures interacting in silent dialogue or quiet activity. The main figures represent Christian leaders: St. Paul pleading the cause of Christ, St. Athanasius addressing the Council of Nicaea (325 A.D.), St. Augustine presenting his book *The City of God* to a Roman official, St. Francis curing a leper, John Wycliffe translating the Holy Scriptures from Latin into English, John Wesley preaching, and Phillips Brooks telling the Christmas story to assembled children. The theme of recognizing important preachers ties the bas-reliefs to the carvings of the memorial pulpit.

The dignified figures in period costume fill the panels, touching and sometimes overlapping the frames. In the scene of St. Paul before King Agrippa and Bernice, the right foot of Bernice steps off the floor and into the viewer's space. As the figures painted by La Farge "exceed the bounds of their frames,"[24] those in the bas-reliefs exhibit a similar dynamism, particularly in the slight movement of the lower robes. The figures are seen mostly in profile, with the exception of Phillips Brooks, whose portraitlike head is turned slightly toward the viewer. The figures in each panel face each other and are completely focused on their conversations. Motion is discernible but restrained. Slight gestures of the hand express a thought or speech. The central panel shows St. Francis with a leper, who is portrayed naturalistically through the musculature of his thin body, the bony left shoulder and concave chest. The theme of the frieze reinforces the spirituality and mystery of the church's teachings, while the bas-reliefs present a period history of the church, including a modern Episcopalian theologian.

Maginnis's original scheme to remove the vaulting in the apse and replace it with a plaster ceiling to be decorated with mosaics was quickly abandoned for reasons of cost. As work progressed on the metal leaf and painting of the upper walls, however, it became apparent to Paine and the committee that substantial work was needed to clean the soiled vaulting and restore the deteriorating plaster. Following rapid deliberations, it was decided to accept Maginnis's recommendations

10-4. Elevation of the Trinity Church sanctuary, Maginnis & Walsh, Architects, 1938. (Maginnis & Walsh Collection, Boston Public Library. Reproduced courtesy of the Trustees of the Boston Public Library.)

concerning repair and cleaning of the cove and ceiling vaulting, and also to remove existing trusses and reinforce the vault with structural steel.[25] Maginnis's desire for a lighting program that would create an ethereal atmosphere and convey "a feeling for the emotional quality of light" was accomplished by the Rambusch Design Studios, a frequent collaborator with Maginnis.[26]

The dominant feature of Maginnis's design is the altar with the cross suspended above it (fig. 10-4). The altar, a solid block of white Montenelle marble with borders of Cosmati work, is set on a base of Galena Siena marble, which is used again in the steps and floor inside the communion rail. (A retable was not required, because the altar was designed to be seen from all sides, standing as it does inside the semicircular communion rail, which is the same shape as the original wooden version by Richardson.)

Two peacocks carved on the front face of the altar flank a central vase from which two branches of a grapevine encircle the birds and flow to either side in three great swirls, diminishing in size and culminating in the lower corners with a flourish. The peacock has traditionally been used in Christian art on tombs and sarcophagi to represent the change from life to immortality, and two peacocks placed symmetrically denote the duality of man—the human and the divine. The grapevine both represents the wine used at the communion service and suggests the Gospel metaphor of Christ as the True Vine.[27] The vine motif is repeated on the sides of the altar and the two marble sanctuary chairs, and it is continued throughout the upper walls and vaulted ceiling decorated with gold leaf and various patterns of the Cross, grapes, leaves, and quatrefoils. These motifs were common in Byzantine art, and, in this case, were copied from the sixth-century sarcophagus of Archbishop Theodore in St. Apollinare in Classe, and a panel in the Reliquary Chapel of St. Apollinare Nuovo, both in Ravenna, Italy, which Maginnis is known to have visited.[28]

The design and execution of the carvings on the front of the Trinity altar make it very similar to the alabaster and onyx altar designed by Maginnis for St. Catherine of Genoa (1907–20), a Roman Catholic church in Somerville, Massachusetts. The Byzantine-inspired interior of that Italian Lombardian Revival building culminates at the altar with a small baldachino set in front of a marble-columned retable. The front of the main altar there, modeled by Hugh Cairns and executed by Irving & Casson, is decorated with flowing vines, peacocks, and other birds also copied from the Ravenna sarcophagus.[29]

The rear of the Trinity altar is also elaborately carved with panels of Algerian onyx marble, inlaid with various exotic marbles and mosaics. The iconography of the carvings, modeled by C. Hiram Hughes of Irving & Casson, relates to the communion service, during which the worshiper experiences Christ's promise of eternal life.

A large wooden cross, carved by Irving & Casson and decorated in gold leaf and polychrome by Pennell, Gibbs & Quiring, hangs above the Trinity altar, suspended from the ceiling by a bronze armature and chains. It is edged with a decorative cable pattern known as cross cablée, which lightens its overall effect. The cross's arms culminate in square panels, each containing a symbol of one of the four Evangelists. A dove in a circle appears just below the vault and above the central window at the juncture of the armature and the chains (fig. 10-4). The dove is an emblem of the Holy Ghost and is most often portrayed as descending in flight and bearing the Seven Gifts of the Holy Spirit.

As a concept, the suspended cross frequently came up for extended discussion because many people felt that a cross standing on the altar with the six candlesticks would be more appropriate; however, the matter was finally resolved in favor of Maginnis's proposal.[30] This aspect of the project presented special challenges to the team of artists, a fact that was acknowledged by Kinsolving in his correspondence with Henry Pennell: "Yours was a difficult task, conditions were hampering and time, so necessary for happy working out of artistic conception, was limited and inadequate. You rose above these cramping limitations, and co-operating cordially with Mr. Maginnis succeeded in producing a result which through coming years will remain an aesthetic triumph."[31]

Maginnis's decoration of the chancel might very well have pleased H. H. Richardson because of his own fascination with the Byzantine style. Henry-Russell Hitchcock notes that during his European travels in 1882, Richardson was undoubtedly humbled by the interior mosaics at Ravenna and St. Mark's in Venice.[32] Exact ideas that Richardson and La Farge may have had for the completion of the chancel are not documented. Maginnis's primary sources for its decoration came from his own lifelong interest in and study of the Byzantine and Romanesque styles.

The apse of the Episcopal Church of St. Bartholomew in New York (fig. 10-5), which Bertram Goodhue (Cram's former partner) was asked to design in 1914, bears some resemblance to the Trinity chancel and may also have inspired Maginnis.[33] He made it clear privately and publicly how deeply he admired Goodhue's work and "brilliant manifestation of versatility": "Known as a designer of rarely sensitive and pictorial imagination, it was his skill in rendering . . . in . . . opulent pen style, . . . which captured the professional interest for the distinction of his subjects from the very beginning." Later, in an obituary for Ralph Adams Cram, Maginnis wrote that "the prolific enterprise of his [Cram's] pen had carried him to a prominence that from the beginning shadowed the figure of the bril-

10-5. Apse of St. Bartholomew's, New York, Bertram Goodhue, Architect, 1914. (Photo by Bob Johnson; Courtesy of St. Bartholomew's Church.)

liant Bertram Goodhue up to their separation, when Goodhue's genius came to its own revelation."[34]

In a way, Goodhue and Maginnis faced similar problems with the St. Bartholomew and Trinity commissions because they both had to work within certain design parameters determined by their predecessors. Goodhue had to incorporate the triple-arched entryway of the 1872 Romanesque building by Renwick & Sands.[35] Maginnis had the daunting task of refocusing the energy of the Trinity interior in a building he considered "sturdy but exotic," and one that had turned away from the Gothic Revival influence in America emanating from England. Both men were highly successful at their tasks. In a personal letter, Kinsolving commended Maginnis's ability to work within the Richardsonian context: "You brought to the task a rare appreciation of the present fabric of Trinity Church and a remarkable sympathy with our spiritual hopes for this new Chancel. . . . You have not only solved an intricate architectural problem but have lavished upon it an out-pouring of your creative genius. Recognizing that you receive no financial remuneration commensurate with your labours, we trust that the completed Chancel will prove a yet further adornment of your reputation and a complete satisfaction in your memory. We are confident that it will be regarded by the multitudes of visitors from near and far as a work of artistic genius immeasurably enhancing this Church."[36]

Maginnis, working within the belief that art and Catholic religion complement each other, supported views similar to those stated in the conservative Catholic periodical *Ecclesiastical Review* in 1890: "Christian art . . . teaches not only the fact of Christianity, but also aims at convincing the beholder of the supernatural character of that fact."[37] With regard to church architecture, Maginnis cited "two principles which call for recognition,—the optical and the aural. . . . Worship of God at the altar . . . is the fundamental one [principle] in its demand on the architecture. The lines of the interior must contrive to secure a befitting aspect of solemnity—an atmosphere which shall stimulate religious emotion." Later, he pointed out the implicit irony that modern Catholic worship is confounded by the practice of "advancing the altar into intimate touch with the congregation." He applauded the Episcopalian trend of "more and more emphasizing their attachment to the medieval idea," whereby the Divine Presence in the tabernacle of the altar is recognized and respected architecturally.[38]

One of the techniques Maginnis used most effectively in ecclesiastical spaces in order to concentrate such a focus was to set a block altar in shades of white and gold against a darkened background. This dramatic use of chiaroscuro may be seen in two important Maginnis commissions that preceded Trinity and bear some relation to it in both overall conception and altar details: the Crypt Church of the Basilica of the National Shrine of the Immaculate Conception, Washington, D.C. (1920–24) and St. Catherine of Genoa in Somerville. The main altar in the Byzantine-style Crypt Church is raised on a three-stepped base and stands in the center of the crypt, with fifteen subsidiary altars in chapels radiating off the main space and illuminated by lunette windows. The primary decorative program, executed by Bancel La Farge (the son of John La Farge) from 1925 to 1931, consists of mosaics loosely based on the sixth-century interior of San Vitale in Ravenna. The altar, carved of semitransparent golden onyx from Algiers, is resplendent with designs in soft golden mosaics. The mosaics shimmer under low rounded vaults covered with dark gray and brown Guastavino tiles, suggesting the atmosphere of early Christian places of worship. The altar, dedicated to Our Lady of the Catacombs, appears to give off its own light as it stands in the deep shadows of this setting.[39]

At St. Catherine of Genoa, Maginnis set the altar apart by means of several devices (fig. 10-6). A baldachino with a gold dome gives height to the tabernacle of the Blessed Sacrament. The white, cream, and gold altar is placed high on a predella, backed by the deep hues of purple and gray Fleur-de-Pêche marble used in a freestanding curved colonnade. Book-matched slabs of the same marble, strongly veined with white, line the walls of the apse. The colonnade with its heavy cornice creates a shadowy passageway behind, further setting the altar apart. Although the overall sumptuous apse decoration at St. Catherine bears a resemblance to the original Maginnis proposal for Trinity, both the proposal and the final outcome are greatly simplified, producing an even more powerful and dramatic effect. Maginnis was probably aware of both the simplicity and the contrast of marble in the Byzantine apse of St. Bartholomew, where Goodhue reversed the use of contrasting colors by setting a black marble altar against an apse wall sheathed with narrow slabs of amber-colored marble. A tall, elegant cross inlaid in the central panel of the revetment with a black border visually joins the cross with the altar.

The approach to the Trinity altar and the chancel space consists of a sequence of three floor levels, beginning at the nave, with symbolic import.[40] The choir level is defined by the choir rail itself. The chancel space is separated from the choir level by the communion rail which, with its book-matched panels of Morocco red flammé marble, not only provides a break in the rhythm of the ascent but also creates a prominent visual base for the white altar. The dark red, heavily veined marble panels also tie the chancel space coloristically to the reddish tones of the interior walls. The expansive horizontal elements serve as an anchor to the apse as a whole, and the powerful curves of the elaborately stenciled and gilded trefoil vaulting rise and curve inward as an animated backdrop for the suspended

10-6. Apse of St. Catherine of Genoa, Somerville, Massachusetts, 1907–20, Maginnis & Walsh, Architects. Restored by J. W. Graham Inc. (Photo courtesy of J. W. Graham Inc.)

cross. Maginnis would have experienced the effect of such strong horizontal components from his visit to the Cappella Palatina (1143) at the palace of Roger II in Palermo, Sicily. In that fine example of a private chapel adorned with mosaics, the choir rail with open carving and a solid marble communion rail are staggered and lead to the altar space deeper within the chancel. The layering of the horizontal elements controls the dynamic quality of the colonnade and bold geometric patterns of the chapel apse.[41]

Maginnis succeeded in reorienting the chancel space at Trinity toward the altar and the suspended cross by highlighting the white elements against the dark green marble and shimmering gold of the surrounding wall. This refocusing is strengthened by the direct visual connection, on axis, with the *Christ in Majesty* window by John La Farge above the entrance, binding entrance and chancel together.

The new priorities within the chancel space were related to the ecumenical movement within the Episcopal Church, 1927–37, during which the church turned forward and outward, and a major revision of the liturgy brought its worship up to date in the twentieth century. In 1937, three Episcopal Church handbooks were published: one relating to the history and use of the *Book of Common Prayer*, a homiletic guide, and a guide to the hymnal and liturgical song.[42] The rector's pastoral response to the ideas presented in these books was to put them into practice at Trinity by reaching out to the broader Boston community, particularly to students and visitors. He also expressed his concern that the liturgy should be an instrument to enhance both private spirituality and communal worship.[43] Maginnis brilliantly resolved the challenge that Kinsolving set for himself and his church. As climax to the liturgy, the new chancel preserved the traditional priority of the sacrament of communion, yet at the same time, its visual radiance provided a welcoming ambiance for worshipers new and old.

## NOTES

I am deeply grateful to Professor Keith Morgan for his support during the course of my research on Maginnis & Walsh. My sincere thanks to John Woolverton, James F. White, and Richard Candee for productive conversations about various aspects of this project. John Clift, Director of Facilities at Trinity Church, extended his most gracious hospitality and gave generously of his time and expertise. The staff at the Fine Arts Department of the Boston Public Library and at the Basilica of the National Shrine, Kathy Flynn at the Peabody Essex Museum, Rev. Brian F. Manning, Rev.

Robert M. O'Grady, and Bishop Richard G. Lennon were most helpful; and many others contributed to the project.

1. Quoted in "Bishops Lawrence and Sherrill Help to Dedicate Trinity Chancel," *Boston Globe,* December 19, 1938.

2. Charles D. Maginnis, "The Movement for a Vital Christian Architecture and the Obstacles—The Roman Catholic View," *Magazine of Christian Art* 1, no. 1 (April 1907): 24.

3. Sullivan left the office in 1907, and the firm was known as Maginnis & Walsh from 1908 to 1954.

4. Donna M. Cassidy, "The Collegiate Gothic Designs of Maginnis & Walsh," in John R. Zukowsky, ed., *Studies in Medievalism in Architecture and Design* 3, no. 2 (Fall 1990): 153–85.

5. Charles D. Maginnis, "History and the New Architecture," *Journal of the AIA* 9, no. 4 (April 1949): 178, 177; Charles D. Maginnis, "The Artistic Debate," *Liturgical Arts* 12, no. 4 (August 1944): 82.

6. See chap. 1 of Richard Longstreth, *On the Edge of the World: Four Architects in San Francisco at the Turn of the Century* (Cambridge, Mass.: MIT Press), 9–39. Walter C. Kidney also mentions the Gothic and Romanesque work of Maginnis & Walsh in *The Architecture of Choice: Eclecticism in America, 1880–1930* (New York: George Braziller), 42. In his discussion of domestic architecture, Mark Alan Hewitt refers to a process he calls "genre application," whereby an architect assimilates a style so thoroughly that he is able to apply it consistently while putting his own mark on the building and not merely imitating the original archeologically: *The Architect and the American Country House, 1890–1940* (New Haven, Conn.: Yale University Press, 1990), 38–42.

7. Maginnis, "Artistic Debate," 82.

8. Anne Farnam, "H. H. Richardson and A. H. Davenport: Architecture and Furniture as Big Business in America's Gilded Age," in *Tools and Technologies: America's Wooden Age,* ed. Paul B. Kebabian and William C. Lipke (Burlington: Robert Hull Fleming Museum, University of Vermont, 1979), 80–92.

9. On the Arts and Crafts movement in America, see Marilee Boyd Meyer, ed., *Inspiring Reform: Boston's Arts and Crafts Movement* (Wellesley, Mass.: Davis Museum and Cultural Center, Wellesley College; New York: dist. Harry N. Abrams, 1997); T. J. Jackson Lears, *No Place of Grace: Antimodernism and the Transformation of American Culture, 1880–1920* (Chicago: University of Chicago Press, 1994), 59–97; Margaret Henderson Floyd, *Architecture after Richardson: Regionalism before Modernism—Longfellow, Alden, and Harlow in Boston and Pittsburgh* (Chicago: University of Chicago Press, 1994), 372–74; Richard Guy Wilson, "Ralph Adams Cram: Dreamer of the Medieval," in *Medievalism in American Culture: Papers of the Eighteenth Annual Conference of the Center for Medieval and Early Renaissance Studies,* ed. Bernard Rosenthal and Paul E. Szarmach (Binghamton: Center for Medieval and Early Renaissance Studies, State University of New York at Binghamton, 1989): 193–214. Also important is Susan J. White, *Art, Architecture, and Liturgical Reform* (New York: Pueblo, 1990). Representative examples of American liturgical arts are elegantly presented in the recent exhibition catalogue *Sacred Spaces: Building and Remembering Sites of Worship in the Nineteenth Century,* ed. Virginia Chieffo Raguin and Mary Ann Powers (Worcester, Mass.: Trustees of the College of the Holy Cross, 2002).

10. Archives of Trinity Church, Boston (hereafter cited as ATC), Robert T. Paine to the Committee on Chancel Decoration (hereafter referred to as the Committee), April 5, 1937.

11. ATC, William Hall, Attorney, to Robert T. Paine, November 30, 1915.

12. ATC, Robert T. Paine to the Committee, April 5, 1937; Robert Bull to Robert T. Paine, December 27, 1938.

13. ATC, minutes of the Committee, March 24, 1937; "Architectural Competition Trinity Church" (1937), 6, 1; C. K. Cummings to Robert T. Paine, March 17, 1937.

14. ATC, minutes of the Committee, February 8, 1937; "Architectural Competition Trinity

Church" (1937), 6; Robert T. Paine to Harold E. Miller, April 15, 1937. A sentiment shared by many is that the loss of the tower chandelier was a sad legacy of the changes made in this campaign.

15. Descriptions of the chancel may be found in Bettina A. Norton, ed., *Trinity Church: The Story of an Episcopal Parish in the City of Boston* (Boston: Wardens and Vestry of Trinity Church in the City of Boston, 1978), 52–62; and Edgar D. Romig, *The Story of Trinity Church in the City of Boston* (Boston: Wardens and Vestry of Trinity Church in the City of Boston, 1952), 54–59. La Farge's unexecuted concepts for the decoration of the chancel are described by H. Barbara Weinberg in "John La Farge and the Decoration of Trinity Church, Boston," *Journal of the Society of Architectural Historians* 33, no. 4 (December 1974): 323–53. For a comprehensive contextual discussion of the mural painting, see Kathleen Curran, "The Romanesque Revival, Mural Painting, and Protestant Patronage in America," *Art Bulletin* 81, no. 4 (December 1999): 693–722.

16. ATC, William Emerson to Jury, June 1, 1937; Kinsolving to Ralph Adams Cram, June 9, 1937.

17. ATC, "Report of the Jury," 1–2; statement accompanying Maginnis submission, May 1937; Charles D. Maginnis to Rev. Arthur Lee Kinsolving, June 11, 1937.

18. William Emerson, "Charles Donagh Maginnis," *Journal of the AIA* 23, no. 5 (May 23, 1955): 213.

19. Excellent sources for medieval architecture are Roger Stalley, *Early Medieval Architecture* (Oxford: Oxford University Press, 1999); and Hans Buchwald, *Form, Style, and Meaning in Byzantine Church Architecture* (Aldershot, U.K.: Ashgate, 1999), esp. 306–13 on geometry. Suggestions for further reading are J. Arnott Hamilton, *Byzantine Architecture and Decoration* (London: B. T. Batsford, 1933, 1956); and Richard Krautheimer, *Early Christian and Byzantine Architecture* (1965; Harmondsworth, U.K.: Penguin Books, 1986).

20. Cosmati work is a combination of Venetian gold glass, colorful marble mosaics, and gilding arranged in polychromatic patterns and set in marble.

21. Peter W. Williams, "The Medieval Heritage in American Religious Architecture," in Rosenthal and Szarmach, *Medievalism in American Culture,* 171. See also Sacvan Bercovitch, "The Biblical Basis of the American Myth," in *The Bible and American Arts and Letters,* ed. Giles Gunn (Philadelphia: Fortress Press; Chico, Calif.: Scholars Press, 1983), 221–32.

22. ATC, Kinsolving to Robert T. Paine, June 21, 1938; Kinsolving to the Committee and Charles D. Maginnis, June 25, 1938. The relationship between the written word and the symbolic images is analyzed by Rev. William E. Gardner in *Trinity Church, a Fortress of God* (Boston: Trinity Church, 1938), 8–16.

23. See Gardner, *Trinity Church,* for details.

24. Weinberg, "John La Farge," 337.

25. ATC, Robert T. Paine to the Committee, July 15, 1938, concerning a taller scaffolding and cleaning; minutes of the Committee, August 2, 1938, approving repair of ceiling, removal of transverse and radial truss members, and addition of structural steel. The steel framing is shown in Maginnis's drawing #9—dated March 24, 1938, revised August 3, 1938—in the Fine Arts Department, Boston Public Library.

26. ATC, Charles D. Maginnis to Robert T. Paine, January 19, 1938; "A Tribute to Viggo F. E. Rambusch," *St. Ansgar's Bulletin,* no. 94 (April 1998): 20–21.

27. George Ferguson, *Signs and Symbols in Christian Art* (New York: Oxford University Press, 1959, 1967), 9, 21.

28. These carvings were illustrated in a book that many ecclesiastical architects of this period used as a reference: F. R. Webber, *Church Symbolism* (1927; Cleveland: J. H. Jansen, 1938), 302–4; the symbolism of peacocks is discussed on 76–78.

29. Milda B. Richardson, "St. Catherine of Genoa," *Sacred Architecture,* no. 6 (spring 2002): 14–15.

30. ATC, the Committee's request to see rough models of the suspended cross and candlesticks (June 8, 1938) and vote to approve the plan (June 20, 1938).

31. ATC, Rev. Arthur Lee Kinsolving to Henry Pennell, November 24, 1938.

32. Henry-Russell Hitchcock, *The Architecture of H. H. Richardson and His Times* (1936; Hamden, Conn.: Archon, 1961), 246–47.

33. Christine Smith, *St. Bartholomew's Church in the City of New York* (New York: Oxford University Press, 1988).

34. Charles D. Maginnis, introduction to *The Work of Cram and Ferguson, Architects, including Work by Cram, Goodhue, and Ferguson* (New York: Pencil Points Press, 1929), n.p.; Charles D. Maginnis, "Ralph Adams Cram," *Commonweal,* December 4, 1942, 162. In a letter sent to Goodhue following his separation from Cram, Maginnis wrote, "Your identity is not so nebulous. You now stand quite clear and clean-cut in the artistic firmament, shining perhaps a little too brilliantly for the rest of us." Quoted in Richard Oliver, *Bertram Grosvenor Goodhue* (Cambridge, Mass.: MIT Press, 1983), 123 n. 62.

35. At fifteen years of age, in 1884, Goodhue had become an apprentice in the office of Renwick, Aspinwall, & Russell and stayed for almost eight years—his only formal training in architecture. Smith, *St. Bartholomew's Church,* 31.

36. Maginnis, *Work of Cram and Ferguson,* n.p.; ATC, Dr. Arthur Lee Kinsolving to Charles D. Maginnis, November 23, 1938.

37. Quoted in John Dillenberger, *The Visual Arts and Christianity in America: The Colonial Period through the Nineteenth Century* (Chico, Calif.: Scholars Press, 1984), 70.

38. Charles D. Maginnis, "Catholic Church Architecture," *Architectural Forum* 27 (August 1917), 35; Charles D. Maginnis, "Architectural Modernism and the Church," pt. 1, "Architectural Design," *Architectural Forum* 50, no. 3 (March 1929): 419–20. Bishop Albert Rouet makes a similar point, "Sacred space presupposes precise limits," in *Liturgy and the Arts,* trans. Paul Philibert (Collegeville, Minn.: Liturgical Press, 1997), 94.

39. Frank DiFederico, *The Mosaics of the National Shrine of the Immaculate Conception* (Washington, D.C.: Decatur House Press, 1980), 2–8. See also Gregory W. Tucker, *America's Church: The Basilica of the National Shrine of the Immaculate Conception* (Washington, D.C.: Basilica of the National Shrine of the Immaculate Conception, 2000), 62–67.

40. Gardner, *Trinity Church,* explains the symbolism of the sequence of three floor levels at Trinity.

41. Between 1890 and 1910, Maginnis made three extended trips to Europe, including Sicily. J. Arnott Hamilton, *Byzantine Architecture and Decoration* (1933; London: B. T. Batsford, 1956), 242–43.

42. Massey Hamilton Shepherd Jr., *The Reform of Liturgical Worship: Perspectives and Prospects,* Bohlen Lectures, 1959 (New York: Oxford University Press, 1961), 8–9. The three books were *The American Prayer Book* by Rev. Dr. Bayard H. Jones, *The Eternal Word in the Modern World* by Professors Burton Scott Easton and Howard Chandler Robbins, and *Church Music in History and Practice* by Canon Charles Winfred Douglas. See also Massey Hamilton Shepherd Jr., ed., *The Liturgical Renewal of the Church* (New York: Oxford University Press, 1960); James F. White, *The Cambridge Movement: The Ecclesiologists and the Gothic Revival* (Cambridge: Cambridge University Press, 1962); Christopher Webster and John Elliott, eds., *The Church as It Should Be* (Stamford, U.K.: Shaun Tyas, 2000). For further background, see Robert W. Prichard, *A History of the Episcopal Church* (Harrisburg, Pa.: Morehouse, 1991); James Thayer Addison, *The Episcopal Church in the United States, 1789–1931* (New York: Charles Scribner's Sons, 1951); and William Wilson Manross, *A History of the American Episcopal Church* (New York: Morehouse, 1935).

43. Rev. Arthur Lee Kinsolving, "The Future of Trinity Church," in *Trinity Church in the City of Boston, Massachusetts, 1733–1933* (Boston: Wardens and Vestry of Trinity Church, 1933): 167–74.

# CONTRIBUTORS

KEITH BAKKER is a furniture conservator based in Albuquerque. He was trained at the Smithsonian Institution and received a master's degree from Antioch College. His study of the Trinity furnishings was commissioned by the church.

DAVID B. CHESEBROUGH, Illinois State University, emeritus, holds advanced degrees in history, theology, and sociology and is a specialist in American religious history. He is the author of seven books, four of which are part of the Great American Authors series, including his *Phillips Brooks: Pulpit Eloquence*.

KATHLEEN A. CURRAN, Trinity College, Hartford, holds a Ph.D. from the University of Delaware with a dissertation on the Romanesque Revival in Germany and America. She is the author of *The Romanesque Revival: Religion, Politics, and Transnational Exchange*.

ERICA E. HIRSHLER holds degrees from Wellesley College and Boston University. She is Croll Senior Curator of Paintings, Art of the Americas, at the Museum of Fine Arts, Boston. Among her many publications is *A Studio of Her Own: Women Artists in Boston, 1870–1940*.

KEITH N. MORGAN earned his Ph.D. at Brown University and is now professor of the history of art at Boston University. He is the editor of the forthcoming *Buildings of Massachusetts: Metropolitan Boston,* a volume in the Buildings of the United States series sponsored by the Society of Architectural Historians.

James F. O'Gorman is Grace Slack McNeil Professor of the History of American Art at Wellesley College. Among his numerous books are *H. H. Richardson and His Office: Selected Drawings; H. H. Richardson: Architectural Forms for an American Society; Three American Architects: Richardson, Sullivan, and Wright, 1865–1915;* and *Living Architecture: A Biography of H. H. Richardson.*

Thomas M. Paine is a practicing landscape architect and president of the Robert Treat Paine Historical Trust, which assists the City of Waltham, Massachusetts, in safeguarding Stonehurst, a house by H. H. Richardson, and its archives. His great-grandfather, General Charles J. Paine, was a brother of Robert Treat Paine.

Virginia Chieffo Raguin, a medievalist with a doctorate from Yale University, is an expert on nineteenth-century American stained glass. A professor of art history at the College of the Holy Cross, she is the author, among other works, of *Glory in Glass: Stained Glass in the United States* and *Reflections on Glass: 20th Century Stained Glass in American Art and Architecture.*

Milda B. Richardson is a Ph.D. candidate at Boston University. Her publications include contributions to *Sacred Spaces: Building and Remembering Sites of Worship in the 19th Century* and *Buildings of Massachusetts: Metropolitan Boston.*

Theodore E. Stebbins Jr. was for a quarter century curator of American art at the Museum of Fine Arts, Boston. He is currently Distinguished Fellow and Consultative Curator of American Art at the Fogg Museum, Harvard University. Among his many publications is a seminal study of Trinity Church: "Richardson and Trinity Church: The Evolution of a Building," *Journal of the Society of Architectural Historians* (1968).

Charles Vandersee, associate editor of the six-volume Harvard University Press edition of *The Letters of Henry Adams,* was associate professor of English at the University of Virginia. He died in January 2003.

# INDEX